THE 12 RULES OF *Smart* MANAGEMENT

SMART MANAGEMENT
FOR EFFECTIVE MANAGERS

Systematic Methods And Response Techniques

PAUL BOOTH

This book is available in an electronic format and in paperback format through print-on-demand distribution.

Paperback: ISBN 978-1-54394-579-9

Diagrammatic Plan of the Contents

Chapter 1
Introduction
SMART MANAGEMENT

Chapter 2
Systematic Methods And
Response Techniques
Question, Decision &
Action Planning Models

Chapter 3
Perfect Time Management

Chapter 14
Managing Your Health &
Stress Levels

Chapter 13
Making Powerful Presentations

Chapter 12
The Complete Negotiation

Chapter 11
Ideal Monitoring & Control
Methods

Chapter 10
Managing Effective
Decisions

S
M
A
R
T

M
A
N
A
G
E
M
E
N
T

Chapter 4
Discussion Skills to Avoid
Misunderstanding

Chapter 5
Executive Writing Made Easy

Chapter 6
Recruiting Your Team

Chapter 7
Coaching &Reviewing for
Success

Chapter 8
Handling Complaints,
Discipline, Change &
Delegation

Chapter 9
Managing Groups Productively

CONTENTS

Chapter 5: Executive Writing Made Easy 78

The Third Rule of Smart Management: Develop an executive writing skill to educate, sell, convince, motivate or influence your reader.

Chapter 6: Recruiting Your Team 90

Fourth Rule of Smart Management: Recognize and identify what makes certain employees stand out from the crowd.

Chapter 7: Coaching and Reviewing for Success 110

The Fifth Rule of Smart Management: Establish an
effective method for coaching and reviewing individuals
for success and correcting failing performance.

Chapter 8: Complaints, Discipline, Changes and Delegation

The Sixth Rule of Smart Management: Learn how to handle complaints professionally, discipline effectively, make changes that work and delegate successfully.

Chapter 9: Managing Groups Productively

The Seventh Rule of Smart Management: Develop your own specific applications, concepts and skills to manage groups productively.

Chapter 10: Managing Effective Decisions

The Eighth Rule of Smart Management: Focus on what makes an effective decision and put your decisions into action using simple conventional processes.

Chapter 1: Introduction

Section: 1.0. What this Book is All About

Managers continually face tough decisions and challenges. Effective managers are those who carefully analyze the problem or opportunity, identify and create value decisions and implement those decisions towards successful results in a systematic way.

Smart Management will provide you with the skills; the Systematic Methods And Response Techniques to develop quality management decisions and strengthen twelve areas of management, which are essential to the effective manager and management of resources for positive results.

You will be able to cover the principles and processes of management; highlight problem areas, challenges and opportunities and address management responsibility and accountability that organizations and business require of you.

In simple words, this book can show you how to develop your own management and career strengths and you will get the skills to take control of your job ... You get concise information in a modular format that you can use immediately! You will learn from years of management experience... about how management works, it will be uncomplicated and easy to understand as it is applied practically, in the real world.

The most important activity in which managers engage is decision-making; it is the common thread that runs through all management activities. Many managers must make decisions in very competitive business environments under difficult conditions and on occasion under considerable time pressure.

Smart Management focuses on all the skills necessary that are an integral part of the decision-making process and more, to take you from the immediate issues of time management to the longer term issue of managing your health and stress levels. The book's emphasis is on how the use of systematic processes can provide you with a competitive advantage in your field, recognizing that the correct assessment, decision-making and implementation of skills are a part of your everyday activity.

Why SMART Management?

S M A R T Management is quite simply the application of **S**ystematic **M**ethods **A**nd **R**esponse **T**echniques; these simple methods and techniques can be employed in your work environment immediately to make you more efficient and more effective.

S M A R T is the acronym of
Systematic **M**ethods **A**nd **R**esponse **T**echniques

The Objective of Smart Management

To prepare the manager with an understanding of the systematic methods and response techniques, models and skills to analyze any problem or opportunity, identify and create value decisions and implement those decisions and actions.

The 12 Rules of Smart Management

The twelve rules of smart management provide you with a set of basic guidelines and principle elements applied to management. These fundamental elements offer you the rules and the associated management skills which all knowledgeable managers should know.

The rules of Smart Management are highlighted in the forthcoming chapters: -

> **Rule #1:** *Create focus and organize your life in a sea of interruptions.*
>
> **Rule #2:** *Recognize and understand what makes certain discussions successful and which lead to misunderstanding and conflict.*
>
> **Rule #3:** *Develop an executive writing skill to educate, sell, convince, motivate or influence your reader.*

Rule #4: *Recognize and identify what makes certain employees stand out from the crowd.*

Rule #5: *Establish an effective method for coaching and reviewing individuals for success and correcting failing performance.*

Rule #6: *Learn how to handle complaints professionally, discipline effectively, make changes that work and delegate successfully.*

Rule #7: *Develop your own specific applications, concepts and skills to manage groups productively.*

Rule #8: *Focus on what makes an effective decision and put your decisions into action using simple conventional processes.*

Rule #9: *Learn what makes focused managers develop appropriate monitoring and control methods that work.*

Rule #10: *Understand how negotiation is a skill which requires you to be aware of issues, positions and strategy to ensure all the parties reach agreement.*

Rule #11: *Build confidence and professional presentation skills at every opportunity.*

Rule #12: *Reduce your stress levels and improve your health and wellbeing when you are under pressure.*

Smart Management provides the reader with: -

1. **Twelve Rules**

    The twelve rules of **Smart Management** will guide you to produce the results and most important management skills used by successful managers. The text is written from the manager's perspective, based on content that leads the manager through a management key skills programme anticipating that the manager will become fully functional and effective.

2. **S M A R T Perspective**

    This book draws on **Systematic Methods And Response Techniques** to provide the fundamental tools and concepts for seeking positive results in the use of your own skills and the resources available to you.

3. **A Systematic View**

Presents classical and generic models and methods for analyzing immediate and recurrent problems in management and illustrates well proven management methods, principles and techniques.

4. **A Universal Approach**

    The book applies management thinking for mangers in all organisations, industries and markets.

5. **An Integration of Information, Theory and Practice**

    Management information and theory has been refined to a minimum and the book focuses primarily on the practical application of information in the work environment, advocating the use of more practice and less theory.

6. **Managerial Approach**

    The book focuses on the decisions and key skills that management executives and top management have to face daily to guide the resources of the company towards positive results.

7. **Practical Manager Oriented Exercises**

    The exercises and self assessments are provided for ease of use, they are kept to a minimum and in a modular format so that the manager is able to absorb the information quickly and relate it to a personal work environment immediately.

8. **Features**

    The book features end of chapter summary reviews and quick guides for future use. These summary reviews and quick tips and guides distil the wisdom of this book into simple clear statements, to explain the logical methods and processes used by successful managers and how they are employed in practice.

9. **Wisdom**

    The book contains quotations of wisdom from various leaders, philosophers, writers, politicians, sportsmen, physicists, generals, professors and businessmen which relate to modern management.

10. **Content**

    The content covers all the key skills and topics that an informed and effective manager needs to know and succeed in a modern business environment.

The systematic methods and response techniques and the twelve rules of management discussed can be applied in your work environment immediately.

A Word about the Importance of Positive Work Behavior

Many effective and successful managers develop positive work behavior models of their own and the summaries and quick guides provided will assist you in the retention of the methods, techniques and processes and instill a positive approach towards finding solutions to problems, challenges and opportunities, which are presented to managers daily.

Remember..........

Management Wisdom

Victory comes from finding opportunities in problems.

*Sun Tzu

However, **Smart Management** is not intended to dictate your path or prescribe the course of action you should take – as the manager this is your decision – based on the information and tools you have to hand at the time and the particular circumstances for each problem, opportunity, area or company.

The methods and techniques provided however will focus your thoughts towards rational and creative solutions for your company's objectives and your own career objectives.

Section: 1.1. Who was this book written for?

Smart Management will enable you to become a more effective manager it will equip you with understanding and knowledge. It lays down basic guides for the overworked executive, the supervisor, the manager and the businessman. It is for self-motivated managers at the start of their careers or for those more battle hardened mature managers who want to re-evaluate and perhaps improve their management skills. So, whether you're new to the field or a seasoned executive this book will give you insights into what it takes for you to perform effectively.

If you feel you are overworked or underpaid then surely it's time for you to get on top of your job... and this book will help you.

If you are an aspiring manager the best possible way to learn is to make a serious commitment to use the skills you have learned, assume responsibility for the results of 'your' company where you are directly involved, ***before*** it is bestowed on you. The objective is to look after the company's interests; grow your company and your own stature will grow as a result.

Section: 1.2. Why was this book written?
In the field of management there is a requirement for a broad scope of management skills in many different industries from highly commercialized businesses to non-profit based businesses. The range of manufacturing and service businesses spans many industries agricultural, mining, financial, government, electronics, education, energy, utilities, health and medical industry to name but a few. This book was written to serve all managers in all industries.

The Smart Management programme is designed to cater for this broad spectrum of managers and particularly to: -

1. Examine how to structure systematic methods of problem or opportunity assessment, problem solving, decision-making and implementation through action planning using systematic methods.

2. Explain how resources can be used at all levels of the decision making process in functional areas in a participative and interactive way.

3. Strengthen twelve key skills areas of management, which are essential to the effective manager and the management of resources for positive results.

4. Illustrate how effective management skills can be used to support the organization's strategy objectives.

5. Fill any gaps in a manager's learning and experience, sometimes left by insufficient time for practical management training, not enough management experience or rapid promotion.

Section: 1.3. What makes an effective manager?
The effective manager; is many things – to many people.

If you want to become an effective manager you must pursue the skills and training which will allow you to become an entrepreneur, be creative, motivated, specific, optimistic, ambitious and above all things you must be seen as fair and reasonable and if this sounds like a lot of work – **it is!** But, you will become the type of person who gets excited about your project successes and accepts your failures with dignity and learns from them. You will improve your strengths and skills and reduce your shortcomings to become an effective manager who refrains from being cynical or negative. So read on, because this book will provide you with the means to improve your skills and training to make you unstoppable and take you forward in management and in life.

Remember.........

Management Wisdom

A man is great not because he hasn't failed; a man is great because failure hasn't stopped him.

*Confucius

Reactive versus Proactive

In business one of the differences between a manager and an ***effective*** manager is that effective managers do not wait for plans and planning to be handed down from their manager and adopting a ***reactive*** approach. Effective managers consider the task at hand, the problem or opportunity and apply their minds to plan ahead adopting a ***proactive*** approach.

As a proactive manager you need to ….

1. Know that, the higher up the company hierarchy you go the more you have to plan.
2. Know that, if you want to climb the corporate ladder you have to plan – continually.
3. Learn to accept responsibility before it is bestowed on you.
4. Learn to ask:
   a. What do I contribute to the company's profitability?
   b. How can I develop myself?
   c. How can I minimize the costs to the company?

      d.   How can I minimize the risks to the company?

      e.   How can I save the company money?

      f.   How can I improve overall efficiency?

      g.   How can I develop my personnel?

  5.   Accept that – no plan – equals – no discipline.

Do so, and you will become top in your field.

Remember........

Management Wisdom

It's tough at the top, but its hell of a crowded at the bottom.

*Unknown

Management Ability and Systematic Processes

Effective managers continually develop their management ability and processes to ensure quality management decisions through systematic methods and response techniques.

The following is indicative of managers with different management abilities and systematic processes:

	Type Three Manager	Type Two Manager	Type One Manager
Performance Expected	**Ineffective**	**Efficient**	**Effective**
Management Ability	Limited	Limited	Developed
Systematic Processes	Limited	Developed	Developed
Results Anticipated	Poor -Average	Good	Best

From the table above, it can be seen that: -

Type Three Manager – Ineffective Managers

Ineffective Managers have not developed their management ability and have limited systematic processes to cope with the work environment – the performance expected could be classed as 'Ineffective', the results expected would be poor to average at best.

Type Two Manager – Efficient Managers

Efficient Managers have not developed their management ability fully, but have developed systematic processes to cope with the work environment – the performance expected could be classed as 'Efficient', the results expected would be good.

Type One Manager – Effective Managers

Effective Managers have developed their management ability and have developed systematic methods, processes and response techniques to cope with their work environment – the performance expected could be classed as 'Effective', and the results expected would be the best possible.

Section: 1.4. Why develop SMART Management?

Management isn't easy or it would be applied more successfully. Many management problems left unattended in production, service, resource and finance areas often do not surface until the problem is out of control.

Poor management and the inability to handle management problems effectively affect the quality and cost to the business directly. Competition, attitudes, morale, training, misunderstanding and internal conflict can play a major part in the loss of revenue.

SMART Management uses classical **S**ystematic **M**ethods **A**nd **R**esponse **T**echniques to identify a problem or an opportunity and provide the means to guide and define quality decisions and the associated key skills.

Management must make decisions at times with insufficient data and information about dynamic operational processes that may be difficult to address. Nevertheless, this is not advocating 'reactive' or 'quick fix' decision making, on the contrary, it is indicative of the need to improve methods and responses which properly analyse management decisions in a systematic way and avoid crisis management.

It can be said that most managers will respond to their environment in a reactive way when things don't go according to plan or when there are new problems or opportunities developing. The manager's reaction will take the form most likely to meet the immediate needs and drives of the manager and the company. On the other hand, this response may not always be in line with the best practices of management.

If a manager has a tendency to take on too much at once, the manager's immediate environment can become somewhat overloaded with personal needs, opinions, ideas, standards and expectations from both internal and external sources. This may create confusion and interferes with a manager's clear thinking.

This is due to **NOISE**, an acronym generated from **N**eeds, **O**pinions, **I**deas, **S**tandards and **E**xpectations explained as follows: -

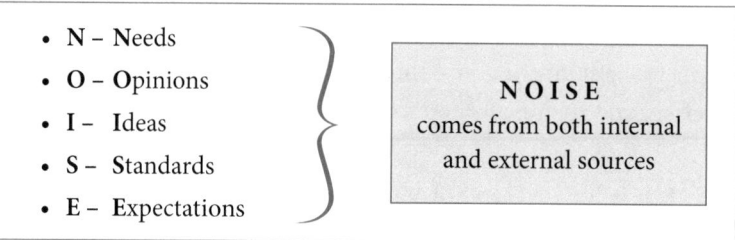

- **N** – Needs
- **O** – Opinions
- **I** – Ideas
- **S** – Standards
- **E** – Expectations

N O I S E
comes from both internal and external sources

NOISE – interferes with clear thought and results in Crisis Management

All these inputs can distort or modify a manager's response to the situation; although the manager's response may be impulsive it is an attempt to get back to the standard or the plan. The response varies greatly from manager to manager according to the level of the manager's personal NOISE and the needs and drives of the manager and the company.

The negative result of continuing to react to situations is that the manager may remain in a state of anticipation or crisis management.

The Objective: is to reduce the NOISE level in a 'systematic' way and stop the manager from going into crisis mode. This is achieved through applying **Smart Management** and selected classical support models, systematic methods and response techniques to different problem situations and making this systematic approach second nature for the manager.

Section: 1.5. Application rate and results

Please, don't believe the pursuit of a management career is easy. Management responsibility is a profession and mastery of any profession requires commitment, patience and hard work, and your success in business management takes determination, diligence and practiced systematic methods and response techniques.

Although management advice can sometimes appear complicated and confusing; '**Smart Management**' is simple... it will get you up and running quickly. You may make mistakes along the way, but learn from them, accept them with dignity and move on.

Remember.........

Management Wisdom

Opportunity, is missed by most people because, it is dressed in overalls and looks like work.

*Thomas Edison

Find the right sections or chapters for you, in your world   and make this book work for you!

If you are prepared to enjoy your job and to invest in your future, then this book will take you to a higher level of understanding of management in less time than it takes to complete a management course of equal content. And if you invest the time; this book will guide you through a straightforward no nonsense management programme which you can: -

- ❏ Work through, at your own speed.
- ❏ Work when you want to.
- ❏ Start using the programme guides and see the results, immediately.
- ❏ Use as a reference handbook.

Sound too good to be true?........ It's not! It's easy to start, easy to complete and you, your colleagues and your operational team will observe the improved results in your performance.

At this point, you own the keys to your own destiny and you have every-thing to gain!

A management career offers you the opportunity to create an excellent income and it can open up interesting job opportunities. When the components of management are understood management will no longer be a grey area.

Section: 2.0. Why you will succeed

You will succeed because; you will be able to apply the knowledge you have learned, immediately.

Having spent years analyzing and distilling all the management techniques 'Smart Management' was created for determined, self motivated people who want to re-evaluate and enhance their skills through continuous improvement.

The creation of management training products is nothing new. The principles are as old as the principles of mathematics or science; however, the test of a successful management programme is in the application rate and speed with which the manager can use the knowledge learned. You will be able to use 'Smart Management' and apply the knowledge contained in this book right away.

The sections are designed specifically for ease of use. The following sections will teach you the essential core components of management and provide you with comprehensive system that produces results......*fast.*

Only one person can make it happen – YOU!

Remember.........

Management Wisdom

The will to win, the desire to succeed, the urge to reach your full potential. These are the keys that will unlock the door to excellence.

*Confucius

Section: 3.0. How to get on Top of Your Job

Many people sometimes struggle for years on their own, trying to grasp the intricacies of management with little support and guidance ... you can now select from the sections of this book that show you how to get right on top of your job, quickly and easily, here's how.

It is important that you: -
1. **Read** all the following sections carefully.
2. **Decide** how the sections apply to your work situation.
3. **Answer** the questions in the book by using the self assessments.
4. **Apply** the models, systematic methods, checklists and quick guides provided and the solutions you have written down and turn them into action in your environment.

Your objective:
> Is to make the management skills presented in this book, <u>equal</u> your management practice.

The Basics: Implementation of Smart Management
The following Do's and Don'ts are presented as a guide to good work habits: -

The Do's
1. **Do prioritise your actions** – identify everything that needs to be done. Evaluate every aspect of the job or task and allow yourself additional time for selection of the most appropriate solution and a quality decision, based on the facts to hand and in the time available, so that you can be sure that the objective is accomplished on time and accurately.
2. **Do make a checklist and an action plan** – Write it down; don't try to keep infinite details in your head irrespective of how good you believe your memory is. You should have a written checklist and an action plan to follow, to avoid repeating steps.
3. **Do be flexible** – For sure, your day will not always go as planned, try to build flexibility into your daily work programme.

4. **Do communicate clearly** – Control personnel by communicating clearly. Make sure your personnel and other interacting departments, subcontractors etc. involved understand what is required of them and by when.

5. **Do delegate** – Make sure you have personnel you can delegate to, if not, train them. Learn to say 'no', sometimes you have to say 'no' and delegate the work to avoid over-loading yourself.

6. **Do work when it's time to work** – and switch off and rest when it's time to stop work.

7. **Do take a break or even multiple breaks** – You need time to rest both your body and mind. After concentrating on a particular problem or task for an hour or two, take a break.

8. **Do rest well** – Working 12 to 18 hours a day is not sustainable. At some point your focus and concentration cannot be maintained which leads to careless and unnecessary mistakes. Ideally, you should be getting six to eight hours of restful sleep every night.

The Don'ts

1. **Don't procrastinate.** Check your daily routine work, correspondence and emails once per day and allocate a specific time for it, plan your day and avoid checking and rechecking.

2. **Don't Multi-Task.** – avoid the multi-tasking myth, as you often get less done switching back and forth between tasks and multi-tasking under time pressure often leads to mistakes.

3. **Don't accept new information, changes and re-direction automatically**; question and re-evaluate new information, changes and redirection in terms of the objective originally envisaged to avoid future problems.

4. **Don't over complicate the task.** If the task is becoming over complicated – step back and re-evaluate the task and compare it to the ultimate objective originally envisaged and bring it back to the simplest process to meet the objective.

5. **Don't take shortcuts** – Often management decisions are under considerable time pressure. Evaluate your work methods in terms of effectiveness, not speed of completion which may undermine the quality of your decisions.

6. **Don't work yourself to the point of exhaustion.** Recognise when you are tired. Protect your health and wellbeing. Working yourself to exhaustion will make you more prone to mistakes. When you realise you are taking too long to complete the job, stop and rest or take a nap and refresh.

7. **Don't accept bad or poor quality decisions** – You will know when a decision is inferior so don't be pressured into 'quick fix' decisions that you are not comfortable with, because the decision is under time pressure.

Participative Management Style

Smart Management advocates a participative management style and process. By bringing together the assessment, decision making, planning and controlling functions with the involvement of personnel in a participative way Smart Management can overcome many of the barriers to implementation.

In essence, Smart Management seeks to establish common objectives by management and personnel in their areas of responsibility, drawn up in a measurable and quantifiable action plan. These common objectives are then used to plan the work of the manager and personnel. Progress towards these common objectives is monitored in the form of performance feedback and reviews to ensure that progress towards the original objectives is still on track and if necessary corrective action can be taken in good time.

Consider the following factors to aid implementation of the Smart Management programme: -

❏ **The Manager's Commitment**: is to stay on track and be fair and reasonable in all decisions.

❏ **Company Objectives**: it is important that the manager and personnel understand the overall objectives of the company.

❏ **Manger's Objectives**: it is important that the manager and personnel understand how the manager's objectives relate to the overall objectives of the company.

❏ **Participation and Support**: assessment, decision-making and implementation must be participative, in other words the manager and the manager's personnel are actively involved in setting and therefore supporting their own objectives for the task or project at hand.

❑ **Autonomy in Implementation and Achievement**: the manager must give personnel the necessary autonomy and control and allow contribution to the problem or opportunity solution, with the means to implement the tasks.

❑ **Frequent Monitoring and Feedback**: should be both formal and informal to allow the manager to compare performance to the original objectives. Try to keep most of the monitoring and feedback informal and participative.

Remember.........

Management Wisdom

Be just as enthusiastic about the success of others as you are about your own.

*Christian D. Larson

The Immediate Advantages of Smart Management

1.1   Improves communication.

1.2   Individuals are more aware of the company's objectives.

1.3   Individuals are more aware of the manger's objectives.

1.4   Individuals know what is expected of them.

1.5   Improves managers' behavior, from authoritarian or prescriptive to that of participative and assisting or guiding.

1.6   Aids planning and control.

1.7   Provides immediate feedback on performance of tasks and objectives.

The Smart Management Process

The Smart Management process has been developed and refined to provide you with all the essential information and skills you need and has been developed primarily for the individual..... *You the manager.*

In Summary

Smart Management focuses on all the skills necessary that are an integral part of the decision-making process and more, which will take you from the immediate issues of Time Management to the long term Management of Health and Stress. The book's emphasis is on how systematic methods and processes can provide you with a competitive advantage in your field, recognizing that the correct assessment, decision-making and implementation skills are a part of your everyday activities and your own personal growth.

Remember.........

Management Wisdom

A true leader has the confidence to stand alone, the courage to make tough decisions, and the compassion to listen to the needs of others. He does not set out to be a leader, but becomes one by the equality of his actions and the integrity of his intent.

*Douglas MacArthur

You will find this book easy to get into practice, with reviews and quick guides you can copy and use in your work environment immediately.

Chapter 2: Systematic Methods and Response Techniques

The models, methods and techniques that follow will show you how to focus on the three most important skills of management and develop systematic methods and response techniques to various problems and opportunities you will be faced with daily.

Section: 1.0. The Three Most Important Management Skills

Each step in the problem-solving and decision making process revolves around three main management skills: -

(1) **Assessment:** *of a problem or opportunity*

(2) **Decision Making:** *the development of a solution or decision*

(3) **Implementation:** *of the solution or decision into action*

These skills normally have to be carried out within a predetermined time, whether it is a task, a problem or an opportunity and for the effective manager the word task, problem, or opportunity are interchangeable.

When carrying out the Assessment, Decision and Implementation process it is important to note that: -

❏ **Appropriate Problem or Opportunity Objectives** come from the manager who has the wisdom to look past the symptoms of the problem to the cause; what is going on and why.

❏ **Creative solutions** come from the manager who has the perception to look at the long-term effect of the solution; what to do if plans go wrong and where must the solution lead and what end result do we want.

❏ **Strategic action** comes from the manager with a sense of the present, when to do things and how and who should be involved.

But first, let's discuss some of the classical models and more importantly the methods used by successful managers on which to build your Assessment, Decision-Making and Implementation skills.

Remember.........

Management Wisdom

A person's mind stretched to a new idea never goes back to its original dimensions.

* Oliver Wendell Holmes

Section: 2.0. The Classical Support Models

The following support models presented will assist you to think through the problem or opportunity to be addressed and provide you with the necessary systematic methods and response techniques.

Section: 2.1. An Overview of the Skills and Support Models

In a sea of information and data, the support models will help you to sift through the information and data collected, assess and evaluate the situation, determine whether it is a problem or opportunity, decide on the solution and clearly implement an action plan.

The following diagram presents an overview of the interaction between the three management skills [Assessment, Decision and Implementation] and the three support models [Question Model, Decision Model, Action Plan Model].

This will lead you from the identified problem or opportunity objective through to the end result with feedback from the end result to the original objective for monitoring progress, comparison and evaluation of the end result on completion.

Diagram: 01. Skills and Support Models

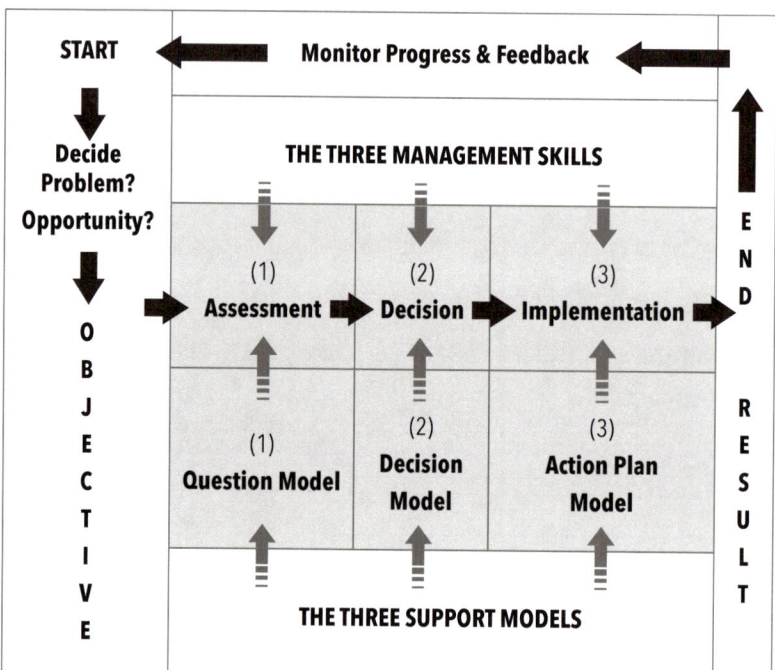

It is essential to understand the simple yet important methods and processes, which these models provide, as you will be able to revisit these models and their use in your day to day management role. The **systematic processes** described will help you overcome any uncertainties and address problems and opportunities effectively.

The purpose of the models is threefold: -

(1.) **The Question Model**: *generates information and ideas.*

(2.) **The Decision Model**: *processes information and ideas towards a decision.*

(3.) **The Action Plan Model**: *turns the decision/s into action.*

Quick Tip: *In order to be efficient and effective, one must continually plan ahead and allow for the ranking of priorities.*

Depending on the complexity of the problem or opportunity, you could use the Question Model as a stand-alone model for simple non-complex tasks, problems and opportunities to reach a decision and implementation, as the tasks, problems and opportunities increase in complexity and strategic importance to the company, you may add the Decision Model and the Action Plan Model as required.

Now let's consider the support models, firstly the Question Model: -

Section: 2.2. Description of the Question Model

Your first approach is the question model; to assist you in eliminating the many uncertainties and moving you quickly to ***the root cause of the problem or the opportunity***. The following questions are indeed your Primary Seven Key Questions and should become second nature to you as an effective manager.

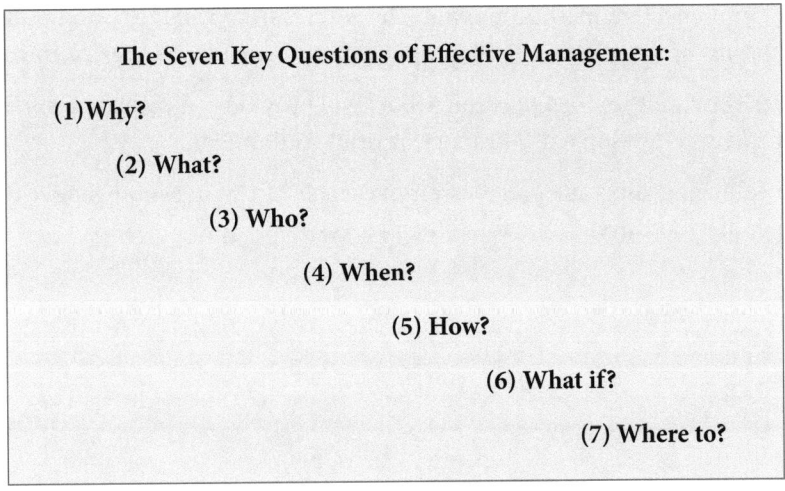

The Seven Key Questions of Effective Management:

(1) Why?

    (2) What?

        (3) Who?

            (4) When?

                (5) How?

                    (6) What if?

                        (7) Where to?

For Example: -

1. Why do I need to take action in a particular area?
2. What objective/s and action plan, shall I set?
3. Who will be involved in the objective/s and action plan?
4. When are my objective/s and action plan dates to be completed?
5. How are my objectives and actions to happen?
6. What if a problem develops, what will I do?
7. Where (to) should my objective/s and action plan lead me?

Remember.........

Management Wisdom

The man who asks a question is a fool for a minute, the man who does not ask is a fool for life.

*Confucius

The Question Model of Management is a time honored and universally recognized management tool to '***systematically focus***' management thinking towards creative problem or opportunity objectives. It is the most efficient and effective method possible, by ***not wasting time*** focusing on the ***symptoms of the problem***, and guiding you to the ***root cause or causes***.

Note: The results of the Question Model will provide you with ***information and ideas*** to develop a preliminary or draft Action Plan.

The following diagram presents an overview of the question model that will guide you through the four step process.

Diagram: 02. The Question Model

THE QUESTION MODEL			
A Simple Four Step Development Process			
Step One: Focus on the objective.	**Question:** (1) Why: is action necessary? What: Objective is to be achieved? And is there a Problem or Opportunity here?		
Step Two: Focus on the Action Plan, actions, responsibilities and timing for resources.	**Question:** (2) What: action has to be carried out?	**Question:** (3) Who: would be responsible for carrying out the action?	**Question:** (4) When: is the action to be carried out?
Step Three: Focus on the method/s to achieve the action plan.	**Question:** (5) How: are the tasks of the action plan to be carried out?		
Step Four: Focus on monitoring and measuring the current feedback to the original objective and on the contingency plan, if the current plan fails. And compare the end result or final position with the original objective.	**Question:** (6) Monitor and measure the current progress and feedback to the original Objective for comparison. What if: a problem or obstacle arises or the opportunity is lost?	**Question:** (7) Where to: feedback to compare result or position with the original objective on completion evaluate the action plan in terms of the Objective accomplished.	

A Simple Four Step Process to Develop the Question Model

The Question Model contains a simple four step process to *generate information and ideas* towards assessing a task or an opportunity or solving a problem quickly and effectively.

Step One: **Focus on the Objective:** Firstly, you need to consider Question: (1) WHY is Action necessary? And Question: (2) WHAT Objective is to be achieved? Is there a Problem or an Opportunity here?

Step Two: **Focus on the Action Plan for Resources:** Now apply some thought to a preliminary Action Plan, the Question: (2) WHAT, Question: (3) WHO would be responsible for the Action plan and Question: (4) WHEN - the time-frame, determine the approximate start and end dates as a guideline, before personnel are finally allocated to the action plan, this is crucial to the productivity and the methodology of problem solving.

Note: *Without specific actions, times and people to carry out the actions, implementation often remains just <u>good intentions</u>!*

Step Three: **Focus on the Method/s to achieve the Action Plan:** The Methodology, detail Question: (5) HOW the action will be carried out and if the action is allowed to move, and determine if it is critical or flexible?

Step Four: **Focus on monitoring and measuring feedback to the original Objective:** The Feed-Back & Contingency, this takes care of the Question: (6) WHAT IF a problem or obstacle arises or the opportunity is lost? Also consider the Question: (7) WHERE TO, provide feedback to compare the end result, or current position with the original objective?

Section: 2.3. Description of the Decision Model

The effective manager starts by applying the Question Model which *generates information and ideas* by asking the Seven Key Questions and then applying the Decision Model which *processes the information and ideas into a decision.*

By carrying out this assessment you are clearly defining your objectives and action plans and firming up and fixing your target dates to ensure achievement.

The Decision Model is a simple **four-step process** with **seven actions** to be carried out. It is a systematic and classical method, which is a thorough and logical process to *turn information and ideas into a decision.*

The Purpose of the Decision Model is fourfold: -

> **Step: 1.**   **Generation:**
>
> Action: (1) Define the Problem/ Opportunity
>
> Action: (2) Collect and Collate Information & Data

> **Step: 2.**   **Comparison:**
>
> Action: (3) Specify the Boundary Conditions, Limitations and Challenges
>
> Action: (4) Compare Alternative Solutions from the Information & Data

> **Step: 3.**   **Selection:**
>
> Action: (5) Rank & Prioritize the Best Tentative Solutions
>
> Action: (6) Select the Best Solution

> **Step: 4.**   **Implementation:**
>
> Action: (7) Implement the Decision though an Action plan

The following Decision Model is a logical procedure to ***define the problem/ opportunity, process the information and data, specify the boundary conditions, select the best solution, implement an action plan and determine the end result/s required***. It can be applied to almost every problem (or opportunity) you may come across. The Decision Model is used in conjunction with the Question Model above.

Let's study the Decision Model below: -

Diagram: 03. The Decision Model

THE DECISION MODEL			
DECISION MAKING METHODS ➡			➡
Step 1: **Generation**	**Step 2:** **Comparison**	**Step 3:** **Selection**	**Step 4:** **Implementation**
Action: (1) Identify & Define the Problem/ Opportunity	**Action: (3)** Boundary Conditions, Limitations and Challenges	**Action: (5)** Rank & Prioritize the Best Tentative Solutions	**Action: (7)** Implement the Decision though an Action plan
Action: (2) Collect and Collate Information & Data	**Action: (4)** Compare Alternative Solutions from the Information & Data	**Action: (6)** Select the Best Solution	
⬅ **Monitoring & Feedback on Progress**			

The steps of the decision-making model are described, as follows: -

Step 1: Generation

Action: (1) - Identify & Define the Problem or Opportunity: The problem / opportunity and reason for making a decision is identified and defined and a solution objective formulated.

Action: (2) - Collect and Collate Information & Data: This process collects all the information at hand and gathers facts & opinions that are thought to be relevant to the problem identified.

Step 2: Comparison

Action: (3) - Boundary Conditions Limitations and Challenges: Boundary conditions refer to the clear definition as to what the decision must accomplish. Specifically, they must state the objectives the decision must reach, the minimum objectives the decision must attain and the conditions the decision must satisfy to resolve the problem identified in Step 1. Action: (1) The boundary conditions take into account all the observed events, issues and facts. They must also consider where challenges or limitations may exist.

Action: (4) - Compare Alternative Solutions: Make a list of alternative solutions from information collected, collated and then evaluate and compare them in relation to the boundary conditions in Step 2. Action: (3).

Step 3: Selection

Action: (5) - Rank & Prioritize the Best Tentative Solutions: Rank and prioritize a short list of the best solutions from the alternatives, and flexible enough to be changed, or modified later, if necessary. They are the best solutions that you can make at that point of time from the alternatives.

Action: (6) - Select the Best Solution: Review the shortlist of best solutions and 'Select' the best solution/ decision and eliminate the alternatives before moving to implementation.

Step 4: Implementation

Action: (7) - Implement the Decision though an Action plan: Break down the decision into its component parts or tasks and incorporate them into an action plan.

Section: 2.4. Description of the Action Planning Model

You now bring all the information, tasks, resources and timeframes together in the action plan. The purpose of the Action Plan is *to turn the decision into action* leading to a positive result.

1. Developing an Action Plan

Action plans specify *what* the actions or tasks will be and *who* will complete each task in a certain time to reach each of the *target dates* (*when*) for example: increase sales revenue by '*x*' 000's pounds, reduce production downtime by '*y*' hours or improve return on investment by '*z*' percent, each task is carried out over a specific time period to meet the overall timeframe of the plan and accomplish the company's problem or opportunity objective. Ideally, the manager and personnel directly involved in their area would contribute to the action plan and the task/s that are to be carried out for example: -

    i.   What tasks need to be carried out?

    ii.   When will the results be achieved for each task to meet the overall timeframe of the problem or opportunity objective?

    iii. How will each task contribute to the company's problem or opportunity objective?

    iv. What specific results must be achieved to reach the company's problem or opportunity objective?

    v.   How will those results be achieved?

2. Developing the Company's (Problem or Opportunity) Objective and Timeframes

The company's problem or opportunity objective should contain quantifiable and measurable results which are produced when tasks are implemented and completed (e.g. '*x*' increase / or decrease by '*y*' time).

    i.   Ensure the tasks contained in the action plan are monitored, compared and reviewed.

    ii.   Remember the task start and end dates are 'guidelines' for completion, and these where possible should be flexible with the ability to move these dates, if necessary, rather than being rigidly structured.

    iii. Alternatively, if the company's problem or opportunity objective **is not flexible**; due to circumstances outside the control of the company; you may need to build in contingencies or have additional resources available to meet the company's overall objective timeframe e.g. overtime, additional resources, etc.

    iv. Any delays or deviations to the company's overall objective timeframe contained in the action plan should be reported by the manager and personnel involved so that alternative action can be taken in good time.

3. Developing Tasks and Timeframes

The manager and ideally each employee directly involved in his/her area should contribute to the development of the action plan tasks, and the company's overall objective. The action plan should illustrate how <u>all</u> the tasks will be implemented.

 i. Firstly, break down the solution / decision into its component parts for each independent task.

 ii. The action plan should reflect in specific detail how each of the tasks will be accomplished, from start through to completion.

 iii. Any possible 'known' delays or deviations to the tasks contained in the action plan should be fully understood by the manager and the manager's personnel so that alternative action can be built into the action plan or action taken prior to commencement.

 iv. Each task should relate to the company's overall problem or opportunity objective.

 v. The format of the action plan depends very much on the nature and needs of the company and can be modified to suit the situation.

Diagram: 04. The Action Planning Model

Consider the following action plan.

By using this action plan model as a template you can develop an action plan to achieve the problem/opportunity objective identified; make sure you break down the overall objective into simple specific tasks or action steps. Place each of these tasks into the action plan in sequential date order and fill out the fields across the form.

The Action Planning model is a simple three step process, as follows:-

 1. **Headline Information**

  *To detail a description of the action plan.

 2. **Task Information**

  *The allocation of tasks/time/ resources and responsibilities.

 3. **Monitoring Progress and Completion Information**

  *The evaluation of the action plan and the end result.

All three steps can be compiled onto one form on completion.

ACTION PLANNING MODEL

1. Headline Information

(A.)	**Compiled by:** **Date:**
(B.)	**Description of the problem/opportunity:** [enter a brief description of the problem/ opportunity?]
(C.)	**Aim / Outcome of the Action Plan:** [enter the overall aim or outcome of the problem or opportunity?] **e.g.** Cost Savings, Productivity improvement, Increase market share, Performance improvement, Return on Investment etc.
(D.)	**Barriers or limitations:** [enter: What barriers, limitations or challenges are anticipated and How these barriers or limitations and challenges will be or have been overcome and What the review dates are to ensure the barrier/s and or limitations do not reoccur?]
(E.)	**Overall Action Plan Start Date:** [enter the target date the plan commences?]
(F.)	**Overall Action Plan End Date:** [enter the target date the plan finishes?]
(G.)	**Overall Critical completion date:** [enter the deadline date?]
(H.)	**Communication / reporting structure:** [enter how /when and to whom the action plan will be communicated?]

2. Task Information

Task No.	Column (1)	Column (2)	Column (3)	Column (4)	Column (5)	Column (6)	Column (7)
	Tasks	Responsible Person	Estimated Start & End Date	Resources [The 5xMs]	Additional Resources [internal/ external]	Date the Task is Completed	Comments on the Task Result
#1.	[enter task to be carried out]	[enter responsible person]	[enter estimated start & end date]	[enter resources required] *Personnel? *Funding? *Equipment? *Procedure? *Materials?	[enter additional resources required from internal or external sources]	[enter the actual date of completion]	[enter the comments on the Result on completion of the task]
#2.	[enter task to be carried out]	[enter responsible person]	[enter estimated start & end date]	[enter resources required] *Personnel? *Funding? *Equipment? *Procedure? *Materials?	[enter additional resources required from internal or external sources]	[enter the actual date of completion]	[enter the comments on the Result on completion of the task]

3. Monitoring Progress and Completion Information		
I.	**Evaluation:** [Enter the quantifiable measures that will determine if the overall objective has been accomplished and successful here].	
J.	**Monitoring & Feedback on Progress** [Enter the progress towards the overall aim of the problem or opportunity in quantifiable and measurable terms: Cost Savings, Productivity improvement, Increase market share, Performance improvement, Return on Investment etc.]	**On Progress** [Enter the progress here]
K.	**On completion of the action Plan – Was the objective accomplished?** [Enter your evaluation regarding completion of the Overall Objective of the Action Plan as a percentage of the Original Objective.] [Enter the overall outcome / or next step]	**On Completion** [Enter your evaluation here]

Notes to the Action Plan:

1.0 Headline Information

(A.) **Compiled by and Date**: Enter the name of the originator of the action plan and commencement date.

(B.) **Description of the problem/opportunity**: Enter a brief description of the problem or opportunity?

(C.) **Aim / Outcome of the Action Plan**: Enter the overall aim or outcome of the problem or opportunity? For example: Cost Savings, Productivity improvement, Increase market share, Performance improvement, Return on Investment etc.

(D.) **Barriers or limitations**: Enter: What barriers, limitations or challenges are anticipated and how these barriers or limitations and challenges will be or have been overcome and what the review dates are to ensure the barrier/s and or limitations do not reoccur?

(E.) **Overall Action Plan Start Date**: Enter the target date the plan commences.

(F.) **Overall Action Plan End Date**: Enter the target date the plan finishes.

(G.) **Overall Critical completion date**: Enter the deadline date.

(H.) **Communication / reporting structure**: Enter how /when and to whom the action plan will be communicated?

2.0 Task Information

1. **Task No:** Firstly, give each task an Identifying number #1. #2. #3. etc.etc.

2. **Column (1) Tasks:** Identify specifically what will be done to take each task to completion and enter task to be carried out.

3. **Column (2) Responsible Person:** Enter the name of the Person Responsible or team leader responsible for each task.

4. **Column (3) Estimated Start & End Date:** Enter the 'Estimated' Start and End Date for each task and build in some flexibility, if possible.

5. **Column (4) Resources – 5xMs:** Consider and allocate resources in terms of the '5 Ms', required to complete each task.
   - 5.1 **MEN:** Personnel
   - 5.2 **MONEY:** Cost / Funding
   - 5.3 **MACHINES:** Equipment
   - 5.4 **METHODS:** Procedure
   - 5.5 **MATERIALS:** Raw and other materials

6. **Column (5) Additional Resources:** [internal/external] Detail the additional support resources, (who/what!). Additional resources that the responsible person would require to complete the task/s and where these internal or external sources will come from.

7. **Column (6) Date the Task is Completed:** Enter the 'actual' date the Person Responsible (or team leader) completes the task.

8. **Column (7) Comments on the Task Result:** On completion of a task – ask, what will the task accomplish towards the overall objective? Is it on time? Are there any delays? Is this a movable date or critical?

On completion and allocation of all resources and time frames, the action plan is now ready for implementation.

3.0 Monitoring Progress and Completion Information

The action plan provides a means to monitor progress and give feedback to management and personnel. And at completion, the action plan provides a means of evaluating the extent of accomplishment and success of the overall objective.

(I.) **For Monitoring & Feedback on Progress and Evaluation on Completion:**

Enter the quantifiable measures that will determine if the overall objective has been accomplished and successful.

(J.) **Monitoring & Feedback on Progress:**

Enter the progress towards the overall aim of the problem or opportunity in quantifiable and measurable terms, for example: cost savings, productivity improvement, increase market share, performance improvement, return on investment etc.

(K.) **Evaluation of the Action Plan on Completion:**

When the action plan is complete, it is important to evaluate the end result on completion by asking – What position are we in now? - What result/s did we achieve in terms of the Original Problem or Opportunity Objective? Compare the quantifiable measures of the original problem or opportunity objective with the current position and establish if it was accomplished and successful. Then enter your evaluation regarding completion of the Overall Objective of the Action Plan (perhaps as a percentage) of the Original Objective and comment to the overall outcome / or next step.

Quick Tips:

- ❏ *Modify the form as you need; to fit your specific requirements.*
- ❏ *Encourage personnel to get involved in contributing to the solution / decision.*
- ❏ *Make sure you break down the objective into simple, specific action steps.*
- ❏ *Ensure any additional resources / high cost items are budgeted into the plan.*
- ❏ *Keep copies handy for use in meetings for progress reviews and updates.*

Section: 3.0. Developing Systematic Methods and Response Techniques

The benefits of Smart Management's systematic methods and response techniques are to:

- ❏ Produce systematic methods for objective setting and develop automatic response techniques and discussion skills to problems and opportunities.
- ❏ Establish a fundamental process for solving day to day problems.
- ❏ Combine theory and practice for immediate use.
- ❏ Provide a basis for management meetings, discussions and group problem solving techniques.
- ❏ Focus attention towards efficient and effective management decisions.
- ❏ Focus on forward planning.
- ❏ Serve as a guide for the future.
- ❏ Increase or improve your management skills.

Section: 4.0. What are the Rewards?

Being well paid is one of the highest compliments a manager can receive. Even the most highly paid managers at the top of their profession continue to improve their skills. Management knowledge and experience is the prime requirement of most companies, therefore, you hold the key to your own future!

The following chapters have been carefully separated and each contains its own core skills, knowledge and wisdom which you can use immediately in your job and you will be able to address the future with a broader appreciation of the requirements of management.

Remember.........

Management Wisdom

The journey of a thousand miles begins with one step.

*Lao Tzu

You have the power to succeed in the future.... Success is in your hands. .....and whatever your objectives in life we wish you every success!

Chapter 3: Perfect Time Management

The First Rule of Smart Management:
Create focus and organize your life in a sea of
interruptions.

Section: 1.0. Time Management

Time waits for no man....

Time is the one commodity that is in short supply for all of us. This chapter will show you how to manage your time more efficiently and effectively... and make your job much easier.

As a manager, people make great demands on you and your time. Most managers' jobs are characterized by:-

- ❏ High energy levels.
- ❏ Fragmented workload.
- ❏ Lack of resources.
- ❏ Intense activity.
- ❏ Work overload.

If this picture is familiar to you, it is taking you away from your primary management focus. The problem with time is that it cannot be stored, stretched or shrunk; once it has gone – it has gone. And in one year you will have used up 525,600 minutes!

How well do you manage your time?

What can be done to use your time more effectively?

Right now you are using precious time, but it is positive time towards improving the quality of your management environment.

The objective of this chapter, quite simply is to get the most out of your time at work without the stress!

The process is to identify ways of saving time and then implement them in your job - to achieve maximum results in your priority areas.

Remember.........

Management Wisdom

Don't tell me how hard you work. Tell me how much you get done.

*James J. Ling

The whole purpose of managing your job and leisure time is that they must balance. You need to balance the time you spend satisfying the demands of the company and the time taken from your personal life with your family, your hobbies and your relaxation. How can you achieve this?

Firstly, your job must be managed in such a way that you receive the maximum from the time you invest in your work activity. Therefore, you will look at ways of maximizing your investment in time, particularly on those tasks crucial to the success of your job.

Where do you start?

Start by completing the following self assessment of your current situation: -

Self Assessment: - What helps you and what hinders you.

Purpose: The following will help you to focus on how you spend your time and why you spend your time on certain issues, and what you spend your time on. This will help you to clarify what helps you in your job and what hinders you.

What Helps and What Hinders.

Answer Yes or No to the following statements.

1. My work objectives set by the company are clear to me.
2. I know what standards I have to achieve for the company.
3. I concentrate on work tasks which bring results for the company.
4. I determine how I spend my time.
5. I get regular feedback to avoid potential problems.
6. I do not spend most of my time in crisis management.
7. I plan tasks well in advance.
8. I always handle important issues on time.
9. I do not forget to carry out assigned tasks.
10. I delegate my work regularly.
11. My personnel share my work load.
12. I have a training system in place for my personnel
13. I do not take work home.
14. I balance my time between work and leisure.

If the answer to these statements is **yes**, well done!

If the answer to any of these statements is **no**, then ask or find out what is causing the problem and hindering you and work towards rectifying the situation.

Important Note:
Your primary consideration is to be **absolutely sure about the objectives, standards** and **tasks** of your job.

Section: 1.1.Barriers to Time Management
Are you Reactive or Proactive?

- ❏ Do you get side tracked due to phone calls, clients, your manager and personnel interruptions or procrastinate when a crisis is pending?
- ❏ Do you plan your day's activities and do you stay on track? If not, then it's time to do something about it.

Remember.........

Management Wisdom

Whatever you set out to do, something else must be done first.

*Murphy's Law

You are now on your way to take care of time constraints in your job; to practice and to achieve, to filter out interruptions and use your time more effectively. You have identified areas you needed to look at. Now you must consider your objectives and look at those areas which may present obstacles to successful completion in your major result areas.

Your Major Result Areas

Our objective here is to identify those aspects of your job, which you should be focusing on to produce maximum results both for the company and for yourself.

First: **Where are your major result areas of your job?**

Now Consider: Primarily, what must you achieve in your job?

What major tasks must you undertake?

What tasks and results are you accountable for?

Secondly: **Prioritize your major result areas in order of importance.**

Now Consider: What must you do that will make the greatest impact on your major result areas?

Who will measure your effectiveness?

How will they do it?

Thirdly: **What must you do and what can you leave?**

Next Consider: What must you do?

What can you leave without an impact on the end result?

You are now far ahead of most managers who have never done this.

Self Assessment: – The Barriers

Now look at some of the barriers which stop you from attaining your important objectives. In deciding what is stopping you from concentrating on your major result areas, the following will help you to focus on what helps you in your job and what hinders you.

The Problem Barriers

Take a look at some of problem barriers and answer yes or no to these statements: -

1. I have enough time during the day for planning.
2. My time is not being taken up by others.
3. I don't have too much urgent work on my desk.
4. I have trained personnel.
5. I have enough support personnel.
6. I am aware of unscheduled changes inside the company.
7. There are no major personnel clashes or friction.
8. I take care of any minor issues.
9. I handle tight deadlines and schedules systematically.

If the answer to these statements is yes, well done!

If the answer to any of these statements is no, take note of what is causing the problem, and work towards rectifying the situation.

You have seen what your major result areas are and where your focus should be and you have also seen what barriers stand in your way.

Remember your objective; you want to save time so that you can get **maximum results** in your **major result areas**.

You are now in a position to look at the area of SAVING TIME in order to focus on your major result areas.

Section: 1.2. How can You Manufacture Time

Previously, you looked at the way you use your time and then identified what you should be spending your time on and the barriers to your major result areas. Now you need to look at how to 'Save Time'.

The Two Ways of Saving Time

There are only two ways of saving time. The systematic methods and response for saving time are either do less work or work more effectively as follows: -

Either Do Less Work – or – Work More Effectively	

1. Do Less Work
 This means you have to do two things
 	
    1.1 Say No
    1.2 Delegate
	2. Work More Effectively
	 This means you have to do three things
	
	    2.1 Set Priorities
	    2.2 Filter out Interruptions
	    2.3 -Develop a Paper
	         Flow System

Do Less Work
Saying – "No"

Let's talk about the first action of **Do Less Work** and saying **"No"**.

Some managers have difficulty saying "no" to added responsibilities and tasks. This may be because of ego, appearances, self-image, pride, ambition, or even as a courtesy, nevertheless the result is the same; the person may be perceived as effective because they appear to be time pressured and loaded with work and the problems of the company. However, most effective managers know this is absolute nonsense!

Saying "No" Politely, but Firmly

It takes a professional and assertive manager; a manager aware of the result areas and job priorities, says "no" politely but firmly to avoid lower priority tasks and responsibilities, for example, you would use your high priority jobs to explain why you cannot assist with the lower priority work.

The result of not saying "no" often enough is that you acquire tasks which are secondary to you making a success of the major result areas of your job for the company. And you may also get the reputation for accepting any low priority task that has to be assigned. The effect is obvious – your time on your major result areas gets eroded.

So what can you do about it? Consider a situation in your current work-load, where you do not want to assume a task or a responsibility. Write down **what** you would say and **how** you would explain that this time would be taken away from your priorities.

Start practicing immediately and remember saying "**No**" politely, but firmly, is the quickest way of manufacturing time!

You have covered a way of Doing Less Work, by ensuring that your time is not eroded by having low priority tasks passed to you. You have planned how to say "no" to such situations and you should practice saying "no" regularly.

Consider, how much time you can save – as a result?

Delegating

You now look at another way of **Doing Less Work** and **Delegating**.

As you move up in your company so you must delegate more.

It is important to note that 'delegation is not abdication', you can delegate the authority for the task BUT the responsibility remains with you!

A manager's skills can be measured by the level of success achieved in effectively delegating tasks. The professional manager recognizes the need to delegate, carefully considers **what** can be delegated, **to whom**, by **what completion dates** and introduces a monitoring, feedback and control system.

The benefits of delegation are: -

1. The people working for you are empowered to do better and are motivated by your trust in them to carry out the responsibility.
2. Their jobs are enriched and empowered.
3. Delegation will influence you to improve your planning and management skills.

Self Assessment:

You now need to check your current level of delegation, take a look at some of these problems which occur when a manager is not delegating enough: -

---

Potential Delegation Problems

Answer the following statements with Yes, No or Not Sure.

1. I don't take work home regularly.
2. I don't work through the weekends.
3. I don't have many jobs/tasks incomplete.
4. My personnel are adequately trained.
5. My personnel have good work experience.
6. My personnel complete tasks well.
7. My personnel could handle my tasks.
8. I don't work harder than my personnel.
9. I spend time on planning and controlling.
10. I don't miss deadlines.

If the answer to any of these statements is yes, well done!
If the answer to any of these statements is no, take note and work on it.
If the answer to any of these statements not sure, then find out.

Almost every manager under delegates, so if you are not satisfied with your delegation don't worry. Plan to delegate at least one task or responsibility of your workload – and do it now!

Here's how: -
Describe the item to be delegated and why you are delegating it and what has to be achieved. Then detail how and what has to be done, describe the limits of authority for the delegate and the support resources available to the delegate. Record the date when it is to be completed and the progress reports required, also detail possible problems or obstacles that might materialize and the means by which the delegate is to monitor and report them back to you. Then define the follow up procedure for the completed task/s, to compare where you wanted to be with the result achieved.

Section: 1.3. The Key to Focus
You have looked at Time Management from the point of view of Doing Less Work by saying 'No' and 'Delegating'.

Set Priorities

Now you need to look at saving time by **Setting Priorities** to **Work More Efficiently and Effectively**

You have set your major result areas in your job. And you have listed barriers to the achievement of these major result areas.

A Word about Pareto's 80 – 20 rule

It can be reasonably assumed that 80 percent of your major result areas will be accomplished in 20 percent of your time. To manage your job effectively therefore, you must spend **at least** 20 percent of your time working directly on those areas. If on the other hand, you are spending more than 80 percent of your time handling routine activities, then you can be considered a **reactive** manager, you are therefore more likely to be fire fighting than managing.

Efficient and Effective

The words 'efficient' and 'effective' are often used in management. What do they mean and how do they differ? Simply put, a manager who deals promptly with every task; returns calls promptly, completes the projects on time is **efficient**. However, the **effective** manager also completes day to day activities promptly; but, the focus here is on those actions which produce results that may have an impact on the company in the medium to long-term. The effective manager is therefore ensuring that critical and sometimes strategic results are achieved for the company.

Setting priorities

Effective managers focus on ensuring attainment of major result areas by being proactive in setting priorities and by allocating **at least 20 percent** of available time on major result areas.

Four Focus Areas

Your workload can be placed into four focus areas:

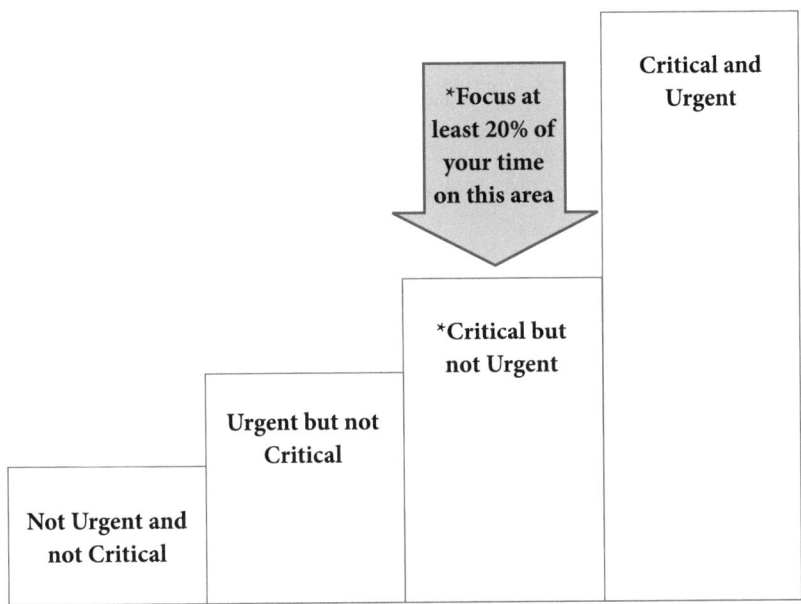

The most important area is *Critical but not Urgent.

You have to focus on those critical issues so that they don't become urgent and suddenly become a high priority, and erode your time. If you are able to achieve this, then you will become a **proactive** manager rather than a **reactive** manager, **and manage your own performance.**

Now, assess your major result areas in terms of how **urgent and critical** they are according to what you have read so far.

Detail **how** you will spend **at least 20 percent of your time** on those areas and **when** you will do this. Consider **who else** will be delegated to support you when you do not have the time available and **how** you will monitor your major results areas to compare actual against planned. This will ensure you are focusing on the right areas and getting control of critical but not urgent issues first.

Remember.........

Management Wisdom

There's never time to do it right, but there's always time to do it over!

*Meskimen's Law:

By setting these priorities some of the problem barriers you listed will be overcome.

Filter out Interruptions

The second way of **Working more Efficiently and Effectively** is that of **Filtering out Interruptions**.

How much of your work time is your own and under your control to determine what needs to be done and then to do it within the time frame you have planned?

As a manager, you have to be freely available. Some managers call this having an **open door** policy.

However, an **ever open door** for you to be interrupted at any time is not conducive to efficient and effective management!

Quick Tip: *a misused open door policy can lead to many wasted hours.*

The two main sources of interruption are people and the phone.

Personnel should not be encouraged to pop in to give you updates and progress reports unless they are scheduled meetings. And you should not allow the phone to interrupt your concentration. Your time would be well spent in briefing your secretary or assistant on filtering or fielding your calls to ensure that you are not interrupted by unnecessary and untimely calls, whilst leaving you accessible to the people who need to get in touch with you.

The skill of handling interruptions is that of 'filtering' them, so that you are only interrupted when it is convenient or you have planned for the interruption. The aim is to filter out the minor issues and focus on important or urgent matters which contribute to your major result areas.

If you have an Open Door Policy – Define it to your personnel

You can now turn your attention to becoming more effective. Detail what you intend to implement, for example, defining your open door policy with those who work for you, to explain that your open door policy is still open – but perhaps more scheduled.

Keep a Daily Time Log for one week – it will surprise you

How many times a day are you being interrupted, ten, twenty times? Test this, by keeping **a daily time log for one week and record EVERY MINUTE** of your activities, the phone calls and visitors you have, and the 'time' taken by each activity. Also, ensure that you objectively record your own 'none productive' time.

Because of the detail required for this exercise, break your time into fifteen-minute sections and ensure you write in the log at the end of each activity – **do not wait or guess it or do it later** – it will most certainly be wrong.

You will be surprised, if not shocked by the result particularly 'none productive' time but you will now know 'where' your time is going.

The Phone - Brief your secretary

Your secretary or assistant should be briefed to take all incoming calls and filter them.

- ❏ Plan how you will do this by considering your objectives and describe **how** they will be stated, **when** and **to whom**.
- ❏ Make a **what if** list of the potential problems that may arise.
- ❏ Determine a monthly review date to compare if you have achieved your objective.

Develop a Paper Flow System

Establishing an efficient paper flow and email system to manage your paperwork and emails is essential to working more efficiently and effectively.

Information overload is here. You can get copies of everything almost instantaneously, and you usually do even when you do not want them. You are wading through reams of emails, reports, reviews, circulars, memos, requests, articles, magazines and junk mail!

How can you manage this problem?

Internal paperwork and particularly emails have become one of the most used or perhaps the most abused means of communication in the business environment. Brief your secretary or assistant on fielding and acknowledging paper and email correspondence for you. So that you do not spend unwarranted amounts of time ploughing through reams of not urgent and not critical emails and paperwork.

Alternatively allocate yourself a set time of day to review and answer your emails to address critical but not urgent issues. You need to focus on those critical issues so that they don't become urgent and suddenly become a high priority and erode your time.

You can manage the problem by using some of the following suggestions: -

Firstly, there are only three categories of incoming e-mails and paperwork, which you have to address, these are:-

1. **Action Immediately** – Take the appropriate action immediately and dispense with the matter right away.

2. **Action Pending** – Take action immediately to obtain more information towards closure and then place in a pending file.

3. **Rubbish** – Read the item, decide on its relevance, and then physically throw it into the waste paper bin, or delete it –but **do not pass it on or file it!**

Now that you are aware that all paper and emails fall into **only one** of the above, you must classify each item and handle each item **only once!**

Note:

1. **Action Immediately** – Primarily for your action.

2. **Action Pending** – Should be the exception, rather than the rule and actioned by your secretary or a member of your personnel, if this is pending longer that one month it should be reviewed for disposal by your secretary or a member of your personnel.

3. **Rubbish** – For your secretary, an assistant or a member of your personnel who should throw it in the waste paper bin.

Plan with your secretary or a member of your personnel – your new classification for incoming paper and e-mails and ask them to classify each incoming item for you as follows:-

1. Action Immediately.

2. Action Pending.

3. Rubbish.

Go through your current workload and decide **how, what and why** you are classifying the e-mails and paper, explain to your secretary or a member of your personnel **how** you or they must action the decision, **when** and to **whom**.

A Word about Deadlines

Your secretary or assistant should keep a duplicate diary either in hardcopy or electronic record of important deadlines and meetings to remind you of their approach. You should plan this implementation with your secretary or a member of your personnel in your work environment – now!

Section: 1.4. Summary Review: Time Management

Excellent! It is time for a quick review.

You started by revisiting your objectives, standards and tasks and detailing your priorities and you listed your major result areas. You went on and considered several barriers to their achievement.

Then you addressed the systematic methods and response techniques to 'save' time by either doing less work or working more effectively. On doing less work you can appreciate the value of saying "No", for good reason, politely but firmly. You looked at delegation and saw that it held benefits both for personnel and yourself. You looked at the need for priority lists; and saw how urgent and important items differed in the attention they needed, and how; 'Critical but not Urgent' items should be handled before they become 'Critical and Urgent.' You looked at how to filter out interruptions from people and the phone. Lastly, you saw the need to develop a paper-flow system by classifying all e-mail and paper items into three categories.

You have assessed the problem barriers to your achievement in your major result areas and those items you feel could be eliminated. For those which have not already been removed, consider **how** you will remove the barrier, by **when** and **who** will be involved.

Also, look at a follow-up on the corrective actions you have undertaken every three to six months; to review your time management and ensure you are maintaining the improvement.

And use the Question Model of Management to assist you with Time Management by asking the following questions: -

1.   **Why** do I need to take action in a particular area?
2.   **What** objectives, action plan, shall I set?
3.   **Who** will be involved?
4.   **When** are my objectives and action plan dates?
5.   **How** are my objectives and action to happen?
6.   **What if** a problem develops, what will I do?
7.   **Where** should my objectives and action plan take me?

Section: 1.5. Quick Guide to Effective Time Management

The following will act as a quick guide to effective time management to help you stay on track prior to your next meeting or deadline. It is always worthwhile to pause and consider how you are managing your time. Sometimes you may get side tracked, but don't worry, this happens to all managers at some time or another. The objective therefore, is to prevent it from happening to you.

A Quick Guide to Effective Time Management:

1. I have identified my result areas.
2. I know what standards are required.
3. I know what time frames are required.
4. I know my tasks and responsibilities.
5. I know my authority levels.
6. Currently, my tasks are for major result areas.
7. My personnel are as busy as I am.
8. My personnel are well trained.
9. I am handling issues on time.
10. I am saying "No" politely but firmly.
11. I am delegating well.
12. I am not being interrupted too often.
13. I have a daily priority list and stick to it.
14. I am spending time on your priorities.
15. My paper-flow system is working.
16. I balance my time well between work, leisure and family activities.

Remember.........

Management Wisdom

Drive thy business, let not that it drives thee.

*Benjamin Franklin

It's your time and having completed this chapter, you are now ready to manage it!

Chapter 4: Discussion Skills to Avoid Misunderstanding

The Second Rule of Smart Management: Recognize and understand what makes certain discussions successful and which lead to misunderstanding and conflict.

Section: 1.0. Discussion to Avoid Misunderstanding and Conflict

These sections will show you how to plan your discussions to avoid misunderstanding and conflict.

Remember........

> ## Management Wisdom
>
> *Leadership and communication are inseparable.*
> *You can't have one without the other.*
>
> ***Claude I. Taylor**

You are now covering one of the most important aspects of a manager's job.

Simply put, one of the jobs of a manager is to get things done with and through people and company resources; therefore a major part of a manager's time is spent interacting with people.

Different management jobs require different levels of interaction; although any managerial interaction with personnel, customers, colleagues and suppliers should be of a high quality.

Consider for a moment, what types and the number of discussions you have with customers, your colleagues, your personnel and your suppliers every day during a normal working week and make a note of them.

All interaction is learned as you grow; from childhood through school, college, university etc. Most people are not taught how to interact with people in business critical situations and as a result, in many instances this may lead to misunderstanding and conflict. However, there are basic systematic methods and response techniques which can guide your thoughts in this area.

A Word on Participative versus the Autocratic Style of Management
Participative management is not new, nevertheless it does work therefore the area you shall cover next will be based upon interactive skills using a participative management approach.

There are many seminars available on participative management theory; however our focus will be on its application. Many managers profess to practice participative management, but often talk to the people who work for them using a very much autocratic approach.

Participative management works, your objective is to put participative management at the forefront of your management style by using: -

1. The basic discussion outline.
2. Discussion skills.
3. A planning method.
4. A way in which to review discussions.
5. The quick guide for future reference.

Firstly, establish the objective for the discussion.

Section: 2.0. Discussion Outline

In the pursuit of improving your interactive skills, the following discussion outline will help guide you from an autocratic style of management and close the gap towards a participative approach to management.

The discussion outline consists of:-

1. **Set your Objective**

2. **Develop the discussion opening**

3. **Clarify any areas of concern**

4. **Listing alternative solutions**

5. **Move to agreeing a solution**

6. **Minimize the risk of failure**

7. **Plan the implementation**

Section: 2.1. Set Your Objectives

For managers the word problem, issue or opportunity are interchangeable to describe the reason for the discussion which necessitates two or more people to collaborate and find agreement on what needs to be done. A quality solution or decision is therefore the objective of this discussion.

With any discussion you need to set your objectives or the end result you anticipate for your discussion.

Discussions could be for any of the following purposes: -

- ❏ Setting Objectives
- ❏ Coaching
- ❏ Problem Solving
- ❏ Buying
- ❏ Selling
- ❏ Appraisal
- ❏ Discipline
- ❏ Etc.

Most discussions have at least one objective in common i.e. shared understanding and clarifying a situation, therefore use the Question Model as a preliminary guide to the discussion: -

Why are you having the discussion?

What is the core purpose of the discussion?

When will the discussion take place?

Who will you be talking to?

How will you get to a best solution?

What if the other party is not in agreement?

Where to in the future, do you wish the results of the solution to be measured?

An objective is specific and stated in terms of the desired outcome of the discussion. Let's look at some examples of discussion objectives.

The objective for your discussion with one of your personnel could be to: -

1. Ensure and check that you both have the same understanding of the cause and effect of a problem.

2. Provide at least two possible solutions that will meet specific criteria.

3. Ensure that your personnel share your understanding of the basic concepts of a new business procedure or introduction.

Try writing an objective for a discussion you are about to have. Ensure that your objective is **quantifiable** and **measurable** and describes **who** you will have the discussion with, **what** you need to share understanding on, and **where** this understanding must lead to and by **when**.

Section: 2.2. Develop the Discussion Opening

Any discussion needs an introduction or an opening to explain the purpose of the discussion, to set the climate and to determine the parameters by which the success of the discussion will be measured, for example **what** was agreed, by **whom** and by **when**?

The introduction should be brief and highlight your objective in a direct and professional manner.

However, for the more potentially volatile discussions you would open perhaps more diplomatically. For example: -

❏ Stressing the assistance required from of the other party to help to overcome the problem.

❏ The current situation in general terms and the reason for the discussion is necessary.

Remember.........
The introduction also sets the climate for commitment to the discussion itself. It should ideally motivate the other party or parties and for this to happen your introduction should be made with empathy, warmth and a genuine concern for the other person's feelings which will help in gaining assistance. Be careful of an insincere comment as it is normally recognized by most people before the statement is finished.

Put yourself in the other person's shoes, for example, think of the feelings of a person who knows they are required to solve a difficult problem or must negotiate the best deal for the company or in for a disciplinary reprimand. The chances are that the other person is feeling some tension so relate to that tension; show that you understand and you care by showing some degree of empathy. This will certainly get you the cooperation and motivation you require for a successful discussion.

Your introduction should reflect that you care about your company, your department's output and the fulfillment of the objectives of your personnel. Your introduction should also show that you sincerely appreciate the contribution of the other party.

Apart from clarifying the purpose – objectives and setting the tone for the discussion; the introduction could also give a brief background, the current status and the reason why the discussion has become necessary.

From your current workload, plan an introduction for one of your next meetings or discussions using the following: -
- ❏ Purpose.
- ❏ Background.
- ❏ Current status.
- ❏ Recommendations or Proposed solution.

Also note separately: -
- ❏ Who you are talking to?
- ❏ What you believe their feelings towards the discussion will be?
- ❏ How will you acknowledge these feelings?
- ❏ Write the end result you expect.

Section: 2.3. Clarifying Areas of Concern

The next step in the discussion outline brings you into the area of clarifying areas of concern. Gathering usable and valid information is of primary concern, in order to indentify and define the root cause. So this part of the discussion refers to covering the basic issues and any areas of concern with the information that has been gathered, organized and supplied by those directly involved.

This also involves getting the facts, figures, motivations and opinions of the parties to the discussion.

In participative companies there is a very positive approach to bottom up information and the contribution and in this regard the quality and content can be invaluable. This method ensures the identification of the cause of a specific problem and the formulation of good solutions.

It involves the formation of a genuine joint problem solving approach by the parties. The information from this approach has its true value in clarifying grey areas which the manager may not have direct access to, other than through a collaborative discussion.

Clarifying areas seeks to answer the questions **who, what, where, when, and how much?** And in this way it defines perceptions and assumptions from both sides.

It looks at the 'actual' versus the 'desired' result and tries to define the reason for any differences. Clarification is therefore needed, to get to the root cause of the problem.

Section: 2.4. Listing Alternative Solutions
As in the classical problem solving / decision-making models discussed earlier you now move into the area of listing alternative solutions.

For more effective thinking you need to develop different points of view and many ideas.

Remember.........

Management Wisdom

Nothing is more dangerous than an idea, when it is the only one you have.

*Emile Chartier

In the clarification stage you organized and gathered information and during the discussion a lot of evaluation is done in order to come up with the real issues or concerns.

Impact on personnel

It is important to consider the implications of change and the impact of a problem on personnel. When implementing a change which affects personnel, it is important to consider the quality of the decision if you do not have sufficient information defer the discussion and decision until you have the appropriate information to move forward with a reasonable level of quality.

Your ultimate purpose is to gather sufficient usable and valid information, therefore you will reach a point where you will be able to consider: -

1. The issues – refined to a few clearly defined ones.
2. A List of probable solutions and corrective actions.

With information and solutions volunteered from your personnel in a participative and collaborative way; you may also consider suggestions from other parties, colleagues and experts in their field when appropriate.

Information and suggestions presented could be used to solve the problem or identify an opportunity.

Remember: As the manager, you will be tested on your ability to check the viability of the solutions proposed by your personnel and other parties, this is your responsibility.

The professional manager looks for as many alternative suggestions/solutions from the other parties as possible irrespective of viability, at this stage. This provides many solutions and flexibility, when determining and agreeing a final solution.

Once you have listed all the possible solutions, each one should be evaluated; the pros and cons of each should be listed. And sometimes the best solution is often a combination of one or more alternatives.

These are some of the questions that the professional manager will ask: -
- ❏ Will it solve the problem?
- ❏ Will there be any negative effects?
- ❏ What will it cost?
- ❏ Who will be against it?

Next, we cover agreeing the best solution.

Section: 2.5. Move to Agreeing a Solution
Agreeing to a solution is one of the main objectives of any discussion.

To move forward both and/or all parties should agree on a solution which they believe, will solve the problem.

There may be many issues during the discussion surrounding the agreement on the best solution. Any obstacles to agreeing to a particular solution can be tested by asking questions.

Here are a few examples of fundamental questions: -
- ❏ What are the pros and cons of the proposed solution?
- ❏ Will the cost / risk justify the results?
- ❏ Are there practical limitations to the solution, money, manpower, methods, materials etc?
- ❏ Does the solution satisfy the objective criteria in the longer term?
- ❏ Does the solution support the company's business values?
- ❏ Do you have the authority to implement the decision, or do you have to seek authority?
- ❏ Is there any impact on personnel?
- ❏ Is there anyone or anything that can reduce success of the solution?
- ❏ Have you checked all the facts available to you - at this time?

The purpose of working through the questions is to arrive at an actionable decision which is acceptable, workable and a low cost and/or low risk solution. Through these questions you may no doubt identify problem areas and unacceptable risks. These problem areas and unacceptable risks may change or modify the solution or cause you to take some other action to minimize the risks and overcome the obstacles.

Agreement is essential in participative collaboration, the initiative coming from the other person or the other parties are important to the solution and commitment to the solution. If you are aware of this during the discussion and ensured the involvement of the other party at each step, you should have no problem at moving towards agreement.

Section: 2.6. Minimize the Risk of Failure

If there is no agreement from the other party, you must go back to the selection of alternative solutions and decide on a best solution to which both parties agree. This may seem elaborate, but the risk of going ahead without agreement and cooperation is a greater risk.

As the discussion process unfolds summarize the discussion and clarify that you have agreement; this provides the opportunity to ask about any reservations or concerns and makes it possible for you to clear them during the agreeing process. In this way you are reaffirming the other party's agreement to a particular solution.

Here are some of the safeguard questions from the Question Model you need to have in mind during your discussions for agreement on a best solution.

1. **Why** are you having the discussion?
2. **What** is the purpose of the discussion?
3. **When** will the discussion take place?
4. **Who** will you be talking to?
5. **How** will you get to a best solution?
6. **What** if the other party is not in agreement?
7. **Where (to)** in the future, do you wish the results of the solution to be measured?

Section: 2.7. Plan the Implementation

The final step of the discussion outline; most discussions on a work-related issue should end up in some form of action and the following from the Question model can be used as the outline for planning implementation: -

❏ **Why** are you taking this action? – State the problem.

❏ **What** is the purpose of the solution?

❏ **When** will it commence?

❏ **Who** will be involved to implement, support, monitor?

❏ **How** will the solution be managed?

❏ **What** if a problem develops?

❏ **Where to** in the future, do you wish the results of the solution to be measured for success or failure?

Section: 3.0. The Discussion Outline Summary

Let's summarize what you have covered so far in the discussion outline.

1. **Objective of the discussion**

   1.1 As the manager, you have to set the objective by which you may measure the success of the discussion and where you want to be.

2. **Introduction**

   2.1 Your introduction explains the reason for the discussion, sets the background and climate for the discussion.

3. **Clarify areas of Concern**

   3.1 By questioning you clarify the areas of concern; obtain facts, figures, opinions and feelings which help you to define the extent of a problem or opportunity.

4. **Listing alternative Solutions**

   4.1 Listing many alternative solutions from both sides gives you flexibility and ensures keeping the other party motivated. Each solution should then be checked against the original objective and the potential risks.

5. **Agree on a best solution**

   5.1 Agreement on the most suitable solution involves checking with the other party, and checking the solution against the objective.

6. **Minimize the risks**

   6.1 This is a precautionary step; once you have decided on a solution, action needs to be taken to minimize the risk of failure.

7. **Planning implementation**

   7.1 The final step of the discussion outline; most discussions on a work-related issue should end up in some form of action and the following from the Question model can be used as the outline for planning implementation.

Section: 4.0. Response Techniques and Discussion Skills

In business, a manager's job is to get things done through other people; therefore the majority of a manager's time is spent interacting with others, which is an ongoing process.

Response techniques encompass; listening, questioning, giving support, sharing feelings, organizing and guiding, summarizing, handling disagreement, balancing control and preventing misunderstandings. The following sections are designed to help you perfect your existing response techniques and discussion skills.

A word about the quality of interaction and trust: Different management jobs require different levels of interaction; however, all managerial interactions with personnel, customers, colleagues and suppliers should be of the highest quality and trust between the parties involved.

Quick Tip: It is important for you to develop your stature through integrity and trust not only throughout these types of discussions, but as an ongoing philosophy. Remember........ Trust can be as fragile as a soap bubble; once it has burst it cannot be rebuilt!

Despite the move towards the electronic office and the e-mail system, people still need discussion and depend on a certain amount of interaction with their managers, therefore and the need for skilful discussion is greater than ever.

You will always need to: -

- ❏ Improve communication channels to motivate people.
- ❏ Help employees relate their objectives to the company's objectives.
- ❏ Encourage personnel to work more efficiently and effectively and to care about what they do.
- ❏ Talk with employees about their work, methods, systems and problems.

Motivation
What is motivation?

It is important for you to realize that discussion forms an essential part of motivation: motivation is getting people to want to do what you would like them to do - willingly.

How do you improve it?

❏ Having a manager who is interested in the progress of personnel; a manager who listens to ideas and helps personnel to find ideas and solutions to problems.

What destroys it?

❏ Managers, who are always too busy, only discuss matters quickly and superficially showing limited interest and not really listening.

❏ 'Superman Syndrome' or managers; who at the slightest indication of a problem criticize those involved and take over the task directing personnel at an operational level, without cognizance of any input from the personnel involved.

Section: 4.1. Listening

A manager must become proficient in the art of communication.

The following will provide you with some thoughts on how to perfect this art: - The most basic essential rule is: **Learn how to listen carefully!**

Remember.........

Management Wisdom

I like to listen, I have learned a great deal from listening carefully.
Most people never listen.

*Ernest Hemingway

Firstly, develop a clear understanding that what you stand for - is worthwhile. Belief in yourself and your values will give you the confidence to become a good listener. And listening is the first and most important skill of communication.

Good listeners – listen, and they show they are listening.

The Do's

Here is your guide to good listening: -

❏ Do prevent outside interruptions.

❏ Do look at the speaker.

❏ Do maintain eye contact.

❏ Do nod approval.

❏ Do encourage the speaker to talk freely, without interruption.

❏ Do make notes.

❏ Do encourage the speaker by your positive body language.

❏ Do ask appropriate questions.

❏ Do stick to the subject.

❏ Do summarize what the speaker has said, when they have finished, to ensure you understand.

The Don'ts

There are many things that actually prevent you from listening or make listening difficult; you should avoid the following: -

❏ Don't leave your telephone or cell phone on.

❏ Don't take a call whilst listening to someone, switch it off!

❏ Don't trying to do two things at once – talking on the phone / talking to another person.

❏ Don't interrupt.

❏ Don't react instinctively or negatively.

❏ Don't exhibit poor concentration or lack of interest.

❏ Don't exhibit poor posture or negative body language.

❏ Don't prejudge ideas.

❏ Don't put up with external interruptions and outside noise.

❏ Don't react negatively to the way the other person acts or looks.

Remember: when you are listening, how will the other person know you are listening? Good listening requires practice and an awareness of the speaker's objective, content and conclusion and more practice.

Quick Tip: *listening carefully is a positive sign of respect.*

Section: 4.2. Questioning

Questioning and good listening are of primary importance. Without the assistance and support of your personnel and other parties, you will never be in a position to make good decisions.

The purpose of questioning is to find the facts that help you define the problem in order to find the right solutions. And in this process you will be utilizing the knowledge of personnel in a participative, constructive and productive manner.

By empowering your personnel to contribute and take responsibility for seeking problem-solving solutions for the company, you will ensure your personnel remain motivated.

Discover Facts

Firstly, there are the questions which will help you discover the facts in order to define a problem or opportunity. These questions start by using the following Question model: -

- ❏ **Why?**
- ❏ **What?**
- ❏ **When?**
- ❏ **Who?**
- ❏ **How?**
- ❏ **What if?**
- ❏ **Where to?**

Quick Tip*: appropriate questions should make people think and not suggest possible answers.*

With these questions you will define the problem and its parameters. Next you need solutions and for that you need another kind of question, as follows: -

Ask for solutions

These questions start with the following: -

- ❏ **What can you....?**
- ❏ **When can we....?**
- ❏ **How should we....?**
- ❏ **When do you....?**
- ❏ **Can we think of....?**

You want original and unbiased proposals from your personnel, because it gives them ownership of the action plan and encourages commitment.

That's the procedure: -

- ❏ **One set of questions to seek information.**
- ❏ **Another set of questions to seek suggestions.**

Section: 4.3. Giving Support

If you question and listen carefully, you may notice a positive change in the reaction from your personnel.

Do not make the mistake of trying to rush this type of questioning with personnel; take your time to develop your style naturally.

If a participative style of management is relatively new for you, gradually prepare your personnel by encouraging their involvement; your personnel will welcome the knowledge you are sharing with them and the trust which you are showing in them to contribute to the decision making process.

Hold back from telling your personnel what to do with regard to problems, opportunities, decisions and ideas. Start by asking your personnel questions on day to day problems and listen for better quality solutions to problems, opportunities, decisions and ideas. If this is unfamiliar ground for you, have patience and continue asking questions and listening. Give your personnel time to consider the content of what you are asking and encourage them to come back to you with facts and ideas.

Give it time and work on it. And don't forget to give appreciation for any contribution from your personnel, however small it may appear.

To recap........
How can you motivate your personnel to contribute: -

❏ **Listen carefully.**
❏ **Be positive towards the contribution.**
❏ **Probe into the core of what is being said.**
❏ **Make notes and write the information and ideas down.**
❏ **Use the ideas.**
❏ **Don't evaluate the information too soon.**
❏ **Don't criticize the contributions.**

Quick Tip: primarily, support is identified through a manager's behavior and attitude far more than what is said.

People need support to encourage them to keep thinking and coming up with good ideas.

This methodology works, so dispel any preconceived idea that the manager is the 'Yoda of all knowledge' and solely responsible for all experience and skill. Utilize and empower your personnel and through their input from open discussion you will obtain a higher level of quality in your decision-making.

Remember: To support an employee's ideas all you need to do is ask for them, and listen.

Section: 4.4. Sharing Feelings

Providing support in an active verbal manner and in non-verbal signals raises the question, how do you support if you do not agree?

Active support should be given when you agree with the concept proposed. Never the less support should still be given for the contribution. When the idea or solution proposed may not be viable, through budget limitations, company policy etc. there is another type of support; the support for the person's effort, enthusiasm and willingness to contribute.

Supporting skills are used to encourage people to give their best efforts and put their trust in the discussion. For this to happen, you need to get closer to your personnel, by revealing some of your feelings on certain concepts. However, you must avoid statements which could be construed as personally directed at the other party.

In negotiations letting the other party in on how you genuinely feel about certain things is a very effective skill, which can free-up a locked discussion.

When the discussion or negotiation threatens to break down, you may want to offer a comment or response such as: -

- ❏ There appears to be certain amount of tension about this particular subject and this is worrying to me.
- ❏ I am concerned about the apparent lack of trust, in this matter, what do you think?

The purpose here is to create an atmosphere of trust and cooperation and when you share your feelings it encourages the other party back into the discussion. Sharing feelings is important to keep the discussion moving forward in a collaborative way.

Section: 4.5. Organizing and Guiding

As a manager, your role in addition to that of a motivator is to organize and guide the discussion.

To summarize, you have looked at various means of encouraging personnel to contribute to discussions, you have noted the importance of listening
and two types of questions namely looking for facts and seeking solutions
and you have considered the role of supporting and sharing feelings.

Organizing: means to arrange, to plan for, to orchestrate or to coordinate.

Firstly, you need to suggest the meeting, its purpose and the sequence
within the discussion the **why, what, who** and **when**. During the meeting
it is your job to keep the discussion focused.

For example: -

❏ We need to discuss the current problem, could we have
a discussion with '*x, y, and z'* including yourself at
9.00am tomorrow?

❏ I suggest we discuss when the problem first occurred and then
move onto the current status and corrective action.

You can also suggest possible agenda and various solutions to the issues.

If no suggestions are forthcoming from your personnel during the discussion, you may want to start by offering one or several tentative solutions or
modifying, expanding on a proposed solution by your personnel without
taking away the initiative of the contribution.

You should prepare for your discussion by constructing suggestions, which
attempt to organize your discussions under the following headings: -

❏ **Opening the discussion**

❏ **Keeping it on track**

❏ **Closing the discussion**

This suggestion technique will assist you in preplanning and organizing
your discussion in the future.

Section: 4.6. Using a Summary

You can use a summary in three ways, to confirm understanding, to confirm agreement and to defuse a situation.

It is for you to focus the discussion and keep it on track. Effective managers make use of summarizing at key points in the discussion to keep the
discussion organized.

A summary is a brief restatement of what has gone before in the discussion and you need to carefully extract and analyze each event or agreement. Your careful listening and your notes will support your summary.
This helps to: -

❏ Bring together the points of the discussion.

❏ Highlight certain facts.

❏ Describe what has been proposed.

❏ Close off an area of agreement within the discussion.

❏ Close the total discussion.

❏ Confirm agreement by the other party.

Note: A minutes of meeting is also a summary.

The Use of a Summary to Defuse a Situation

If you are having a discussion with one of your personnel on a work problem and have reached a point where you have agreed on several issues and one of the issues that you need to discuss become sensitive or the person becomes defensive or even argumentative. To defuse this emotional situation you could summarize the issues already agreed and then clarify sensitive issue for understanding.

❏ This will bring a positive note of mutual problem solving back into the discussion.

A summary also assists in the implementation of agreements.

Quick Tip: start to think in summary, it will assist you to stay focused in discussions

Section: 4.7. Handling Disagreement

So far, you have covered listening, asking questions, giving support, sharing feelings, making suggestions and summarizing.

Whatever transpires in any discussions you should confirm understanding and agreement. You are interested in the outcome because you are responsible for the results. You need it to work, be cost effective and improve the general situation for the good of the company. You may therefore, need to encourage and guide personnel towards a positive end result.

You now have skills to direct and organize most discussions. Through skilful questioning and supporting good ideas you will obtain a good quality result.

But, what do you do when a member of personnel makes a statement which you disprove of, or makes suggestions which are against the company's policies or expresses sentiments which cannot be agreed to?

And how do you handle disagreement and: -

1. **Develop and motivate your people**
2. **Achieve the best business result**

The answer is not easy; many managers have a tendency to react when they hear something that they do not agree with. Unfortunately, it is this reaction that can damage development and motivation you have generated.

When employees hear negative statements against their contributions they normally feel defensive. This can be a sensitive area which must be handled with a positive approach.

You should therefore: -

Listen to the suggestions, facts and opinions.

Unemotionally assess the suggestions, facts, opinions.

Give your reasons, facts, opinion why the suggestions may be impractical.

Avoid the use of the following sensitive words:

❏ **Disagree.**

❏ **Can't.**

❏ **Won't.**

❏ **Wrong.**

❏ **And certainly do not use any words which could be construed as derogatory to the employee.**

Quick Tip: *Listen carefully, do not to react too soon and follow the sequence above.*

Remember.........

Management Wisdom

If you have a job without aggravations, you don't have a job.

*Malcolm Forbes

Section: 4.8. Balancing Control

A way of guiding and controlling a discussion is by providing information.

Here, a good discussion skill means picking the right moment to share your knowledge, opinions or suggestions. Don't be too quick to convey information, as this may give the impression that you are uninterested in the other person's point of view.

An effective manager gauges when and to what extent the facts are made available to personnel and only then does the manager move into the giving advice mode and even then, asks enough questions to make sure that it is not seen as over controlling the personnel.

The exception, is when helping a new employee or helping an employee with a new task.

Note: *If you believe 'telling' is the most appropriate for your personnel, you may have a problem which you will have to work on to avoid over controlling discussions in the future.*

Section: 4.9. Preventing Misunderstanding

A very important skill in any discussion is to prevent misunderstanding. What is the good of any discussion if the parties separate, each with a different understanding of what has been discussed and agreed on?

Remember.........

Management Wisdom

Failing to get them to do it your way might mean they're stupid but it also means you failed to get them to do it your way.

*Cal Keegan

The benefit of mutual understanding for the parties involved in the discussion is that it stops disagreement. Have you ever disagreed with a proposal or suggested plan, only to find out that you really misunderstood what was said?

Therefore, the way to verify information and make sure that you fully understand the details of what has been said is to phrase a statement back to the speaker as a question, as follows: -

❏ Let me see if I understand.........

❏ Are you saying that.........

❏ Are you suggesting that.........

This type of question has many advantages: -

1. Shows your interest.

2. Shows that you have been listening.

3. Clarifies matters for the other party.

4. Helps avoid misunderstanding.

5. Defuses disagreement and differences of opinion.

Section: 5.0. Discussion Skills Summary

The following summary is for your guidance and depending on the nature of the discussion may vary slightly. Importantly, you should maintain a comfortable balance of discussion skills. You can adapt and apply the following to suit the discussion: -

Discussion Outline	Discussion Skills
Introduction	Making suggestions
Clarify areas of Concern	Looking for facts Providing information Supporting Sharing feelings
List alternative solutions	Looking for solutions Preventing misunderstanding Preventing disagreement
Agree on best solution	Listening Summarizing
Minimize Risks	Evaluating solutions
Plan implementation	Balancing control Supporting

Section: 6.0. Discussion Planning

A discussion does not have to be planned in great detail, but it should follow a plan.

What is the objective of management?

- ❏ In simple words: A manager's objective is to achieve the best results for the company through the personnel and resources available.

Therefore, by increasing the knowledge and skills of personnel, they will make better decisions and results for the company.

Remember.........

Management Wisdom

What we need is an enthusiastic but calm state of mind and intense but orderly work

*Mao Tse Tung

The effective manager: -

1. Encourages thinking and problem solving.
2. Provides insight into business techniques.
3. Motivates personnel for sustainable achievement.
4. Increases knowledge about the values of the company.

This happens when you embark on problem solving and include your personnel.

It is the manager's job to define problems. When defining a problem the following Question model outline will assist you in this area.

The Problem Requiring Action: -

- ❏ What is the problem?
- ❏ Who is involved?
- ❏ What are the effects of continuing without action?
- ❏ What are the criteria that a solution must meet?
- ❏ Are there any solutions that must be discounted?
- ❏ What is the value to the company?

❏ What is the urgency and time frame of providing a solution?

Once you have adequately defined the problem, share the decision-making with your personnel, you should feel confident when handing it to your support personnel.

Section: 7.0. Employee Analysis Overview

The first step in planning a discussion is identifying and defining the problem or issue. The problem could be anything from a new company strategy to an employee's work habits.

Part of the manager's job before any discussion with personnel is to assess the other person in general terms of aspirations and motivation. Different people have different experiences, skills, knowledge and aspirations, and the makeup of each person determines their reaction to the discussion.

When you have determined the person with whom you are to have a discussion, you need to assess the person objectively as follows: -

❏ Brief statement of the situation for clarity.

❏ What is your employee's perception of the issue?

❏ What is the background, knowledge, strengths and weaknesses of your employee in relation to this issue?

❏ What motivates your employee?

❏ What reaction would your employee have towards the discussion?

This will give you a clearer view of the discussion and which issues should be emphasized so that you can meet the individual's and the company's needs.

Quick Tip: *effective managers get to know their employees prior to allocating important work.*

Section: 8.0. Summary Review: Discussion Planning

You can help another person grow and become more confident and independent in all your discussions from the disciplinary interview to the promotional discussion, if you care enough to look for the best in that person and expect that person to perform well. When they do perform well show a genuine appreciation and reward them for their performance.

Remember.........

Management Wisdom

Be just as enthusiastic about the success of others as you are about your own.

*Christian D. Larson

When there is sufficient information for discussion planning and it is the manager's job to achieve both the company's objective and the person's objective through the discussion plan.

1. You need to formulate an introduction, where you need to suggest the objective and a sequence for the discussion, at the same time you need to reduce resistance and increase motivation by relating to the employee's strengths and aspirations.

    1.1 Decide what you will say.

2. You must start clarifying areas of concern, which include any concerns you may have about your employee's skills or experience, which may need exploring and / or supporting.

    2.1. Decide what questions you will ask.

    2.2. When the listing of alternative solutions is complete you should keep in mind your employee's experience and knowledge and your own criteria for an effective solution.

    2.3. Decide how you will phrase these questions.

    2.4. Decide how you will bring in your own opinions and ideas.

3. You should agree on the most probable solution and next alternatives.

4. Decide on which employee factors are important to handle the solution.

5. Agree on an implementation plan which minimizes the risks for the company.

5.1. Decide on how you could ensure that your employee is fully committed and understands exactly what is expected.

Effective managers seek out feedback from colleagues, employees and professionals for advice on how to improve. Consider for a moment **what's in it for you**, if you were to improve your discussion skills.

❑ Firstly, accept that you can improve.

❑ Secondly, you must have the motivation and effort to improve.

❑ Thirdly, you need to objectively and constructively compare your current ability with the discussion skill level that you would like to attain and write a measurable objective for improvement.

Feedback should be constructive and consistent if you use an observer. Alternatively: -

❑ You can personally review the discussion, without an observer.

❑ You can get feedback from your employee.

Let's look at the way you review results with an employee. Which questions do you ask to get an employee to evaluate the results of a joint problem solving discussion and how motivated your employee is compared to before and after the discussion?

Your questions should generally be as follows

1. How do you feel about the situation now?
2. Tell me how you feel about tackling this project?
3. What are your reservations?
4. Have we considered all the facts?
5. Have we missed out on a solution?
6. Is there anything you'd like to add?

The answers to the above questions will give you sufficient feedback to help you to review your own discussion skills and plan for some improvement.

There is another way of reviewing discussion skills.

❑ Self Assessment – against preset criteria.

Your Core Objective: is to improve the communication between manager and employee.

Assessing Your Success:

Now give some thought to how successful you were by asking the following: -

1. Did your employee do most of the talking?
2. Did you ask most of the questions?
3. Do you now have a better relationship with your employee?
4. Did you cover the outline discussion skills fully?
5. Did you get your employee's commitment?

If the answer to these questions is yes, well done!

You could review all discussions in this way against a logical discussion outline and the list of discussion skills.

And use the Question Model of Management to assist you throughout this process:-

- ❏ **Why** do I need to take action in a particular area?
- ❏ **What** objectives, action plan, shall I set?
- ❏ **Who** will be involved?
- ❏ **When** are my objectives and action plan dates?
- ❏ **How** are my objectives and action plan, to happen?
- ❏ **What if** a problem develops, what will I do?
- ❏ **Where** should my objectives and action plan take me?

Section: 9.0. Quick Guide to Avoiding Misunderstanding and Conflict

Avoiding misunderstanding and conflict are summarized as follows: -

Management Behavior for Effective Discussion

1. **Understand and follow a logical discussion outline.**
    1.1. Set objectives.
    1.2. Have a clear and motivating introduction.
    1.3. Clarify areas of concern.
    1.4. List alternative solutions.
    1.5. Agree on a best solution.
    1.6. Minimize risks.

    1.7.   Agree on an implementation plan.

2. **Practice all discussion skills in a balanced manner.**

    2.1.   Set objectives.

    2.2.   Listen.

    2.3.   Question, seek facts, and seek solutions.

    2.4.   Give support for ideas and contributions.

    2.5.   Share own feelings.

    2.6.   Make suggestions.

    2.7.   Disagree.

    2.8.   Summarize.

    2.9.   Provide information, facts and ideas.

    2.10. Prevent misunderstanding.

3. **Carefully plan important discussions.**

    3.1.   Analyze the situation and set clear achievement objectives.

    3.2.   Analyze the employee's strengths, weaknesses and motivation.

    3.3.   Design a specific flow to the discussion with questions and statements aimed at total involvement and commitment.

4. **Review all major discussions in order to improve on your skills.**

    4.1.   Organize feedback from other people.

    4.2.   Seek evaluation comments from employees.

    4.3.   Answer the review questions – yourself.

    4.4.   Work on an improvement plan.

Apply these guides and make them specific to your discussions. You now have sufficient skill and knowledge to see you through almost any discussion, successfully.

Chapter 5: Executive Writing Made Easy

The Third Rule of Smart Management:
Develop an executive writing skill to educate, sell,
convince, motivate or influence your reader.

Section: 1.0. An Introduction to Executive Writing

The purpose of writing is to enjoy communicating with people, developing your own style and putting your thoughts into words. You can achieve this using the following sections:

First, let's look at the aspects of business writing, these are normally memos, reports, and letters which come in many forms. A well written memo, report and letter can sell, motivate, influence, record ideas, increase your stature and build your career. Effective managers know just how much can be gained through the written word.

Remember.........

Management Wisdom

It is the quality rather than the quantity that matters.

*Seneca

Writing is a valuable skill, well worth acquiring. Internal memos, emails and correspondence within your company can form attitudes and direct activity.

Through effective writing you will be able to communicate to all levels of the business, generally increase your own productivity and show your ability to solve problems. Even with the advent of e-mail and the electronic office, the ability to write clearly and concisely to convey a message has not diminished. Therefore, the manager who can write in a clear and convincing manner is contributing to the success of the department, division and the company.

The written word has many advantages, it gives you time to carefully apply your mind to the structure and record your thoughts clearly. For the reader it provides all sorts of information and a record for future reference.

Writing, like any other managerial activity should give you a return on your investment in time. Poor writing can waste your time and the reader's time, if the message is not clearly defined in the writing.

Consider for a moment and answer the following: -
- ❏ **Why are you writing your current correspondence?**
- ❏ **What types of written communication do you write?**
- ❏ **Categorize them.**
- ❏ **Where do you send them?**
- ❏ **What do you normally expect in terms of feedback from these?**
- ❏ **How often do you write?**

Section: 1.1. The Required End Result

The purpose is to achieve increased understanding between the reader and yourself, and to have a positive and cooperative effect on your reader.

As you know, achievement of a positive result is not through luck alone.

Remember.........

Management Wisdom

The harder you work, the luckier you get.

*Gary Player

Written communication is a valuable management tool when used wisely and written in such a way that your reader understands your objective and is in agreement with the required conclusion or end result. A clear objective is therefore the means which enables the reader to understand the content.

Business revolves around setting objectives; so the emphasis is on focusing on your objective in your written communication. Writing is a matter of organizing and selecting ideas and facts, which support your objective.

In your correspondence, there may be more than one objective but once you know the objective or objectives of the writer, your reading of emails or reports becomes easier.

The reason for writing emanates from the objective, when you write to a client to present a new product. The objective is to arrange for an appointment where you can present and sell the benefits of your company's product to your client.

Once the objective is clear, you can plan your communication in terms of main ideas and supporting facts which motivate, persuade or convince your reader.

You may want to assess your current incoming and outgoing mail, as follows: -

Exercise - Incoming Correspondence
Take four types of correspondence from your in tray - an email, a memo, a letter and a report and write down the perceived objective of the writers and your assessment as to whether the writers achieved their objective.

	Writer's objective?	Objective Achieved?
1.		
2.		
3.		
4.		

Outgoing Correspondence
Plan your objectives for at least four of your outgoing correspondence and state the readers perceptions or actions you would like to stimulate, keep these in mind when checking your final draft.

	My objective	Readers' perceptions or actions I would like from my correspondence.
1.		
2.		
3.		
4.		

Section: 1.2. The Reader

In developing your thoughts about what must be written, you should be able to assess how much information you need to put into an email, letter or report in order to achieve your objective.

What you will write depends very much on your reader. You will need to assess your reader in some detail: -

1. Who is the recipient/s – title / position / relationship to me, if any?
2. How well do I know the recipient?
3. Can the recipient/s make decisions in my area / or influence the company?
4. Does the recipient have more or less authority than me?
5. Does the recipient/s normally react quickly or slowly?
6. What is the recipient/s background experience to the subject matter?
7. What do I want the recipient/s to do in terms of attitude or action after reading my correspondence?

Once you have assessed your reader or readers you will be in a better position to lead them through a logical thought process or to course of action which coincides with your own thoughts. You could use examples which they can relate to in terms of previous experience. You could appeal to some form of action which is within your reader's authority.

How well do people who have written to you know you? Check some correspondence as follows: -

1. Have they got your job and name correct?

2. Are they over-simplifying or is the writing style too complex?
3. Do they ask for something, which is within your authority to action or support?

Assessing your correspondence and good reader assessments will help you get to the principal content of the correspondence quickly and help you achieve your objectives in your writing.

So now, you know to whom you are writing to, and more importantly - what you expect your reader/s to do.

Section: 1.3. The Principal Content

You can now start planning the content of the written communication and the answers to the following questions will guide you.

- ❏ **Why** am I writing?
- ❏ **What** will catch the reader's attention that you could use in the opening?
- ❏ **What** is the main focus of the content?
- ❏ **What** do you want the reader to do and when?
- ❏ **What** is special about your correspondence from the reader's point of view?
- ❏ **What** will influence the reader – what can the reader gain?
- ❏ **Does** the reader need to know any additional information?

You are now in the process of bringing together the reader and content assessments into an outline for your correspondence.
These assessments will help you to decide on: -

1. An appropriate opening.
2. The main ideas.
3. Supporting information.
4. And how to phrase the communication.

Reports

When you write a report to someone, either to explain an event, plan some actions or make recommendations. Reports demand facts, figures and research and are based on the same reader and subject assessment. But the content and structure may be slightly different as you will see in the various report structures.

Exercise

In the following exercise plan the content for a complex email or short report you need to write. It could be an explanatory report to your manager or to the board, a letter asking for capital equipment, additional personnel or a service etc.

1. **Objective of the Report** (the specific reason for writing)
2. **Outline and Background Information**
3. **Current Status**
4. **Main idea or proposal 1**
   4.1. Supporting information
5. **Main idea or proposal 2***
   5.1. Supporting information
6. **Main idea or proposal 3***
   6.1. Supporting information
7. **Summary and Recommendation**

* Include or remove these items as required

Section: 1.4. The Purpose of an Introduction

You will discover starting your emails, memos and reports will become easier by developing your objective for writing.

Essentially, the introduction should get attention and create interest. Perhaps the most important aspect of those first few words is to – *get attention.*

Instead of: -
- ❏ In response to your......
- ❏ Further to your letter......
- ❏ Please be advised......
- ❏ As requested......

Try a little more creative style: -
- ❏ Could you give me your advice on......
- ❏ I have a problem which you may be able to help me with......
- ❏ Our last discussion produced some interesting solutions......

The subject matter generally dictates the introduction. If you don't like these, use something else ensuring the introduction is appropriate for the occasion. Try a few introductions, write them down and make them your own.

And of course, you can always be more conservative with your introductions, if for example you are writing to the company's managing director or an employee about company policy, a disciplinary meeting or a formal letter of invitation to a board meeting.

By analyzing the techniques and styles of other writers you will develop your own writing style and skill.

Remember the following points: -
1. Your introduction must get immediate attention.
2. Your introduction sets the tone and influences the style you use.
3. Think carefully about the effect you'd like your introduction to have.
4. Consider what you would like your reader to think about you and your subject.
5. Consider what effect or action you want.
6. Consider who else may read this letter.

Section: 1.5. Do You Have Style?
Style can often speak stronger than the content and when used in an imaginative manner, it is extremely effective. Style makes a letter or report personal to you and sets the tone in which you'd like the subject to be handled.

Keep your objective and the reader and the subject assessment in mind to provide a powerful introduction and an appropriate style.

Your writing should be easier and more pleasant to read with the following criteria: -
1. A clear introduction.
2. A definite / distinctive body which creates an atmosphere suitable to the subject.
3. Answers the questions the reader may have, i.e., why and how.
4. Language that reflects your own style.
5. Sentences that are constructed in an easy-to-read manner without too many commas and spelling mistakes.
6. An ending which stimulates thought or motivates action.

Section: 1.6. The Executive Report

You have covered the need to set a clear objective and to assess your reader and your subject matter and you should understand the following: -

- ❏ The objective and reader assessment is to decide on the style to use.
- ❏ Readers can be grouped and assessed even if you are sending out many copies of the same report.
- ❏ To motivate readers you must answer the reader's questions and outline the benefits to the reader.
- ❏ A well-written email or memo reflects the style of the writer.
- ❏ Office emails and memos need a distinctive introduction, body and closure.
- ❏ Formal reports like other written communications need to have a clear objective.

The Formal Report

The many types of progress reports, technical reports, sales reports and financial reports that the manager may be called upon to write, all have a structure or outline. This makes it easier for you to present the facts you have researched and the ideas you have.

At the outset of any correspondence you write, setting the objective, reader and subject assessment should become second nature to you. This process will help you prioritize your information; develop your approach and the extent of support information required.

For example, the general manager may need more technical and financial detail; although the board of directors may not require the full technical detail of a particular decision, but simply an outline or an executive summary.

The introduction to a report should encompass the following: -

- ❏ Describe the background or history leading up to the report.
- ❏ Identify the objective and purpose of the report.
- ❏ Answer the readers' questions regarding why, where, who, and how.
- ❏ State briefly, what is to follow in the body of the report?
- ❏ Determine the style you will follow for the report, i.e. technical, basic, detailed or complex?

Section: 1.7. Build the Structure

The following structures will help you with your report writing correspondence in the future: -

1. **Complex Reports**
   1.1. Title Page
   1.2. Background
   1.3. Synopsis
   1.4. Table of Contents
   1.5. Table of Illustrations
   1.6. Introduction
      1.6.1. Facts and Examples
      1.6.2. Conclusions
      1.6.3. Recommendations
   1.7. Appendix
   1.8. Index
2. **Detailed Report or Memo**
   2.1. Introduction
   2.2. Background Information
      2.2.1. Problems or Reasons
   2.3. Current Situation and Status
   2.4. Recommendation or Proposed Solution
   2.5. Benefits
3. **Simple Email, Report or Memo**
   3.1. Background Information
   3.2. Current Status
   3.3. Proposed Solution

There are many variations on the above outlines which could form the basis for a logical progression of information, examples, conclusions and you will be able to refine the outline to suit your own purposes.

Previously, you looked at the criteria for an effective introduction; this provides a platform for the rest of the report.

From your introduction to get attention you can present your facts and ideas in a clear and organized manner, with: -

❏ A logical flow of ideas and facts.

- ❏ Organized in terms of your thoughts.
- ❏ Keep it simple and direct.
- ❏ Avoid complex expressions.
- ❏ Avoid acronyms.

Section: 1.8. The Conclusion

The facts, examples and illustrations are used to lead your readers easily to a logical conclusion in all your correspondence. A report is perhaps more formal in its style and the closing summary should be clear and concise.

You need to ensure that your reader has come to the same logical conclusion that you have. For this to happen, you must use the following structure: -

- ❏ A summary of your main thoughts.
- ❏ Your recommendations including any alternatives pro-posals and note any cost or company policy implications or limitations.
- ❏ Conclude with a brief summary of the original objective or reason for the report.

Executive Summary

You may be required to provide an executive summary or synopsis of a lengthy report. Such an executive summary normally starts off with the recommendations followed by a clear and logical summary of the main arguments and information.

An executive summary should be brief and to the point as its main purpose is to assist the reader who may not require the all encompassing technical and commercial detail but requires only the salient points of the complete report. It also helps your reader if your report is easy to follow, for example, to have clear headings, bullet points and numbering. This technique makes the writing and reading of complex technical or commercial reports much easier.

To recap: Some basic principles, before you start writing are: -

1) Determine your objective

2) Define the reader and assess your subject matter.

3) Clarify exactly what you want your reader to know or action to take.

4) Write clearly, simply and in an organized manner.

5) Start off in a manner that will get the reader's attention.

6) Make sure that the facts are correct.

7) Make your subject interesting and add your own writing style.

8) Use language which is natural and flowing without acronyms or slang.

9) Appeal to your reader's interest and the benefits to your reader.

10) As a general rule, keep all emails, memos and letters and correspondence of this nature to one page.

Remember, well written memos and reports can also support your career image.

When closing, always get back to the objective making sure that your communication: -

- ❏ **Motivates** if action is required.
- ❏ **Provides alternatives** if decisions have to be made.
- ❏ **Educates** if learning or awareness is required.

Section: 2.0. Quick Guide to Executive Writing

Focus on the techniques and thoughtful application during your writing; this will help you to use your time economically.

As an effective businessman or businesswoman you need to think in outline, plan methodically, write clearly and concisely and send your communication to obtain a worthwhile response, this can be achieved easily with a little practice.

You might want to use the following quick guide below in the future; this applies equally for one reader or many readers.

1. **Decide on your objective and purpose**
   1.1. What is it?
   1.2. What qualifies me?
   1.3. What do I want the reader/s to do?
2. **Assess your subject**
   2.1. How much do I have to tell the reader?
   2.2. What will catch the reader/s attention?
3. **Assess your reader**
   3.1. Who is/are the reader/s?
   3.2. What is the reader/s position or authority?

    3.3. How much time will the reader/s need to decide?

    3.4. What is the reader/s background?

4. **Write the opening**

    4.1. How can I get the reader/s attention and interest?

    4.2. Will the introduction motivate the reader/s further?

5. **Write the body**

    5.1. Does it have a clear introduction, body and close?

    5.2. Do I need to use more headings?

    5.3. Does it clearly define problems and solutions?

    5.4. Does it answer all possible questions?

    5.5. Is it short, concise, and structured?

    5.6. Does it fit my personal style?

    5.7. Will it appeal to the reader/s?

6. **Summary**

    6.1. Does it have a clear and concise summary of your main thoughts, proposals or recommendations?

This completes the chapter on Executive Writing

And use the Question Model of Management to assist you through this process: -

1. **Why** do I need to take action in a particular area?

2. **What** objectives, action plan, shall I set?

3. **Who** will be involved?

4. **When** are my objective and action plan dates?

5. **How** are my objectives and actions, to happen?

6. **What if** a problem develops, what will I do?

7. **Where** should my objectives and action plan take me?

Remember.........

Management Wisdom

The pen is mightier than the sword!

*Edward Bulwer-Lytton

Wield it well!

Chapter 6: Recruiting Your Team

Fourth Rule of Smart Management:
Recognize and identify what makes certain
employees stand out from the crowd.

Section: 1.0. Personnel Selection

The manager is the key to attracting and retaining talented employees; the best managers select their team and cultivate the talents and skills of their personnel, set realistic expectations and motivate them.

You are now embarking on a subject of recruitment; it is one of the most important tasks in management. You may get away with doing one or two things wrong but personnel selection is the one thing you <u>must</u> do right, a mistake with employee selection can cost the company in both cash and morale.

These sections will take you through the process of personnel selection.

Firstly let's consider the conservative costs associated with a personnel selection which fails.

The total cost of personnel selection for advertising, personnel agency, screening, company time interviewing, training, and loss of production if you make a mistake may be more than the annual salary of the applicant, and while you have personnel who are not performing well, someone, somewhere in the company has had to cover any outstanding work.

It is important to understand what make good personnel selections and which make poor selections from the outset. You also need to understand this for your own recognition and success. The bottom line is that poor personnel selections do not help your career!

Formula for Improvement
Because of the many variables in selection, there is no exact formula to select the perfect employee, but you can improve your chances in the selection process.

It is therefore important to 'get it right the first time', the obvious alternative is to make a conscious decision to start with an employee with all the right basic skills and formally train them into the job.

Personnel selections by managers who use a systematic method for selection and who ensure that their selection decisions are certainly more hit than miss.

Selection depends on your perceptions, impressions, feelings and observations of the candidate and because of these variables it takes some practice to get it right. Never the less, by developing simple and effective systematic methods, response techniques and processes you can overcome most of the pitfalls and become somewhat skilled at selecting the right people for the right job. And these selection methods and processes will improve your own perception.

Personnel Selection success can be measured quite simply against the following three criteria:

1. **Can** the person do the job?
2. **Will** the person do the job?
3. **Will** the person stay?

These are the three questions you should be able to answer before making an appointment decision.

When you make these three questions specific to the type of positions for which you have to select people, you should include: -

1. Ability

❏ Some important items describing the **ability** of the person to do the job or at least those characteristics which will ensure trainability.

2. Job Satisfaction

❏ Some realistic **job satisfaction areas** that the job entails. Your work includes matching the person who will be motivated by those areas. Certain items like work difficulty, challenge, a good team, little supervision, flexibility in the decision area, could motivate the right person.

3. Work Environment

❏ Lastly, you should look at **the work environment** within which the candidate will operate and decide if the applicant will fit in well with fellow workers already in the department and vice versa. Consider the characteristics and work habits of the candidate to ensure a good match.

In simple words, ability is only one of the elements of performance and conflicts created through a lack of motivation or personality problems can also be detrimental to the business.

Section: 1.1. The Personnel Department

By all means use the personnel or human resource department, if you have one, but don't leave the final selection entirely to the personnel department. Remember, as the manager, you are ultimately responsible for your employee!

Personnel management like all other specialist functions is there to help you get it right, however, bear in mind that: -

- ❏ You are responsible for output.
- ❏ You decide on the personnel resource investment.
- ❏ You have control of the costs of your department or division.
- ❏ You provide help to new employees at the induction.
- ❏ And you carry the blame if your selection goes wrong.

The final responsibility for the selection decision, the success or failure of an employee will depend on YOU the manager.

When someone is selected for a particular job that person represents an investment made by your company, which requires a return.

Here are some of the things that personnel management, internally or externally can generally provide for you: -

1. Help you to define exactly what you are looking for.
2. Design and place personnel adverts internally and/ or externally.
3. Liaise with personnel agencies and universities, business organizations, schools career planning departments.
4. Test and interview all candidates and select a short list of the best.
5. Once the appointment decision has been made, complete all the required administration work.
6. When appointed, complete the payroll and record functions.

Check with the personnel manager how they see their role in the selection activity, so that you may establish: -

- ❏ What assistance can personnel management give?
- ❏ When should personnel management get involved?
- ❏ What does personnel management expect from you?
- ❏ By when?

Section: 1.2. Question Time

You have gone through a process of identifying applicants and now you need to develop a detailed profile of the applicant.

In the perfect world you are looking for intelligent, conscientious and loyal employees. However, often an applicant does not come with all the qualities to fit the original detailed brief perfectly, but may have other qualities which are equally suitable to the job.

Firstly, think through the criteria to help you and your personnel manager recognize the most suitable applicants. And detail the questions which you need to answer, before recruiting.

Remember, if you don't know <u>exactly</u> what you want, you probably won't get it.

- ❏ **This Personnel Requirements Guide** may help you think through the early part of the process:

Personnel Requirement Guide	Profile Required
1.0. Job Title (of your choice)	

2.0. Achievements
  2.1. Determine the educational band
     Maximum level?
     Minimum level?
  2.2. What experience is required?
     Type?
     Length of time?
  2.3. What kind of success record?
     How many successes?
     What areas?	

3.0. Aptitude
  3.1. What must the person do especially well?
     *List your answer in terms of priorities	

4.0. Interests 　4.1 Would it help you if the applicant had any special interest? 　　*What?	
5.0. Characteristics 　5.1. Describe the nature of the person you are looking for? 　　*Any particular trait? 　　*Anything you do not want?	
6.0.Current and future Circumstances Think here of commitments required from the candidate 　6.1. Location? 　6.2. Overtime / working late requirements? 　6.3. Travel away from home? 　6.4. Staying away from home? 　6.5. Transfer and relocation possibilities?	
7.0. Other special requirement for the job?	

This will help to clarify exactly what you want in the future.

Quick Tip: *identify one of your most valuable employees in a similar position and assess their characteristics to give you a feel for a similar position you wish to fill.*

Section: 1.3. The Do's and Don'ts Guide

The following is a do's and don'ts list to give you some insight into how an effective manager approaches personnel selection will assist you.

The Don'ts of an effective manager: -

1. **Don't rely on appearance**

   While this is important, especially if the person has to deal with customers, the point is, don't rely on it entirely.

2. **Don't over select**

   A mistake often made in search of the ideal candidate. Too much intelligence can be a hindrance in a routine type position. High creativity in certain routine type positions could cause the candidate dissatisfaction with the job.

3. **Don't only measure experience in terms of years**

   Some people only have one year's experience. Others also have one year's experience but have spent ten to fifteen years to obtain it.

4. **Don't appoint in a hurry**

   The question is not whether it is the best applicant of the bunch but whether the applicant fits the standards of the job to be filled.

The Do's of an effective manager: -

1. **Do give plenty of time to select**

   Some companies even employ trainees ahead of the time when they may be needed as production employees. The more time you give yourself, the more alternatives you can consider.

2. **Do consider the applicant's suitability**

   Individualism is all well and good but this could upset the equilibrium of the team and even the company. Consider how easy or difficult it would be to motivate and control such a person.

3. **Do be sure about what the applicant wants**

   It terms of job satisfaction, rewards, longer term objectives, or they may never find it in the position offered or the company as a whole; try to establish exactly what it is the applicant is looking for.

And, if you can think of some more dos and don'ts from your own experience.... write them down and add them to the list.

Section: 1.4. Seek and Ye Shall Find

You can now address the question of where you will find the ideal candidate.

Website Advertising

By far, employment websites are the most popular recruitment method today as this is where most people look for jobs. Also there are specialist websites for executive management, construction, engineering, accountancy these are often used for positions such as directors, project managers, engineers, accountants, consultants etc. It is important to assess which website your ideal candidate is most likely to view, before selecting your recruitment website and placing your advertisement.

Personnel Agency

Specialist personnel agencies, although not cheap they provide a useful service. The right agency can take the pressure off, but to avoid future problems the final decision from a short list of candidates remains with you.

National and Local Press

The newspaper and specialist magazines and news bulletins are often used for positions such as engineers, accountants, architects etc. It is important to think about which publication your ideal candidate is most likely to read before placing your advertisement.

Own Company

The first obvious place to look is within your own company. While the company cannot be regarded as the only source of recruitment, the advantages of appointing a person who you know and who knows your company are numerous.

Universities, Business Colleges and Schools

Here, you can approach the career planning departments for new recruits, which you can train into specific roles within the company. Advertising and interviewing within these facilities is relatively easy and most universities, business colleges and schools are helpful with their pupils obtaining employment on qualifying. This is a longer-term personnel selection solution, but the results are often worthwhile.

Note: A well designed job advert should make your company and job attractive to the candidate plus give enough information about your requirements so that the reader can evaluate their own matching capabilities.

Section: 2.0. Interview Planning & Preparation

Initially, you have two sources of information to plan the selection interview.
1. Your job specification of the ideal candidate;
2. The candidate's application form and/or curriculum vitae

What you need to plan is 'how' you are going to get the information you need for a decision. Assessment starts prior to the interview, with the completed application form and/or the CV which is studied and compared with the job specification. And when you have the application form you can start the interview planning.

Using the comparative technique below; you would complete the facts as presented by the candidate on this form. Assuming the candidate has fulfilled the academic criteria and characteristics of the job specification. This will help you to focus your interview questions.

A simple and typical Job Specification Guideline layout for Project Engineer, which can be modified to suit circumstances: -

Job Specification	Candidates Application	Interview Question Notes	Applicants Answers
Title: Project Engineer			
Achievements • 2 years as a successful Project Engineer	Has been a Project Engineer for 3 years	1. Need to find candidates success rate with projects, during interview?	
		2. How many people, what tasks involved?	
		3. What problems encountered and how overcome?	
Aptitude • Enjoys routine work • Works under pressure at times		4. Candidates general like and dislikes?	
		5. Also interests and hobbies	
		6. Ask about pressure in previous jobs?	
		7. How the candidate coped?	
• References		8. Reference check. Positive? Negative?	
Summary Notes:			

Planning the Interview Time.

Plan how much time to allow for your interviews and the timing in between interviews and for issues such as privacy, no interruptions refreshments etc.

Section: 2.1. The Interview – Setting the Scene

In discussions people need a little time to adjust their thinking and their behavior to one another. This is why it is always recommended to spend a few minutes at the outset of an interview talking about natural non-business subjects. Think about some subjects that you could use to create an amicable climate.

Apart from verbal messages be aware of non-verbal influences to the climate. Things like your dress, your posture, handshake, eye contact, your pace of movement and speech. Consider the 'way' in which you come across to your candidate, a method professional interviewers use is they match the candidate's pace of responses, which tends to put the candidate at ease.

Put the Candidate at Ease

Tension affects different people in different ways. The extremes are that some retreat and become quiet, others talk incessantly and both symptoms interfere with the flow of an interview. It is therefore important to put the candidate at ease. As with any other business meeting you need to 'establish a climate' which is easygoing, yet business like and professional.

A good approach to the employment interview is to consider it as a meeting of two people who each have a decision to make. All good meetings have an agenda and as the senior party you are expected to provide it. People feel more at ease when they know what to anticipate. After the initial opening you need to confirm the contents of the interview and the order in which you would like to discuss them.

For example, to discuss

1. The candidates experience and expectations.
2. Our company/department and answer any questions the candidate may have.
3. The interview timing.

Knowing what is coming should make the applicant feel more comfortable.

And close the interview on a friendly note and thank the candidate for their time and contribution.

Section: 2.2. The Interview – Question Skills

One of the most important skills in interviewing is questioning; the skill of seeking information.

The primary purpose of a selection interview is for you to evaluate the applicant, so we will cover some common questioning errors.

Dichotomous Questions & Questions that Encourage Information

Frequently, questions can be answered by just one word 'yes' or 'no' but this limits the amount of information you receive.

Which of the following questions can be answered in one word yes or no?

1. Do you feel frustrated in your present job?
2. Did you enjoy your most recent job more than the previous one?
3. What aspects of this job appeal to you more than your present job?
4. What were some of the things you liked or disliked about your last job?

Questions 1. and 2. Would tell you very little.
Questions 3. and 4. Would tell you more about the person and his job.

Note: generally avoid one word answers if you need background information, and use dichotomous questions only when a yes or no will suffice.

Encourage Information Flow

Questions stating 'what' and 'how' will encourage the required information

1. What did you study in Business College that would help you in this job?
2. How would you compare this job with your previous one?
3. What were some of the qualities of your last manager?

Leading Questions

Phrasing good questions is a matter of practice.

Now you need to look at avoiding questions which suggest the required answer. Such questions are called leading questions; these should be avoided as they strongly suggest to the listener the required response.

From the leading questions given below, the alternative question will give you the information required: -

❏ I assume you learned about personnel management in your previous job, didn't you?

❏ **Alternative question**: What did you learn about personnel management in your previous job?

❏ Is your health good?

❏ **Alternative question**: Have you had any injuries or illnesses in the past five years?

❏ You would probably prefer a manager who presents you with challenges wouldn't you?

❏ **Alternative question**: What sort of management motivates you?

Note: generally avoid leading questions, as they have limited application in an interview.

Multiple Choice Problem Solving Questions

A useful technique is to use problem solving type questions. To pose a hypothetical situation and ask your candidate to state what they would do in the situation to address the problem.

An example of such a question is as follows: -

❏ How would you handle an emotional outburst from one of your personnel who came to you with a complaint about another employee?

❏ The employee is highly upset about someone and starts to leave after the outburst.

For example: What would you do?

1. Call the employee back and talk about the employee's problem immediately?

2. Let the employee go and then speak to the employee later?

3. Call the employee back and suggest a meeting once the employee has cooled down?

4. Leave the employee to cool off for a day?

5. Bring both employees together in a meeting to discuss the situation?

Such questions are good for gaining insight into the candidate's ability to handling difficult situations.

The Problem Situation Questions

A problem question allows the applicant to tell you how the applicant would handle a particular situation.

The easiest way to construct a problem question is to begin, "What would you do if……? And then present the situation, for example.

❏ What would you do if you were given a project you could not complete by the deadline?

You may consider variations of this question which are acceptable, as it will allow your candidate to describe what they would do in a particular situation.

It is also good practice to make brief notes of your candidate's answers. Any grey areas you identify can be revisited later in the interview.

Many of your questions will start with: -

❏ Why

❏ What

❏ How

❏ When

❏ Who

❏ What if

❏ Where (to)

With endless possibilities of questions and answers.

Section: 2.3. The Interview – Exploring Details

During your interview you will often pick upon certain words that the applicant says and will want to follow these up on these by exploring certain background details.

For example:

❏ The applicant states: Sometimes a different site manager was in charge and my work was always on time.

❏ The word 'sometimes' suggests that the applicant didn't always get along with the site managers and you need to explore why this was.

❏ The applicant states: I enjoyed most of the duties in my last job.

❏ The word 'most' suggests that the applicant didn't enjoy some of the duties of the job and you need to explore which duties were problematic.

The following are good exploratory questions by asking a direct question: -

You can also use certain phrases when you want to explore the details in your candidate's statements. Here are some phrases, which you could use in the previous examples

- ❏ Please tell me more about...............................?
- ❏ What do you mean by....................................?
- ❏ Can you give me an example of.....................?

Remember, this is an interview it is not the third degree, so tend to phrase the questions in a relaxed manner.

Section: 2.4. The Interview – Reassurance and the Calm Down

Candidates will not normally reveal unfavorable situations or information about themselves. Therefore, to build a complete picture you need to know how the candidate would handle certain difficult situations. You will usually have to rely on your own questioning, assessments and observations or references from previous employers for such information.

When a candidate does relate a problem, or a difficult situation to you, you can reassure the candidate by indicating that you realize that this particular problem or difficult situation is common.

You should also make the candidate feel that you would not blame the candidate for the difficulties experienced.

Section: 2.5. The Interview – Information Sharing

You have now studied questioning, open-ended questions, leading questions, problem questions, multiple choice questions, probing questions and reassurance.

While the main objective is to gather enough information for you to make the selection decision, the candidate also needs to decide if the job is right for them and therefore needs information about you, your department and your company.

Good selection interviews include giving information to the candidate.

Your candidate will have questions to ask and you should be prepared to answer them immediately and honestly. The effective manager will prepare for these questions which will be asked.

The candidate will usually ask questions about: -

- ❏ The Company
- ❏ The Working Conditions
- ❏ Job Responsibilities
- ❏ Job Benefits

A lot of this information is fairly standard and should be readily available at the interview.

As the interviewer you should have a copy and also an appropriate grasp of the company's policies and working conditions.

Interview Preparation

In preparation for giving information at your next selection interview, as follows: -

- ❏ **Company:** you would include information items like a brief history of the company, its philosophy, market share, broad long-term plans, products, services, branch offices, number and types of employees.
- ❏ **Working Conditions:** you would specify the workplace, parking, welfare facilities, working hours and pension etc.
- ❏ **Job Responsibilities:** should be discussed in specific measurable terms, exactly what you would expect the jobholder to do and to what standard.
- ❏ **Job Benefits:** you should plan to discuss salary, bonuses, medical and pension funds, holidays, career development possibilities, and personal growth.

The following is a useful list of Do's and Don'ts for giving information: -

DO	DON'T
Know and give information on job requirements and explain thoroughly.	Oversell job opportunities.
Talk about your division, your products and the steady employment offered.	Talk too much.
Answer all the candidate's questions.	Sell the job to the applicant.
Talk on the candidate's language level.	Use involved shop terms (or acronyms) in explaining a job to an inexperienced but worthwhile applicant.
Provide sufficient information in order that the candidate may make an intelligent decision.	Knowingly or unknowingly misrepresent company policy, wages, working conditions, etc.
Give a brief explanation of company operations and objectives.	Moralize or lecture the candidate.
	Tell the candidate your troubles or outline the history of your success.
	Give encouragement to candidates who obviously are not suited to the company.

Section: 2.6. The Interview – Directing and Guiding

So far you have looked at ways to get job applicants to talk more. Often you may come across the opposite problem, the candidate who may talk too much in the interview situation. Without appearing disinterested in what is being said, be polite and redirect the candidate back onto the subject that will help your assessment.

To maintain control of the interview you would: -

❏ Acknowledge what the person is saying.

❏ Pick up a word and note an exploratory question to it.

❏ Listen carefully for words, which would help you to phrase a question.

❏ If necessary, gently remind the candidate politely, that you have a time limit and that there are other things to cover.

❏ Direct and guide the candidate through areas of the interview which require information to be provided by the company.

Section: 3.0. Quick Guide to the Interview Process

You have now looked at the selection process. You have considered the criteria, where you could find your candidate, how to plan for the interview, finding and giving information. It is now up to you to put it all together for a successful interview

The following summary guide will help you: -

1. **Be Prepared**
   1.1. Check your meeting room.
   1.2. Your time.
   1.3. Have a copy of the candidate's application form.
   1.4. Have your planned questions and writing paper available.
2. **Use your time well. Don't waste it on information that the application form provides.**
3. **Listen attentively and summarize regularly what is being said to get all the facts straight.**
   3.1. Summarizing also helps you to listen better; this is a skill in itself.
4. **Let the applicant do most of the talking. You want to get information not give it.**
5. **Control the interview and keep the applicant on track.**
6. **Make notes during the interview. Remember at the end of the interview, you need to know if the person:**
   6.1. Can do the job (has the candidate got the ability?)
   6.2. Will do the job (does the candidate want the job?)
   6.3. Will stay in the job (will the candidate get along with the company and with you?)
7. **Create a climate which is pleasant and businesslike. Above all be relaxed. If you are tense your candidate will pick up on it.**

Section: 4.0. Reference Checking – is Important

Previous employers can provide you with a good indicator on whether your candidate will be compatible with your company for the job to be filled.

An employer doesn't usually have to give a work reference – but if they do, it must be fair and accurate. Workers may be able to challenge a reference they think is unfair or misleading.

Employers must give a reference if:

❏ There was a written agreement to do so

❏ They are in a regulated industry, e.g. financial services.

Important Note: In the event of any doubt regarding the employment laws regarding reference checking, use your personnel department or your recruitment company to carry out the reference checks, on your behalf.

Some companies send out standard forms or questionnaires. However, reference checking is normally done by telephone.

Typically, firms use the telephone method but limit their questions to verification of employment dates and reasons for leaving to obtain the basic information from the exercise.

Note: Reference checking by telephone takes real skill, and no less than those needed for a selection interview. It is advisable to delegate this task to a professional recruiter and ensure that the structure of the reference check is of a high standard!

You <u>MUST</u> have your candidate's permission to do a reference check and please ensure the permission is in writing. You <u>MUST</u> only contact the referee and company named by the candidate.

To be fair on the candidate, explore further if you receive an unfavorable remark. Some employers may be referring to an isolated incident, so discuss the matter thoroughly. However, it is not prudent to discuss contradictions to the candidate's application.

The following Simple 6 Step Reference Check will help you with the structure: -

These first two steps are important in establishing a rapport with the referee. The next four steps are aimed at obtaining the most from the referee.

1. Get the referee's cooperation to do the reference check by advising the referee that the candidate has agreed to your

> phone call and state that any information given will be strictly confidential.

2. Check whether the call is convenient to the referee.

3. State your questions in a clear and unambiguous manner.

4. Listen attentively to what the referee says.

5. Explore the candidate's strengths and weaknesses in relation to the job on offer.

6. Close the interview by thanking the referee for their time.

Finally, you could disregard the information received from previous employers, as ultimately - it is your decision.

Irrespective of what you decide to do with the information you receive, always check for the strengths you are looking for and weaknesses you wish to avoid. This will help you to structure the job and any possible training requirements.

Section: 5.0. Personnel Selection – and the Winner is

You are now at the crucial point in the whole hiring process it's the time to make a decision.

Here you will find the **Classical Decision Making Model,** as follows: -

1. Problem Identification

2. Information Gathering

3. Boundary Conditions

4. Appraise Information

5. Tentative Decisions

6. Review Decision

7. Action.

Decision Making Process: -

Your initial criteria for a successful candidate should be clear and unambiguous. A comparative assessment will be facilitated from your questioning and research. You have evaluated all the likely candidates narrowing them down to a short list that meets the essential criteria. Throughout the selection process you have virtually completed the decision making process, as follows: -

1. **Problem Identification**: When a position becomes vacant or additional positions are required, you identified a problem, which needed solving, by hiring a person.

2. **Information Gathering**: You then gathered information, what exactly will the person be doing? What type of person will be successful? What must the person be able to do to succeed and stay in the job? You went further and obtained information from the candidates. Perhaps you even eliminated some because they did not meet some essential criteria.

3. **Boundary Conditions**: The boundary conditions of the decision were established during the information gathering stage. These are the minimum criteria that the candidate must meet in order to be considered. Remember the job specification characteristics you listed? Those are your boundary conditions against which you should measure your tentative hiring decision.

4. **Appraise information**: Just before checking references you collated information in terms of strengths, weaknesses, concerns and areas to probe further. After the reference check you place the information in order and the reference check helps you to assess and validate the information.

5. **Tentative Decisions**: Selection decisions require an evaluation process to get to a Tentative Decision. Evaluate on the 'personnel requirement guide' and the 'candidates application and interview results' cross referenced to each of the final candidates or 'short list'. At this point you should have a good feel for the No. 1 candidate who best meets all the 'short list' criteria and an alternative selection No. 2 candidate. If the No. 1 candidate has a change of heart or certain weaknesses emerge you have a good alternative candidate.

6. **Review your Decision**: It's against any relative weaknesses or reservations, that you review your final decision. Next, you need to answer several questions to finalize you decision. Can I overcome any apparent weaknesses? Do I have to support the candidate by giving additional training or modifying the job? And lastly, will my No. 1 candidate accept the job offer? Only when you've checked these answers and you are quite sure that your candidate will accept, do you go to the next action.

7. **Action**: This will mean writing an appointment letter of offer for the selected candidate, and after written acceptance, drafting letters advising and thanking the other candidates for their interest and time.

This brings us to the end of the selection process.

Remember.........

Management Wisdom

The best executive is the one who has sense enough to pick good men to do what he wants done, and the self-restraint to keep from meddling with them while they do.

*Theodore Roosevelt

You will have many opportunities in your everyday management job to use these skills. And it will stand you in good stead for future personnel selection tasks.

Chapter 7: Coaching and Reviewing for Success

———————

The Fifth Rule of Smart Management: Establish an effective method for coaching and reviewing individuals for success and correcting failing performance.

Section: 1.0. How to Handle Coaching for Success

Coaching for success, means creating a culture of leadership and guidance and giving up your authority to the individual rather than taking control of the situation; this can be a difficult area for some managers.

Unfortunately, coaching employees is a task sometimes overlooked even by responsible management and creating a culture of followers in a business may result in poor performance, low morale and high employee turnover levels etc.

Management's job is to build confidence!

Good coaching and mentoring skills are becoming increasingly more important in modern fast paced businesses.

Coaching is almost entirely discussion based.
There are three basic steps: -
1. **When?**
    1.1. When do I need to coach, mentor or counsel?
        ❏ When staff seek help in the course of doing a new or difficult job.
        ❏ When you identify an individual who has the ability and motivation to improve, but not the skills.
2. **What to do?**
    2.1. In essence, what do I need to do?

❑ I need to listen, help them think through issues and confirm some action, which also meets company objectives.

❑ I need to help them to see for themselves what should be
done, how and why.

3. What not to do?

3.1. What should I NOT do?

❑ Give instructions or tell personnel how they should do
it - your way.

❑ The result of giving advice or telling only solves a problem in the short term.

For lasting results a manager should help personnel develop their own
problem solving abilities.

*Note: There will be exceptions where you need to go into the advice mode,
such as during a major crisis when the pressure is on, but this is **not** a coaching situation.*

In being proactive and encouraging others to be proactive the effective
manager will coach employees to anticipate problems and adopt a forward
planning approach.

Basically, there are two types of coaching discussions.

1. When your personnel come to you on a specific issue, task
or problem.

2. When you initiate a discussion to help personnel clarify their
long-term objectives.

It would be difficult to plan for the first type of discussion as it is initiated
by the employee, nevertheless it is important to remain approachable and
at ease with these discussions and to encourage them.

Section: 1.1. Coaching Personnel - Outline and Systematic Method
Coaching is an essential part of personnel development and can take many
forms, formal training, special assignments and study teams etc. Coaching
is important to employees because they rely on their manager for information, feedback and recognition.

The effective manager is expected to manage all aspects of the workforce.
You need to develop a basic outline for coaching whether the employee
approaches you for help or you initiate this type of discussion, as follows: -

Basic Outline and Systematic Method for Coaching: -

1.0 The Objectives

1.1 To create and maintain a warm and open atmosphere.

1.2 To improve the relationship and your own credibility.

1.3 To assist personnel to improve their ability to solve immediate problems through questioning and contributing to solutions to problems.

2.0 The Introduction

2.1 Welcome and encourage the employee and listen carefully.

3.0 Clarify Areas of Concern

3.1 Identify any gaps between the existing and desired ability of the employee and invite the employee to clarify what the employee already knows, what the employee understands or what the employee can do.

3.2 Give the employee time to think through a work related problem or issue and encourage the employee to suggest possible solutions.

4.0 List Alternative Solutions

4.1 Where it is the employee who is directly involved in the problem area, the solutions or ideas and implementation should come from the employee.

4.2 It is important – that you do not attempt fix the problem for the employee.

4.3 Remember, it is the long-term problem solving ability of the employee you are developing.

5.0 Agreement

4.1 Together with the employee you should assess the pros and cons of each solution. This same collaborative approach should continue through the risk assessment to an agreement on a best solution and the implementation plan.

6.0 Avoid

6.1 Criticism of any proposed solution.

6.2 Taking the problem away from the employee by fixing it yourself and / or delegating it to someone else.

6.3 Being too prescriptive.

Problem solving discussions such as these increase commitment to the solution.

Remember..........*To be a good coach, one needs to develop trust.*

Quick Tip*: applying good coaching skills and seeing people grow – motivates both personnel and effective managers.*

Section: 1.2. Nine Most Important Discussion Skills for Coaching

You have covered the relationship and support that goes into a good coaching discussion. You now need to consider which discussion skills you need.

Let's look at the nine most important discussion skills you need in a coaching session: -

1. **Listening** in order to get a clear picture of the employee's current problems. Listen carefully to the employee's answers to your questions. The employee should provide most of the information.

2. **Questioning for facts** regarding what action the employee has already taken. How much of the issue the employee understands. Where the employee has had similar experience.

3. **Recognizing and supporting** the importance of the employee's existing knowledge and experience.

4. **Avoid criticizing** actions the employee may have taken already. This will increase defensiveness. Remember that one of management's key objectives is to increase the independence of employees and for this to happen, you should restrict comment to where you know the employee may have done better.

5. **Providing information** – only where the employee needs it to supplement the employee's own knowledge and experience. The whole basis of mutual problem solving is that useful information is shared between the manager and the employee. Therefore, you must resist the temptation to be overly prescriptive in what the employee should do.

6. **Encourage solutions** from the employee during the coaching discussion: -
   - ❏ On the problem the employee approached you with.
   - ❏ On the possible future problems of a similar nature.

7. **Prevent misunderstanding** by checking understanding, by summarizing in your own words what the employee is saying: -

   ❏ Let's check we're on the same page.....

   ❏ Are we saying that…?

   Particularly, when discussing a new concept or procedure to check that both parties have the same understanding on the issue.

8. **Sharing feelings** will help your employee to relate to you better. This works well for relationship building and shows your openness in the discussion.

9. **A summary** is essential to bring the discussion to a logical conclusion. This should include:

   ❏ The major points discussed

   ❏ The solution agreed upon

   ❏ An action plan with dates and responsibilities

   ❏ Follow up review dates.

Section: 2.0. How to Handle the Performance Review for Success

As a manager, you are responsible for quantifiable and measurable results. And you have been allocated employees to assist you in this. They in turn have work objectives and tasks that are expected to provide meaningful results in terms of the company's objectives. You therefore need to review performance of your employees from time to time.

Section: 2.1. The Performance Review – for Progress and Monitoring

The performance review is one of the forms of management control tools to ascertain current progress and status; it is a method that measures the performance of people and company resources towards achieving predetermined objectives. It is also a way of growing people's skills and developing them.

What does the Review do for an employee?

1. **Recognition**: It provides formal recognition for a job well done.

2. **Development**: Progress reviews can often bring new challenges to the job, such as doing something differently or adding tasks. If you can ensure the review develops the employee in this way it becomes motivational and more interesting.

Reviewing Employee Performance
Performance reviews are discussions which you can plan, as follows: -

Section: 2.2. An Outline for Performance Review Discussions
1. **What is the objective of the performance review?**
   1.1. To improve existing relationships.
   1.2. To establish the progress made against objectives and measure performance to improve the employee's ability to meet preset objectives by the due date.

2. **A clear and motivating introduction would state**
   2.1. Why are we having the discussion?
   2.2. How will we format the discussion?

3. **Clarify areas of concern**
   3.1. What objectives were previously set?
   3.2. What are the results to date?
   3.3. Examine the variance and the reasons?
   3.4. Each objective is discussed and positive and negative variances noted.

4. **Listing alternative solutions for:**
   4.1. **Positive variances.**
      4.1.1. Should results or progress be maintained?
      4.1.2. Should new or increased objectives be discussed?
   4.2. **Negative variances.**
      4.2.1. How can we correct the variances?
      4.2.2. What can be done to bring the progress back on track?
      4.2.3. How can we clear the backlog?

Purpose: These questions are asked in order to: -

❏ **Agree on the best solutions.**
❏ **Minimize risks.**
❏ **Agree an implementation plan.**

The entire discussion outline is aimed at finding ways to ensure good performance and your personnel have clear achievement objectives and review dates.

Section: 2.3. Eight Discussion Skills of a Performance Review
A performance review is a problem solving discussion. You now need to deal with the following eight most important discussion skills necessary for an effective performance review discussion: -

1. **Provide information**: in a clear and concise manner. Provide the facts and figures available to you.

2. **Look for the facts from the employee/s:** -

   Typical questions at a performance review:
   - ❏ Were all objectives reviewed to the satisfaction of both parties?
   - ❏ If not, what can be done to correct those?
   - ❏ Were all the problems or obstacles analyzed and overcome?
   - ❏ Do we have sufficient resources to address the problems you have come across?
   - ❏ Do we have complete notes of this session of decisions made?
   - ❏ Is the employee benefiting from the work experience?
   - ❏ Are the employee's skills and knowledge improving?
   - ❏ Is motivation increasing?
   - ❏ Do the reviewed objectives include enough challenge for the employee?
   - ❏ Have new review dates and established methods for providing feedback been set?

3. **Listen:** carefully and make notes to clarifying questions with: -
   - ❏ What helped you?
   - ❏ What hindered you?
   - ❏ What actions have you taken so far?
   - ❏ Were these actions achieved easily?

4. **Provide Support**: for: -
   - ❏ Achievement of the objective.

❏ The employee's willingness to supply facts and information.

5. **Looking for solutions**: is important when you need to formulate a plan to bring poor results back on track or maintain good results. And it is essential that solutions are volunteered by the employee, rather than you providing them.

6. **Make Suggestions**: try not to provide too much information yourself; however, you may have to make suggestions if the employee has a knowledge gap or lacks the experience and only after every effort has been made to elicit a contribution.

7. **Preventing misunderstanding**: is critical during the review sessions as implementing a misunderstood action will not contribute to the company's objectives.

Questions which summarize the understanding of both parties similar to the following are useful to prevent misunderstanding:-

❏ Are you saying that by going the route you have suggested we may actually increase our market share?

❏ Let me see if I understand correctly, the only obstacle is in area 'x', and you believe that a minor change here could achieve a positive result?

Note: A review session can frequently uncover frustration and feelings of inadequacy. If this happens you should be ready to share some of your own experiences and feelings of similar situations with empathy.

8. **Sharing feelings**: is an important skill to develop good employee and manager relationships and encourage good problem solving relations. By sharing your own experiences, thoughts and feelings you will encourage the employee to do the same. Use comments like the following to defuse a sensitive situation: -

❏ I can understand you feeling frustrated.....

❏ I really appreciate how you must be feeling; I've been there myself.....

Section: 2.4. The Performance Review Agreement

Through the performance reviews you are solving problems that may exist within the business and anticipate possible future problems. During the discussion, check your understanding by summarizing the facts presented and then evaluating past problems that have been overcome, the achievements to date and the future action plans to avoid recurrent problems.

A performance review is based on mutual understanding and an agreement going forward which is normally written down.

Start off with a document describing the expected actions/tasks that are set, achievement status at appoint in time and the completion date. As a result of the review discussion, a new documented agreement may be drawn up which describes the reviewed actions and tasks and follow up actions.

Job Objectives and Review Form

Note: your company probably has standard documentation for these progress review discussions, but if not the simple format below may be useful to you.

Job Objectives and Review Form					
Name					
Position					
Work area					
Objective / Action / Task	Result/s Achieved	Problem/s Encountered	Reviewed Objectives	Follow up Action	Date complete

This type of form acts as a summary of the discussion which the employee can take and work to.

Please note, as with all other discussions summaries are crucial at the end of each major task or objective discussion and at the conclusion of the session.

A copy of the document such as the one above should form the basis of your planning and monitoring. Good discussion skills will become second nature to you with a systematic method, planning structure and review technique.

Section: 2.5. Feedback

Feedback should be given on positive and negative results. Handling positive results is relatively easy; it is the negative results which may create sensitive issues. The downside of ignoring a performance problem or negative results undermines employee motivation and may surface in any number of places as poor customer relations, poor attitude and deadlines not being met etc.

And keep the Question Model in focus, as it will help in clearing any difficulties or tension created during the review

1. **Why** do I need to take action in a particular area?
2. **What** objectives, action plan, shall I set?
3. **Who** will be involved?
4. **When** are my objectives and action plan dates?
5. **How** are my objectives and actions to happen?
6. **What if** a problem develops, what will I do?
7. **Where** should my objectives and action plan take me?

Performance reviews; are important discussions because the ultimate aim is to make your employee less dependent on you. Ideally you should be able to structure work objectives for your employees to enable them to review their own progress and performance and make this performance visible within the company.

Section: 3.0. Correcting Failing Performance

Use of the fundamental concepts will allow you to take the lead by providing the climate that makes problem solving and achievement attractive and provide information to help your personnel set their own objectives.

Section: 3.1. Outline and Systematic Method for Correcting Performance

You can prepare by thinking through this outline and use the discussion skills to improve employee/s motivation when correcting performance.

The Objectives for the Discussion are to: -

1. Close the performance gap with an agreed solution.
2. Help and encourage employees to reach their objectives.

3. Handle the discussion calmly and unemotionally and avoid criticism.
4. Motivate for better achievement.

Define a Clear and Motivating introduction

1. Refer to past discussions or agreements.
2. The reasons why it is important to have the discussion.
3. What you would like to achieve during the discussion.
4. Discuss current performance.
5. Discuss current behavior.

Clarify Areas of Concern

1. Explore any obstacles to the agreed level of performance.
2. Discuss the probable causes of the deviation from prior discussion or agreement.
3. Clarify if there are any problems and why.
4. Get the employee's perception of the effects and duration of the problem.

List Alternative Solutions

1. Ask your employee for solutions they could agree and commit to.
2. Make notes on various solutions for each problem identified.
3. Add solutions which motivate your employee.

Agree the Best Solution

1. Refer to the company's objectives.
2. Refer to the original objectives.
3. Explain any restrictions imposed on you through budgets and other controls.
4. Detail criteria for action, which develop the employee and are attainable.

Agree methods to minimize any technical or commercial risks

1. Detail the risks associated with not completing the corrective actions.
2. Minimize the risk by exploring and agreeing technical and commercial support resources to assist the employee.

3. Does your employee exhibit any resistance to the solutions proposed?

4. Is there any resistance from others?

5. The above outline will prepare you for handling these types of discussions comfortably and assist you with your forward planning.

Section: 3.2. Questioning and Listening

You now need to cover the discussion skills; skills that will help you to defuse sensitive situations. Often in a performance problem the real cause of the problem may be vague. And care must be taken by creating a supportive and motivational climate.

All problem solving and especially vague or failing performance problems require extensive questioning. You will identify pending or future problems easily if you set clear objectives and benchmarks for achievement with the following discussion skills.

Discussion Skills: -

1. **Define the problem**: looking for facts becomes critical when you need to define the extent of a deviation, the degree of damage caused, the implications if nothing is done and the reasons why the problem arose etc.

2. **Cause and effect relationship**: when the cause and extent of a problem is unclear, effective managers frequently check their own understanding of what is being said. In this way the manager ensures that both parties understand the cause and effect relationship.

3. **Preventing misunderstanding**: throughout the discussion you can build up a logical progression of facts until you have a clear picture of what is happening and why. In this way you can ensure the discussion or solution will not fail because of a misunderstanding regarding the information supplied.

4. **Listening**: to prevent misunderstanding you have to listen carefully and let the speaker know that you are listening, particularly where your employee may feel that they are being criticized. Looking at the person and making supportive gestures confirms you are listening and this is important.

5. **Share feelings**: the test of good discussion skills in a failing performance discussion is getting a positive response at the various stages without the person becoming defensive, critical or blaming others.

   The following will help you in the event of the employee becoming emotional or defensive. Stay calm and recap to make sure that there are no misunderstandings on either part.

   - ❏ Let's see if we both have all the facts, what you are saying is.......?
   - ❏ I know it's tough for you right now, so let's work together on it.
   - ❏ Could you just summarize the situation for me so far?

6. **Questioning to look for solutions**: you cannot fix a problem until the employee acknowledges that there is one! Therefore it is important the employee acknowledges the problem and agrees: -

   - ❏ That a problem exists.
   - ❏ The employee will play a major part in fixing it.
   - ❏ That looking for solutions requires extensive questioning to make the decision easier.

7. **Support the ideas and contributions**: let people know that you value them and their contributions by letting them know their ideas are good and thanking them for the contribution, which confers respect and courtesy to the employee.

8. **Summary of agreed solutions and actions**: this failing performance discussion may frequently lead to new or different action. The agreed action must be carefully summarized so that both parties know and remember exactly who has to do what and by when.

9. **Actions Required for Planning**: your first objective is to correct failing performance and bring the activities and results back on track. You therefore, need to define failing performance in much more specific terms. You need to know the expected activity and results, exactly what has to be done and by when. And then you must have sufficient facts on the deviation in terms of:

- ❏ What was done?
- ❏ What has not been done?
- ❏ When did it happen?
- ❏ Who was involved?

10. **Motivate your employees**: your second objective will be to guide this discussion in such a manner that you relate to the employee and obtain enthusiasm and motivation from the employee to change or improve - the purpose is not to allocate blame.

Remember.........

Management Wisdom

Fix the problem, not the blame.

*Old Japanese saying

Your research may also uncover other events which may have impacted on performance, as follows: -

- ❏ What has changed recently that could have caused the problem?
- ❏ Is there a new product, system, method or person involved?
- ❏ Have the employee's personal circumstances changed?
- ❏ Are other work areas failing as a result?

Quick Tip: *Keep an open mind and attempt to relate any other event to the variation in performance and do not draw early conclusions or make a definite cause and effect links too quickly, when you are only researching for probable causes.*

In order to be positive, supportive and trusting you must relate to your personnel's strengths and motivation, so that you may build solutions on these strengths. You therefore need to identify your personnel's strengths beforehand; however, discussion on any apparent weaknesses or challenges should be kept to a minimum, if mentioned at all.

Section: 4.0. Reviewing Coaching and Performance Discussions

Effective managers review all major discussions in order to improve their skills. And encouraging evaluation and comment on the success of the discussion directly from the employee is the most appropriate. It will help you conclude discussions in a friendly amicable way and ensure that the person leaves feeling that you value your employee's work, contribution and opinion.

Discussion skills will now seem quite logical to you:
And the answers emanating from the following questions will give you a good idea of the level of commitment from your employee and whether the employee feels part of the solution process.

To recap: -
- ❏ You have assessed the situation.
- ❏ You know what you want.
- ❏ You have assessed the person.
- ❏ You know the employee's skill set.
- ❏ You know what work the employee is good at and likes doing.
- ❏ You can plan the questions and statements that will help you and your employee reach a solution objective.

One final thought on performance reviews: at the end of every discussion, automatically ask yourself the following questions: -

- ❏ Did I ask most of the questions?
- ❏ Did the employee do most of the talking?
- ❏ Did the employee generate most of the solutions?
- ❏ Did I summarize to prevent misunderstanding?
- ❏ Is there an acceptable solution agreed upon?
- ❏ Did I handle sensitive issues tactfully?
- ❏ Did I handle emotion and friction calmly and with understanding?

If the answer to these questions is yes, then you are on track - well done!

Chapter 8: Complaints, Discipline, Changes and Delegation

The Sixth Rule of Smart Management:
Learn how to handle complaints professionally,
discipline effectively, make changes that work and
delegate successfully.

Section: 1.0. How to Handle Complaints Professionally

All managers receive complaints at some time or another and complaints can be embarrassing to the company, but not all complaints are purely negative; you may learn a great deal from customer complaints which can assist you in correcting performance, streamlining you business, getting it right and staying profitable.

Put simply, the customer holds the keys to your success – or failure. Therefore, when you receive a complaint from a customer, remember the following: -

Remember.........

> ## Management Wisdom
>
> *Grasshopper always wrong, in argument with chicken.*
>
> ***Book of Chan**

A Complaint Assessment
Firstly, consider where most of your complaints come from and make a list.
Complaints generally come from different areas: -

- ❏ Customers.
- ❏ Suppliers.
- ❏ Personnel.

❏ Colleagues.

❏ Interdepartmental.

Managers receive complaints about: -

❏ Failures in the product or service. Failures to meet deadlines, unfair treatment, inappropriate behavior, dress and failure to adhere to company policy, etc.

You should not be concerned about a complaint; you should be concerned about a complaint that is <u>mismanaged</u>. In other words, when the complainant is not satisfied with how their complaint has been handled. Sometimes a seemingly minor issue can grow to negatively affect long term client relationships, future contracts, market reputation, trust, interdepartmental relationships, morale, productivity and the profitability of your company.

Effective managers spend time on this vital topic of complaint handling.

Section: 1.1. A Systematic Method for Complaint Handling

The following discussion outline applies to most complaint handling situations.

Apply it to a complaint you are currently handling to answer: -

❏ What can you do about complaints?

❏ How can they be handled so that both parties get to a win-win solution?

Discussion Outline for Complaint Handling

1. **Set Objectives**

    1.1. This is the objective you wish to achieve; it contains the criteria by which you measure your success on completion of handling the complaint.

    1.2. Note this may not be done before the discussion as most often complaint handling is a reactive discussion. The objective you wish to achieve with the complainant once formulated should always be at the back of your mind.

    1.3. Setting objectives is a planning step that can be done either on paper or in your head.

2. **Open Discussion**

2.1. This should state your sincere and genuine desire to resolve the complaint. It should also provide the complainant with the motivation to speak to you without further escalation. Your recognition of the complainant's feelings is an important factor in the success of this discussion.

2.2. Open the discussion by making a suggestion as to the structure of the discussion and how you might handle it. And check that the complainant agrees. Confirm with the complainant that it is your sincere desire to resolve the complaint.

3. Clarify Areas of Concern

3.1. This is the fact-finding area of your discussion. You want to establish the complainant's reasons for bringing the complaint and put yourself into the complainant's shoes. It may be necessary to deal with emotional and sometimes aggressive confrontational statements often with increasing volume. This may be difficult to deal with, but stay calm and show empathy with the complainant. Maintain this calm and sincere tone throughout the discussion and be aware of the level and tone of your own voice – keep it conversational and at your normal pace.

3.2. With this approach it will be possible to get past the emotion to the facts of the complaint. Calmly and clearly question the complainant's views and reason for the complaint.

3.3. It is important to get factual information regarding the complaint. Listen, be sympathetic and speak with empathy, particularly if the complainant is expressing negative or aggressive emotion. Provide information to fill any information gaps that the complainant may have.

4. List Alternative Solutions

4.1. Here you can narrow down any critical issues to a few clearly defined issues and you list possible tentative actions. Ask the complainant for their desired outcome to the complaint, and once this is clear to you. Ask the complainant for alternative solutions that they believe would rectify the situation and then go on to evaluate each solution with the complainant giving clear explanations for your views. Clearly state what you can do and what you may not be able to do.

4.2. Actively look for solutions for the complainant and provide the necessary information to keep solutions positive. Avoid the use of words such as can't, won't, not possible.

5. Agree on the Best Solution

5.1. Remember, you are aiming at a solution which meets the needs of both the complainant and your company. Openness and honesty should characterize your contributions.

5.2. Check the complainant's perception of the solutions as you must get a feel for the complainant's willingness to agree or disagree with different solutions to correct the problem, as you handle this area.

5.3. Jointly agree on the best solution and summarize who will do what and by when.

6. Minimize the Risks

6.1. Here you want to ensure that the action you have jointly agreed upon will:

6.1.1. Resolve the complaint to the maximum extent of your ability and authority.

6.1.2. Satisfy the complainant.

6.1.3. Prevent the complainant's problem from occurring again.

This may involve action steps on your part and possibly the complainant.

6.2. Explore the complainant's commitment to a joint solution to minimize any possible technical and commercial risks.

7. Agree on an Implementation Plan

7.1. Here you agree who does what, by when, with whom, how much and how well. And if appropriate, when the actions will be reviewed.

7.2. Detail and confirm with the complainant who will do what, through summarizing to bring your discussions together and move it forward to closing the discussion to the satisfaction of the complainant and the company.

Section: 1.2. Discussion Skills for Complaint Handling

You have looked in some detail at how to handle complaints using the discussion outline. You now need discussion skills to: -

❏ **Defuse.**

❏ **Reinforce.**

❏ **Show empathy.**

You should focus specifically on the skills necessary under each step in the outline, which are important to smooth the process, as follows: -

1. Set Objective.

2. Open Discussion.

3. Clarify Areas of Concern.

4. List Alternative Solutions.

5. Agree on Best Solution.

6. Minimize risks.

7. Agree on Implementation Plan.

You have seen how specific discussion skills are important at the various stages in the discussion outline. Now we look at some useful discussion skills when handling complaints, which can enhance your approach, as follows: -

1. **Showing Support for the Complainant**

   1.1. It is good to know when people listen to you and are concerned about your problems. So, when you have an incoming complaint, you should make every effort to listen calmly and carefully to the complainant's problems and show your support to the complainant without overly committing the company.

2. **Sharing your Feelings with the Complainant**

   2.1. This skill is particularly important to defuse any complaint. Show your feelings to the complainant; explain how you feel about the complaint and share their feelings to rectify the complaint. It encourages the complainant to calm down and open up. This allows you to deal with any underlying facts and root cause of the complaint.

3. **Prevent Misunderstanding**

   3.1. It is useful to check out your understanding at several specific intervals during the discussion.

3.2. Through understanding it is possible to resolve a complaint satisfactorily. Check your understanding of the complainant's perceptions of the facts and areas of concern and their feelings and perception of the solutions they would like to see to resolve the complaint.

4. Listen carefully to the Complainant

4.1. Above all listening carefully is a vital and active skill; listen to what the complainant is saying, how the complainant is saying it and what the complainant is not saying. Show empathy and summarize to indicate you have listened carefully.

Section: 1.3. Planning for Complaints

You need to plan for complaint handling. Specifically, you need to plan your discussion outline and discussion skills.

There are three aspects to planning for complaints as follows: -

1. Analyze the Situation and Set Clear Objectives

1.1. Complaints can require either reactive or proactive action on your part. You know that complaints arise out of several factors, such as a product or relationship failure, changes in technology or in company policy or legislation etc. You can therefore anticipate many of the complaints you receive. You can therefore, plan how you address these satisfactorily.

1.2. However, there are also those complaints which materialize that are new, both to you and the company. They require you to determine 'reactively' the best solution to the complaint.

1.3. The objective you set yourself should be clear, unambiguous and achievable as described in the first stage of the Discussion Outline, previously covered.

2. Assess the Complainants Root Cause and Motivation

2.1. Specifically, you want to get to the facts of the complaint. During discussions, you can get a feel for the person's motivation for the complaint. If you are able to determine the specific root cause of the problem and what is driving the person you are in a good position to understand the complainant.

2.2. In the case of a complaint from a client about your company, you need to find out the root cause of what is driving the complaint.

It may be difficult sometimes to access the customer's personal motivation. But, if you can get to the facts and root cause it will make your discussion towards a solution easier.

3. **Design a Specific Flow to the Discussion**

    3.1. You have looked at how specific discussion skills can be helpful. For example, sharing feelings is useful to let the other person know what you feel about the situation and by expressing support for the complainant this is useful towards reducing aggression and agreeing a solution.

    Note: Once you have planned how, when, and what you will say; you will be in a position to handle any recurrent complaint and ultimately work towards eliminating the root cause for these problems, for the benefit of the business.

Section: 2.0. Summary Review: Complaint Handling

In order to improve your skills, it is necessary to evaluate and review the discussion, feedback is essential to managing effectively: -

1. **Organize Feedback from Other People**

    1.1. Handling complaints is a difficult and sensitive issue. It is because of that difficulty that it is necessary to get feedback on your performance.

    1.2. This could come from other people in the company

    1.3. Or from asking the complainant how they feel about the discussion. Ask if the complainant is happy and satisfied with the outcome of the discussions. Ask if the complainant will bring complaints to you, in the future. In that way you will certainly get feedback from the most important source - your customer.

2. **Seek Evaluation Comments from Employees**

    2.1. Your colleagues and personnel are useful sources of information about your performance. You will, of course have to prepare or coach them for this role. You may wish to ask them to comment on certain aspects of your discussion.

    2.1.1. Getting to the root of the problem.

    2.1.2. Reducing aggression.

    2.1.3. Handling your own feelings etc.

3. **Self Assessment Review Statements**

 3.1. The following can be used to highlight your success in this area, answer yes or no to the following statements: -

  3.1.1. I asked most of the questions.

  3.1.2. The complainant did most of the talking.

  3.1.3. Your relationship with the complainant has been enhanced.

  3.1.4. I know what I did well.

  3.1.5. I know what I could do better.

  3.1.6. I know which discussion skills I used to good effect.

  3.1.7. I know which discussion skills I could have used more.

   ❏ If the answer is yes to the above statements, well done!

4. **Draft an improvement plan**

 4.1. As a result of your review, and answering the above, what should you do next time to improve the discussion?

Remember.....

 ❏ Handling complaints is critical to the business.

 ❏ The discussion outline is the basis for such a discussion.

 ❏ The discussion skills suggest the methods of handling each step in the outline.

 ❏ The discussion should be pre-planned, where possible.

 ❏ The discussion and the outcome should be reviewed.

Section: 3.0. Quick Guide to Effective Complaint Handling

You could use the Quick Guide to ensure efficient and effective complaint handling: -

1. **Set clear unambiguous and achievable objectives for the discussion.**

 1.1. And determine what outcome you want.

2. **Detail the complainant's root cause and motivation.**

 2.1. Decide what the complainant's root cause, facts, reasons and motivation are.

3. **Work out what questions you will use.**

    3.1. Decide how you will get the complainant's involvement and commitment.

4. **Work out how you will use each of the discussion outline steps in the sequence proposed.**

    4.1. Determine how you will ensure you maintain this plan.

5. **Determine which of the discussion skills you will use with each of the discussion outline steps.**

    5.1. Decide which will be the most difficult to use.

    5.2. Decide which will be the most critical to use.

6. **After the discussion arrange for feedback on your skills.**

    6.1. Decide

        6.1.1. Who?

        6.1.2. How?

        6.1.3. When?

        6.1.4. And against what criteria?

7. **Use the review questions suggested.**

    7.1. Consider what others you can add.

8. **Work out an improvement plan for yourself and determine.**

    8.1. How?

    8.2. When?

    8.3. Where?

Remember.........

Management Wisdom

Better than a thousand hollow words, is one word that brings peace.

*Buddha

You are ready to take on any complaint that might come your way, now and in the future and more importantly you can now assist other personnel who may be experiencing problems in this area.

Section: 4.0. How to Handle Discipline and Difficult People

As a manager, you will undoubtedly have to handle discipline and difficult people from time to time.

The discussion is not an easy one it requires preparation and planning. The consequences of ineffective handling of such a discussion or not addressing these discussions are serious for the company.

Remember.........

Management Wisdom

Left to themselves, things tend to go from bad to worse.

*Unknown

Typical in-company problems are generally related to some form of disciplinary action the results of which can be: -

- ❏ **Union action.**
- ❏ **Arbitration.**
- ❏ **Legal action.**

The ineffective handling of the preliminary disciplinary discussion can be problematic. Therefore it is important for you to be able to handle such discussions in a fair and reasonable manner, and maintain the discretionary power and authority to take disciplinary action to the next level, if required.

The following will guide you through handling a discipline discussion and difficult people for the company and yourself appropriately.

The purpose of the preliminary disciplinary discussion is to jointly agree a solution to the current situation.

It is not intended to cover the many procedural aspects of disciplinary hearings, including formal reprimands, warnings, letters, disciplinary meetings, hearings, dismissal, arbitration and legal actions that could form part of this topic; which would normally be handled through reference to your legal and/or employment law department personnel.

In order to start the process, think of a situation when you may have to have a discipline discussion with an employee for a recent action which is outside company policy or you have identified a need for performance improvement or there is an opportunity for improvement.

You know how important a disciplinary discussion can be for you, your personnel and your company. Firstly, you need to look at what can be done when conducting the primary disciplinary discussion, as follows: -

Section: 4.1. A Systematic Method for Handling Discipline

The following discussion outline is for handling a discipline related discussion: -

1. **Set Objectives**

   1.1. The first step enables you to decide what you want to achieve; to correct, reprimand or take disciplinary action against the individual.

   1.2. For example, you want to get the individual back on track, therefore: -

      1.2.1. Formulate your objective.

      1.2.2. Ensure it is quantifiable.

      1.2.3. Ensure it is measurable.

      1.2.4. Set a review date.

      1.2.5. Decide where you will have the disciplinary discussion.

2. **Have a Clear and Motivating Introduction**

   2.1. Once you have the individual in a setting where you will not be interrupted: -

      2.1.1. Clearly explain why you have called the person in and the nature of your concern.

      2.1.2. Give information on what has led to the discussion becoming necessary.

      2.1.3. Begin the discussion by recapping the circumstances which led up to this discussion and provide information. Make suggestions as to how you would like to handle the discussion.

3. **Clarify the Areas of Concern**

   3.1. Explain why you are concerned and ask for the individual's help in solving the problem.

   3.2. Ask for the individual's open response.

3.3. Clarify any concerns the individual may have.

3.4. Ensure that all the information and facts presented are correct.

3.5. Ensure that the individual does the same from their side.

3.6. Share your feelings; it is useful to explain your concerns and providing information is important to support your concerns.

3.7. Look for facts to establish the individual's reasons and concerns regarding the problem.

4. **List Alternative Solutions**

4.1. Ask the individual for their solution to the situation.

4.2. Write down these solutions as it shows your intent to solve the problem and becomes a reference document.

4.3. Add your solutions, as applicable.

4.4. Look for solutions and find out what the individual perceives can be done to prevent a recurrence of the problem.

4.5. Be prepared for disagreement, as you may not agree with all the individual's solutions.

5. **Agree on the Best Solution**

5.1. Jointly review each solution with the individual and test them to see if they will solve the problem in the future.

5.2. Jointly agree on the best and most practical solution.

5.3. Decide what action the individual has to take to ensure that the solution works.

5.4. Decide what action you need to take to ensure the solution is working.

5.5. Summarize the discussion to ensure everyone is in agreement regarding who will do what and by when.

5.6. Decide how you will handle the summary.

6. **Minimize the Risks**

6.1. Ensure what you have to do to make the solution work.

6.2. Decide what actions are appropriate for you to take with the individual. Here you should spell out exactly what disciplinary steps you have to take, their nature and whether they will be withdrawn at a later stage and/or the effective date for their implementation, if the situation does not improve.

6.3. You don't want this situation to recur, therefore you must indicate for the record the disciplinary action you are presently taking and what future action you will take if there is no improvement or a recurrence of the problem.

6.4. Record how you will do this.

7. **Agree on the Implementation Plan**

7.1. Summarize the entire discussion by restating, for the record: -

7.1.1. The action plan to resolve and overcome the problem.

7.1.2. The disciplinary action you will be taking now or in the future.

7.1.3. The plan going forward on completion of the action plan.

7.2. Summarize all-important issues to spell out who does what, how, by when.

Section: 4.2. Discussion Skills for Handling Discipline
To continue to support the process: -

1. Have a clear and motivating Introduction.
2. Clarify areas of concern.
3. List alternative solutions.
4. Agree on the best solutions.
5. Minimize the risks.
6. Agree on the implementation plan.

You saw how important it is to use specific discussion skills for each step during the discussion outline.

The Four Discussion Skills
The discussion skills you will use are listed as follows: -

1. **Supporting**

1.1. This is useful to indicate and stress areas of agreement between you and the individual. It is necessary to clearly differentiate between where you agree and disagree and close these gaps.

2. **Sharing Feelings**

2.1. You will probably elicit negative feelings from the individual when you indicate the nature of this discussion. You should be prepared to express your sincere feelings on the matter, as this creates openness and promotes trust.

3. Preventing Misunderstanding

3.1. Summarize; this skill is necessary to ensure you are in possession of all the relevant facts. It enables you to show that you are listening to the individual's arguments and the facts presented.

4. Listening

4.1. You must listen carefully and calmly and plan when you will speak and when you will listen.

Section: 4.3. Planning For Discipline

To have the discussion you must plan. At the end of this section you will be in a position to hold the discussion concerning discipline.

Planning: -

1. Analyze the Situation and set Clear Objectives

1.1. There is a need to set objectives for the discussion.

1.2. Consider your objectives for such a meeting.

2. Analyze the Employee's Strengths, Weaknesses and Motivation

2.1. You must consider the individual with whom you are going to be dealing.

2.2. Firstly, the individual's strengths.

2.2.1. What strengths can you build on?

2.2.2. What strengths can you count on?

2.3. Secondly, the individual's weaknesses.

2.3.1. You should try to avoid a lengthy discussion on the weaknesses, if at all.

2.3.2. Set strict deadlines for any of the issues.

2.4. Thirdly, the individual's motivations you can appeal to?

2.4.1. Stress the need for high quality results, standards, excellence etc.

3. Design the Discussion Flow

3.1. How to use the discussion outline.

3.1.1. Ask specific questions.

    3.1.2. Decide when.

    3.1.3. Get the individual involved.

    3.1.4. Get the individual to commit to an action plan.

You are now well prepared for the discussion.

Section: 5.0. Summary Review: Handling Discipline

And now you must consider reviewing the disciplinary discussion.

1. **Organize Feedback from Other People**

    1.1. With your manager.

    1.2. Review the discussion with a colleague.

    They can often give good feedback and suggest alternative ways of handling comments / situations.

2. **Evaluation from Employees**

    2.1. Sometimes depending on the sensitivity it can be difficult. But, the most obvious person to seek evaluation from is the individual. You could ask questions directly at the end of the discussion to obtain some feedback, as follows: -

    ❏ How do you feel about the discussion?

    ❏ Do you feel you have been treated fairly?

3. **Self Assessment Questions**

    Ask self assessment questions as follows: -

    3.1. Did I achieve my objective?

    3.2. How well did I use the discussion outline?

    3.3. What did I learn from its use?

    3.4. How well did I plan?

    3.5. How satisfied am I with the feedback I obtained on my discussion?

    3.6. How could I obtain more / better quality feedback next time?

    3.7. What could I do better next time?

4. **Work on Improvement Plans**

    4.1. Having reviewed your discussion.

    4.1.1. What can you do to improve your skills next time?

Section: 6.0. Quick Guide to the Effective Handling of Discipline

You have reviewed the need to plan and carefully execute a preliminary discipline discussion. This Quick Guide for such a discussion will help you through this sensitive area.

1. Set an objective for the discussion, which is quantifiable and measurable.
2. Make sure you have all the correct facts.
3. During the planning of the discussion decide what the important facts are.
4. Establish a climate which is relaxed, yet business like and professional.
5. Determine and list the questions you plan to ask during the discussion.
6. All discussions should be perceived as fair and reasonable and as corrective measures, not as a punishment.
7. Anticipate the sensitive areas of the discussion and attitude you may encounter.
8. Decide which discussion skills will be particularly important to use to handle the sensitive areas and attitude.
9. Decide how you will use the discussion outline.
10. Determine how you can motivate the individual and take the time and action you require.
11. Decide how you will obtain feedback on your skills.
12. Through feedback, determine if you have been successful or not, and determine what you will do if you need to correct it.

Quick Tip: *ensure all discussions of this nature are fully recorded and dated for future reference.*

Remember.........

> ## Management Wisdom
>
> *In order to carry a positive action we must develop here a positive vision.*
>
> ***Dalai Lama**

Section: 7.0. How to Make Changes that Work

The following sections, deal with the aspects of communicating change. We live in a time of ever increasing change. It has become a part of our lives.

Remember.........

> ## Management Wisdom
>
> *The only person who likes change is a wet baby.*
>
> ***Roy Z M Blitzer**

What is established practice today may become outdated tomorrow with more and quicker changes likely to occur in the future.

Change in business is inevitable for survival. Computer hardware replaces employees; electronic equipment regulates the pace and quality of work, the flow of electronic information moves instantaneously and emails, contracts, graphs, plans and drawings are now rapidly available between departments, companies and countries.

How do you handle these changes? First, you will be faced with more situations where you have to communicate change effectively to your personnel.

The result of managers communicating change badly is: -

- ❏ **Insecurity.**
- ❏ **Poor morale.**
- ❏ **Low motivation.**
- ❏ **Job insecurity.**
- ❏ **Distrust.**

The result of managers communicating change effectively is: -

- ❏ **Open communication.**
- ❏ **Reduced resistance.**
- ❏ **Less obstruction.**
- ❏ **Empowering people.**
- ❏ **Building trust.**
- ❏ **Support for the change.**

Your job is about communicating change in the most effective manner, to minimize the negative consequences and build positive responses to change.

Remember.........

Management Wisdom

The secret of change is to focus all your energy, not on fighting the old, but on building the new.

*Socrates

Section: 7.1. Systematic Method for Communicating Change

How do you communicate the change?

The answer is contained in the following systematic methods and discussion outline. By using the outline you will be able to make changes work for you.

Discussion Outline for Communicating Change

1. **Set Objectives**
   1.1. Where do you wish to be once the change is complete?
   1.2. Specific objectives revolve around making the change work, introducing the change without resistance, testing reaction to the change, obtaining commitment to making the change work.

2. **Give the Introduction**
   2.1. When communicating change it is vitally important to be clear and unambiguous.

2.2. You will need to clearly identify the areas that will be affected. Explain why the change has been necessitated and how it is to be implemented. Hold nothing back from the employees and be transparent on this issue; they will need all the facts for you to reduce resistance and gain commitment to the changes you have to make.

2.3. In introducing your subject you need to provide information about the change. You need also to make suggestions about what structure and format you think the discussion should follow.

3. **Clarify Areas of Concern**

3.1. The secret for success here is to be completely open and honest. Tell people openly who will be affected by the change and how it will affect them. Anticipate questions and give facts to clarify any areas of concern.

3.2. Look for facts about how it will affect your personnel, provide information about the change, and include the positive and negative versions.

4. **List Alternative Solutions**

4.1. There will no doubt be opposition and objections and problems raised. You will ask the people who are affected for their honest commitment to make the change work. Your skill is to ask them diplomatically and calmly how they would overcome any objections and problems, list their solutions in a way that everyone can see them and ensure you obtain all solutions giving everyone the opportunity to voice their solution.

4.2. Look for solutions from your personnel. If you disagree with a solution state your difference in opinion and support it with facts.

5. **Agree on the Best Solution**

5.1. Here you will be required to call upon your group handling skills to agree on the best solution to each obstacle or problem raised.

5.2. Ensure that you summarize the discussion regularly to avoid misunderstanding.

6. **Minimize the Risks**

6.1.1. Your solutions may have to be checked out with other departments, people or a higher authority for feasibility. However, this is normally acceptable to advise your personnel that you will come back to them once you have assembled more information or obtained the appropriate authority to implement the proposed solution, and you would carry this out quickly.

    6.1.2. The open climate which you have established during this discussion will assist you in bringing the risks, obstacles and problems into the open.

7.   Agree on the Implementation Plan

    7.1. Decide and agree, **who** is going to do **what, why, where, how** and by **when?** It is most important to close off your agreement to the plan correctly, the more difficulty you foresee at this stage the more time you require clarifying the areas of concern, listing alternative solutions and if necessary, revisit those steps.

    7.2. Summarize your discussions to establish **who** does **what, when, where**, and **how**.

Section: 7.2. Discussion Skills for Communicating Change

You know from experience that it is not what you say, but how you say it that counts.

The following discussion skills will help support the systematic method for communicating change, which can help you ensure success: -

The Four Discussion Skills

The following four discussion skills are essential and used throughout your discussions. You can apply these skills to effectively communicate change or changes you have planned.

1.   Supporting

    1.1. You must show that you are supportive. When someone was supportive to you, you felt trusting, committed. Well, that is the positive attitude you are seeking and you can obtain a positive attitude by being genuinely supportive with your personnel.

2.   Sharing Feelings

    2.1. By telling others how you feel about the change shows your openness and trust in sharing with them. It helps create trust and is particularly useful in this type of difficult discussion.

3.   Preventing Misunderstanding

3.1. This skill should be used throughout the discussion to ensure that you adequately and correctly understand what has been expressed and how personnel feel.

4. **Listening Carefully**

   4.1. With this skill you will be able to clarify areas of concern, which requires careful attention to what's been said and what is required of you.

You have considered the outline and discussion skills. Next is planning for change.

Section: 7.3. Planning for Change

Let's go through the planning process below: -

1. **Analyze the Situation and Set Clear Objectives**

   1.1. This revolves around ensuring the change works, gaining commitment to the change, ensuring minimal organizational resistance to the change.

2. **Analyze the Employees Strengths, Weaknesses and Motivation**

   2.1. You must know your employees:

      2.1.1. Their strengths, which you can build upon.

      2.1.2. Their weaknesses which you must take cognizance of and avoid during discussion.

      2.1.3. And what motivates your employees or what should you stress to coincide with their motivation.

3. **Design the Discussion Flow**

   3.1. Planning when to introduce certain facts is essential. You should also plan what questions to ask – when and what solutions to the problems and obstacles you feel may come up.

In order to ensure you are fully prepared for your discussions, review the previous sections to check that you have everything organized.

Section: 8.0. Summary Review: Making Changes

Review your discussion and determine your strengths and improvement areas.

There are four areas to consider: -

1. **Organize Feedback from Other People**
   1.1. You could call in a consultant to assist.
   1.2. A trusted colleague or mentor to comment and test ideas with.
2. **Seek Evaluation from Employees**
   2.1. Seek the opinion of the employees to whom you are communicating the change.
   2.2. Ask personnel for their comments on how things went.
   2.3. Your questions should be informal even casual, yet unambiguous.
3. **Self Assessment Review Statements**
   3.1. The following can be used to highlight your success in this area, answer yes or no to the following statements: -
      3.1.1. I followed all the systematic methods in the discussion outline.
      3.1.2. I used the discussion skills.
      3.1.3. I know which skills I could improve on.
      3.1.4. I know what I should do differently next time.
      3.1.5. I know what went well with my planning.
      3.1.6. I know what did not go well in the planning.
      3.1.7. I know what I can do better next time.
         ❏ If the answer is yes to the above statements, well done!
4. **Work on an Improvement Plan**
   4.1. Identify from your review what you want to capitalize on.
   4.2. Identify what you would do differently next time.

Section: 9.0. Quick Guide to Communicating Change

At the conclusion of this section on communicating change, it will be useful to have a quick guide to use before such a discussion:

1. Set an objective for the discussion, which is quantifiable and measurable.
2. Use the systematic methods and discussion outline.
3. Make sure you have all the correct facts.
4. Communicate all the facts about the change clearly.

5. Determine how you can motivate individuals and take the time and action to support the change.

6. Consider and list what obstacles and problems you may encounter.

7. Make a note of how you will deal with obstacles and sensitive areas using the discussion skills.

8. List the questions you plan to ask during the discussion.

9. Decide who will be for the change and who will be against the change and how you will handle those for and against the change.

10. Ensure you have everything in place, before the discussion.

11. Decide how you will obtain feedback on the discussion.

12. Through feedback, determine if you have been successful and determine what you will do to correct it, if necessary.

Remember.........

Management Wisdom

Nothing is more constant than change.

*Unknown

Section: 10.0. How to Delegate Successfully

Firstly, delegation is an essential part of your job as a successful and effective manager and these sections will show you how to delegate successfully.

Remember.........

Management Wisdom

Don't put off till tomorrow what you can delegate today..

*Unknown

The fact that delegation is interpreted differently by different people and sometimes incorrectly can lead to some confusion. Therefore, two areas require clarification: -

1. It is important to note that **delegation** is not **abdication**.
2. You can delegate the **authority** for the task but the **responsibility** remains with you!

As you move up in your company, so you must delegate more.

Remember.........

Management Wisdom

Responsibility always exceeds authority..

*Kinkler's First Law

Good managers can be measured by their success in effectively delegating their tasks. The professional manager recognizes the need to delegate carefully and considers **what** can be delegated, **to whom**, by **what completion dates** and introduces a monitoring, feedback and control system.

Delegation if used well, can improve your own efficiency and effectiveness and it can have a very positive impact on personnel training and personnel motivation for the company.

Self Assessment: Please consider the following self assessment to see if any of the statements fit your profile: -

---

My Profile

Answer true or false to the following statements?

1. All my jobs or tasks are completed on time.
2. I never miss a deadline.
3. I do not take work home.
4. I do not work harder or longer than my personnel.
5. My personnel are adequately trained.
6. My personnel can complete tasks well.
7. I tend to spend more time on planning and controlling rather than on details.
8. I am confident in delegating my tasks.

If the answer to all of these statements is true, well done!

If the answer to any of these statements is false, take note and work on them. This should give you some indication that you should be delegating at least a portion of your work to your personnel.

Section: 10.1. A Systematic Method for Delegation

The following systematic method and outline is the most effective way to show you how to delegate.

To start with, please consider a task or small project from your current workload which you can delegate, as you become more confident with experience, delegate whole projects rather than individual tasks.

Use this section to plan delegation.

Discussion Outline for Delegation

1. **Set Objectives**

    1.1. Decide what you want to achieve by delegating a particular job, for yourself and for the delegate.

2. **Have a Clear and Motivating Introduction**

    2.1. Introduce what you want to delegate clearly, explain your objective for the employee's growth, competence, etc.

    2.2. Provide information about what you want to do, why and how.

2.3. Make suggestions to the format for the discussion and what you will say.

3. **Clarify Areas of Concern**

   3.1. Clearly state your areas of concern for the content details, quality levels, dates of completion etc., of the job to be delegated. Share your feelings on these areas to show your trust in the delegate.

   3.2. Allow the delegate to voice areas of concern, it is important to elicit concerns and explore how the delegate feels about taking on the delegate role.

   3.3. By providing information you will be able to explain and detail any concerns you may have.

4. **List Alternative Solutions**

   4.1. Ensure that both you and your delegate generate as many solutions as possible.

   4.2. The list should contain all the various ways of ensuring that your concerns are met. Applying this to the job at hand.

   4.3. Looking for solutions will enable you to draw out your delegate's alternatives, this is vital for commitment. Discuss each solution and be prepared to handle disagreement, both yours and your delegates.

5. **Agree on the Best Solution**

   5.1. Each solution must be evaluated in the light of the information you have, the information the employee has and the concerns of both parties.

   5.2. The best solution is the best way of delegating the work and ensuring its effective completion, given the constraints on you, the delegate and completion of the job.

   5.3. Having discussed each alternative solution, choose the best solution. Summarizing is useful to avoid misunderstanding and in deciding who will do what and by when.

6. **Minimize the Risks**

   5.1. To ensure that all goes well with the job delegated, schedule feedback meetings and reports back to ensure that the delegation is effective.

5.2. Ensure that the employee is committed to the solution. Seek confirmation of the delegate's commitment and ask what the delegate will do to complete the job.

7. Agree on the Implementation Plan

7.1. Summarize who is going to do what, by when and to what standards, determine a periodic monitoring and feedback system.

7.2. Summarize all the actions agreed. Record the agreed points in writing and give the employee a copy of your notes of the outcome of the discussion.

Section: 10.2. Discussion Skills for Effective Delegation

You have looked at specific means of handling effective delegation discussions by using the systematic methods and discussion outline: -

1. Have a Clear and Motivating Introduction.

2. Clarify areas of Concern.

3. List Alternative Solutions.

4. Agree on the Best Solution.

5. Minimize the Risks.

6. Plan Implementation.

The following are useful skills for the discussion outline. Consider how you would plan to use them in your delegation.

The Four Discussion Skills

1. Supporting

1.1. Supporting is an important skill; it shows your genuine and sincere concern for the viewpoints of your delegate. It is particularly useful in instances when you want to demonstrate your agreement to your delegate's suggestions in the process.

2. Share Feelings

2.1. Particularly useful to show areas of concern, and to bring out difficult concerns which you may have e.g. quality, deadlines etc.

3. Preventing Misunderstanding

3.1. By summarizing, you ensure that you fully understand what has been discussed and particularly when you explore any concerns the delegate may express.

4. Listening

4.1. It is extremely important to listen carefully! Ensure good eye contact, note taking and use of the above three skills to improve your listening ability. You must listen and be seen to listen by the delegate.

Section: 10.3. Planning for Delegation

You are now ready to plan the discussion: -

1. **Analyze the Situation and Set Clear Objectives**

    1.1. Determine what the employee's level of commitment is to the job you want delegated.

    1.2. Decide how pressurized the individual is with current work loading.

    1.3. Decide what you want to achieve for yourself and for your delegate.

2. **Analyze the Employee's Strengths, Weaknesses, and Motivation**

    2.1. Decide what really motivates the delegate.

    2.2. Determine what your delegate's reaction will be to the delegation.

    2.3. Consider the ways you can build on the delegate's strengths.

    2.4. Consider what you must do to avoid weaknesses.

    2.5. Consider how the employee reacted to delegation before.

3. **Design a Discussion Flow**

    3.1. Use the systematic methods and discussion outline as your agenda for the discussion.

    3.2. Determine how you will explain the structure of the discussion to your delegate.

    3.3. Decide on what facts, opinions you should assemble before the discussion which your delegate may require.

    3.4. Prepare questions and statements needed for you to get commitment and show your confidence in the delegate.

Section: 11.0. Summary Review: Delegation

Let's look at a typical review, in order that you may learn what was done well and not so well, in the future.

1. **Organize Feedback from Others**

    1.1. Discuss the delegation discussion with a colleague or mentor

2. Seek Evaluation from Employees

2.1. A valuable source of evaluation is from the delegate. Obtain an evaluation in the form of feedback comments from the delegate.

3. Self Assessment Review Statements

3.1. The following can be used to highlight your success in this area, answer yes or no to the following statements: -

3.1.1. I followed the systematic methods and discussion outline.

3.1.2. I used all the discussion skills.

3.1.3. My planning was good.

3.1.4. I know what didn't go so well.

3.1.5. I know the discussion went well.

3.1.6. I can repeat my successes.

3.1.7. I reviewed my discussion.

3.1.8. I know what I will do differently next time.

❏ If the answer is yes to the above statements, well done!

4. Work on an Improvement Plan

4.1. From all of the above, you should have a good idea about what you should do differently next time.

Section: 12.0. Quick Guide to Successful Delegation

You have gone through delegation in detail, it's now appropriate to look at a quick guide which you can refer to in future delegation discussions to develop your future successes.

1. Work out how you can apply each of the discussion outline steps.

2. Use the discussion skills.

3. Anticipate the delegate's attitude to you and to the job being delegated

4. Decide how you will handle this.

5. Plan and anticipate questions or objections from the delegate.

6. Plan feedback to obtain an evaluation of your handling of the discussion.

7. Determine the level of reliability of this feedback.

8. From previous delegation discussions assess your strengths and how to capitalize on them.

9. Determine your minimum and your maximum objective for the discussion.

10. Decide what you can do to ensure that you achieve your objective.

11. Decide what factors worked to your advantage and to your disadvantage in the discussion and determine what you should do, to improve in the future.

Remember that the Question Model can be used throughout these difficult areas: -

1. **Why** do I need to take action in a particular area?
2. **What** objectives, action plan, shall I set?
3. **Who** will be involved?
4. **When** are my objectives and action plan dates?
5. **How** are my objectives and actions, to happen?
6. **What if** a problem develops, what will I do?
7. **Where** should my objectives and action plan take me?

Remember.........

Management Wisdom

An idea is not worth much until a person is found who has the energy and the ability to make it work.

*Unknown

Chapter 9: Managing Groups Productively

The Seventh Rule of Smart Management:
Develop your own specific applications, concepts
and skills to manage groups productively.

Section: 1.0. How to Run a Meeting

The purpose of these sections is for you to cut down the amount of time spent in meetings, and to make those meetings you attend more structured and productive with clear objectives and ultimately to assess your itinerary of meetings objectively to eliminate some of those meetings, where possible.

As a manager, you probably spend a great deal of your time interacting with other people; your personnel, colleagues, customers, clients and other departments etc. Consider all the meetings you currently attend and decide if you are satisfied with them.

Much of your time may be spent in meetings of one sort or another; however, meetings are an important part of your job. It is also important to review them from time to time to assess their contribution to the business.

Remember.........

Management Wisdom

If a problem causes too many meetings, the meetings eventually become more important than the problem.

*Hendrickson's Law

These sections will help you focus on how to run and use meetings effectively. You firstly need to, classify the purpose of your meetings into the following areas: -

1. **Information Giving**: coordination type meetings; the purpose of which is to communicate, concerns, policies, procedures, results and changes.

2. **Persuasive**: information, facts, and opinions used for change management in order to convince attendees regarding imminent changes.

3. **Information Gathering**: information solicited for use by the manager, the management team or the director etc. Examples are progress meetings of a project or a critical task and meetings to assess employee reaction to changes or potential changes.

4. **Problem Solving**: typically a chairperson may have to elicit opinions and suggestions from group members and then guide the meeting to a joint decision. Problem identification and recommendations and project development teams and quality team meetings, fall into this category.

Section: 1.1. Check the Group Dynamic

You have noted the types of meetings you attend, now you need to understand why handling personnel in a group is different from handling personnel individually and some of the implications.

Handling personnel individually on a one to one basis can be difficult and particular skills are necessary to work with individuals. Bear in mind that all the difficulties and enjoyment of working with individuals are compounded when working with a group.

Group Meeting Factors to Consider

If one looks at an average meeting consisting of about six to twelve people the implications for you and the company are: -

1. **Hidden Agendas**: Individuals have their own agendas and with them hostility and friction can surface; however, you will be able to handle these incidents skillfully by defusing the situation, by remaining calm and professional.

2. **The Showmen**: Some individuals like to talk too much. To handle such individuals, acknowledge the point they are making and then move onto the next person, item or topic.

3. **The Non Participant**: Some individuals don't like to talk in meetings this can make life difficult. Ask them specific questions and ask for their opinion on appropriate issues.

4. **The Cost of Meetings**: a one-hour meeting once a week with eight managers is one day's time. Four management days per month taken out of the calendar. This comes with a high cost to the company; plus the work lost on other activities. For an adequate return on this management investment in time these meetings must be efficient, effective and productive!

Section: 1.2. Develop the Agenda

A properly constructed agenda can speed up and clarify your meetings. An agenda serves to categorize what is expected and how long each item is estimated to take.

An effective agenda should detail: -

❏ The item for discussion.

❏ The purpose of the item for: -

○ Information.

○ Discussion.

○ Decision.

❏ The estimated length of time for each item.

Placement and Timing of Items

Next, matters related to the general placement and timing of items: -

1. **Providing information**: particularly background information should be circulated before the meeting with the agenda to save time during the meeting.

2. **Span of Attention**: most people's span of attention is +/- twenty minutes on a topic, meetings should ideally not run longer than two hours; otherwise people's attention lags to the detriment of the meeting. Where circumstances force you to exceed the two hour limit then split the meeting up with short breaks.

3. **Early Items**: requiring low priority and little thought should be placed early in the agenda so that they can be discussed and dealt with quickly when everyone is fresh.

4. **Common Interest Items**: with a high level of interest to everyone should be placed next, while their attention is high.

5. **Sensitive Items**: Sensitive items which may cause conflict should be placed next but not too late in the meeting to avoid over running the time. Also have a fact sheet drawn up ahead of the meeting of the pros and cons of the issue to be decided on and make it available to all attendees at the meeting. This avoids the facts being lost in discussion or repeated and keeps everyone on track.

6. **Non-Sensitive Items:** Ensure you have some non-sensitive items towards the end of a meeting - to end the meeting on a positive note.

7. **AOB**: 'Any Other Business' on the agenda is normally a time waster, therefore leave it off.

Section: 1.3. Preparation

To ensure your meetings are effective and don't hear the comment "Not another meeting!" you need to prepare, so that they are efficiently organized and conducted.

You must: -

❏ Prepare before a meeting.

❏ Prepare during a meeting.

❏ Prepare after a meeting.

Let us look at each one in turn: -

1.0 Preparation before a Meeting

1.1   Detail your objective - the purpose of your meeting should be clearly noted.

1.2   Ask yourself if a meeting is the best way of achieving your objective, or is the meeting necessary?

1.3   Detail the agenda.

1.4   Consider the individuals who should attend the meeting. Consider the opinions and information they can contribute.

1.5 List the individuals who you believe should be invited and then assess if they need to be present.

1.6 Consider the amount of notice needed for the meeting.

1.7 The date.

1.8 How long personnel have to prepare.

1.9 Send out the invitations in good time.

2.0 Preparation during a meeting

2.1 Decide who will be taking notes and arranging the minutes.

(This can also be carried out prior to meeting).

2.2 Decide and agree how many breaks are needed and timing between agenda items.

(This can also be carried out prior to meeting.)

2.3 Arrange for refreshments, if necessary.

(This can also be carried out prior to meeting.)

2.4 Date and time of next meeting, if a follow up is necessary.

3.0 Preparation after a meeting

3.1 Good minutes will indicate who has to do what and by when.

3.2 Consider when the minutes will be distributed and if extra copies should go to anyone else in the company.

3.3 Distribute minutes as soon as possible immediately after the meeting.

This planning can be used to set up all of your meetings, whether they involve the clients, personnel, other departments or suppliers.

Section: 1.4. Organizing a Group Meeting

The following factors are considered for group management.

1. Location:

When looking at the location of the meeting, and what is required.

1.1. Your prime concern is that the meeting is easily accessible to all of the participants.

1.2. Consider the cost to the company of the meeting and the return on this investment.

1.3. In-house meetings are less costly than outside venues.

2. Venue:

You should choose an appropriate venue.

   2.1. You will require a well-ventilated or air conditioned room with good lighting and perhaps presentation facilities, white board, projector, screen etc.

   2.2. The venue should be conducive to the type of meeting you wish to hold, and there should be easy access to refreshments, bathroom facilities during the breaks.

   2.3. The venue can become critical when negotiating, but that is covered under a different section.

3. Seating:

Seating is important at a meeting.

   3.1. You will need a table or tables and reasonably comfortable chairs.

   3.2. The table should be large enough to accommodate all the people who are to attend the meeting and the people should have enough room so that they don't feel restricted.

   3.3. You should really avoid seating people on opposite sides of the table to each other when they have opposing views on an agenda issue. For example, when strong debate is a possibility, avoid seating known opponents directly facing each other; space them away from opposing positions.

   3.4. In the absence of a round table, oval board room tables are the best and tend to create an atmosphere conducive to problem solving and cooperation.

4. Atmosphere:

You may make the atmosphere of the meeting formal or informal.

   4.1. This depends on factors such as the size of the group. As the group becomes larger, so the need for a formal meeting becomes greater. A formal approach is appropriate for stockholders' meetings, board meetings and committee meetings. The formal atmosphere is established by means of formal procedures, order of speaking and addressing the members of the meeting by their formal titles etc.

5. Follow up and outcome:

   5.1. If follow up correspondence is required ensure collection of all members' contact details.

5.2. Finally, consider and compare the results and success of the meeting against your original objective.

Section: 1.5. The Effectiveness and Quality of a Group Decision

So far, you have covered managing people in groups, in general terms.

Now, you must decide when it is appropriate and even necessary to use a meeting for making a group decision and when it is not.

There are two factors which when combined create the effectiveness of a group decision.

These are: -

1. The Objective Quality of the decision taken in terms of logic and judgment. This is determined by supported facts and how well the decision making process has been carried out.

2. Support for the Decision is determined by the level of acceptance and cooperation by those who are to carry out the decision, number of votes in favor of the decision or show of hands.

This process can be fairly subjective, but it gives you a process for categorizing and comparing the effectiveness of several decisions by taking the: -

Objective Quality of the Decision - multiplied by – **the Support for the Decision**

By using these two factors you can classify problems into four basic categories and then you are able to assess whether using a group discussion is the most effective method for obtaining a solution.

This is explained as follows: -

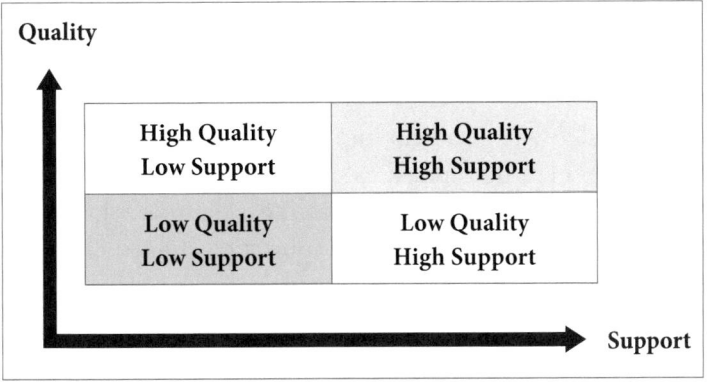

The diagram is explained as follows: -

1. **High Quality/Low Support**. These problems require qualified and experienced personnel and do not necessarily reflect personal interests.

    ❏ Examples are typically found in the operational areas of companies, decisions on marketing activity, new product launches and pricing structures where backing from personnel is seldom crucial in these matters.

2. **Low Quality/High Support**. When there are several solutions to a problem and the solutions affect individuals that would indicate a need for high support. When the solutions produce a similar quality decision, then the need for experts in the decision is low. Here the perception of a fair and reasonable decision is important.

    ❏ An example: who should work on a particular high profile project?

3. **Low Quality/Low Support**. Decisions such as these may not require a meeting and a management directive is sufficient to decide among the alternatives.

    ❏ An example: who should compile a generic monthly report schedule?

4. **High Quality/High Support**. Here you must be careful, as skill is required on the part of the discussion leader to ensure that the need for a good decision is adequately covered by the decision and confirmation of acceptance and support by those carrying out the decision.

    ❏ Examples are: work procedures, setting company budgets and service levels to customers etc.

Section: 1.6. Management Action to Decision Types

A group discussion will have a positive effect on the quality of a decision in cases when you listen to an exchange of ideas rather than asking each person individually.

A group discussion will also help improve backing for the decision when those people who are nominated to carry it out are actively involved in the decision. Through contribution it becomes their decision. Ownership by those carrying out the decision is important as ultimately they will be responsible to ensure it is carried out.

When involved in these four types of decisions, it will determine four kinds of management action as follows: -

Decision Type	Management Action
High Quality/Low Support.	❏ **Inform.**
Low Quality/High Support.	❏ **Consult.**
Low Quality/Low Support.	❏ **Delegate.**
High Quality/High Support.	❏ **Influence.**

This is explained as follows: -

1. **High Quality/Low Support Decision: Inform**.

    Management Action: When experts or specialists are involved it is appropriate to simply **inform** your personnel of their decision. For example, decisions involving computer systems, financial procedures, production methods or legal requirements.

2. **Low Quality/High Support Decision: Consult**.

    Management Action: You would **consult** with the group; you will need to ensure you obtain all their ideas and suggestions by listening carefully and summarizing your understanding of what has been said and how the people feel about the decision.

3. **Low Quality/Low Support Decision: Delegate**.

    Management Action: It may be appropriate to simply **delegate** these decisions to the group for them to make. A relaxed attitude is required when neither quality nor support is uppermost.

4. **High Quality/High Support Decision: Influence**.

    Management Action: Your skilful handling of this group is essential if this type of decision is to be effective. You will need to **influence** and guide the group, and balance their individual and collective requirements with the need to make a good high quality decision.

Section: 1.7. Presenting Problems

So far, you have looked at groups from the types of meetings you have to manage, the agendas and when to use groups. Now you are ready for presenting a problem to the group.

There is a specific process to follow, which you can apply to a specific meetings that you are currently planning.

1. **What**

1.1. What you should do before the meeting.

    1.1.1. First, identify the real problem and decide how it should be classified according to Quality and Support. This will give you your behavioral approach.

    1.1.2. Plan the discussion.

    1.1.3. Arrange the location of the meeting.

2. **How**

2.1. How you should introduce the discussion.

    2.1.1. First clarify your objective. State it in clear, unambiguous terms.

    2.1.2. Then go on to stimulate interest, by suggesting the approach which should be used, and get agreement on this before moving on to the actual discussion.

3. **When**

3.1. What you should do, when involved in the discussion.

    3.1.1. You must ensure that no person in the group, including yourself is allowed to dominate the discussion.

    3.1.2. Then move the discussion on trying to prevent people from becoming sidetracked or involved in personal agendas or on their favorite subjects.

4. **Where to**

4.1. You will conclude the discussion by summarizing the progress and decisions agreed, and check this by asking the people at the meeting if you have accurately summarized the discussion. Clarify what action has to be taken and by whom.

Always have a well-planned process, try to anticipate what will come out of the meeting and detail your response.

Section: 1.8. The Expected Behavior of the Discussion Leader

You have looked at the process of presenting problems to a group and in following that procedure the four key behaviors you should use are: -

❏ Stimulate.

❏ Guide.

❏ Move.

❏ Check.

You can use these key behaviors for the benefit of the discussion as follows: -

1. **Stimulate**

    1.1. The effective manager must first stimulate group members to take part and contribute, by initially defining the problem / situation being discussed. This includes giving basic information or facts.

    1.2. Successful leaders ask for more information than the information they give.

    1.3. Successful leaders ask personnel to supply information to stimulate discussion and get commitment.

2. **Guide**

    2.1. It is important for the meeting leader to guide and control the discussion

    2.2. In order to do this you must make suggestions regarding procedure, for example, by starting with the known facts and moving the discussion on when necessary.

    2.3. The effective leader does not make too many suggestions regarding the information and content of the discussion. Most of the suggestions should be provided by the other participants in the group to allow them to feel their contribution is important.

    2.4. Essentially, you must concentrate on leading and contributing through the control and guidance of the process and procedures.

3. **Move**

    3.1. Move refers to moving the discussion forward. You will need to summarize continually to give clarity and aid the participants' understanding of the discussion and once agreed move to the next topic.

    3.2. You should neither overly disagree with nor support other participants' views.

    3.3. Remember, you are the facilitator; you may not use the meeting to establish your own opinions onto the group.

4. **Check**

    4.1. You will continually check for understanding of the following, by summarizing at key points in the discussion: -

       4.1.1. Decisions.

       4.1.2. Viewpoints.

       4.1.3. Agreements.

This enhances your status as a discussion leader and also ensures that you don't misunderstand what is being said.

Section: 2.0. Quick Guide to Productive Group Discussions

You are now looking at the area of establishing a relaxed but businesslike and professional atmosphere in your meetings, which: -

❏ Enhances the company's and your own objective.

❏ Encourages an open and honest exchange of views and feelings.

This is important in all your meetings, whether they involve company employees or clients.

You will achieve the company's objectives and encourage an open and honest exchange of views by using the following points, during your meetings: -

1. **Try to understand other people's thoughts and feelings.**

    1.1. Never interrupt ...... listen carefully to the speaker.

    1.2. Check that both you and other participants in the meeting understand what is being said.

    1.3. Ask for the participant to summarize principal arguments, particularly arguments that they are not in agreement with. This will test whether they have listened carefully to the opposing view.

    1.4. Ask the speaker to give supporting examples of their argument this will also help you to understand.

2. **Listen for guarded expressions or resentment.**

    2.1. Listen carefully for them and bring them out into the open by seeking information from the participant and checking your understanding.

3. **Accept other people's feelings.**

    3.1. Do not argue or try to convince people they are wrong, feelings are very important to people and should not be challenged.

    3.2. A good strategy is to reflect the feeling, by saying

    ❏ You feel . . .

❏ Try to label the feeling - *skeptical, unconvinced, frustrated* etc. This shows people you understand how they feel and that you have been listening.

❏ A word of warning, void any comment which could be construed as derogatory.

4. Involve everyone in the discussion.

4.1. Don't single out people in order to spread the discussion. Individuals can sometimes feel a little pressurized if you question them too closely or repeatedly, on a particular issue. Rather ask general questions inviting contributions to broaden the discussion. A good method is to ask: -

❏ What facts have we got on the situation so far?

❏ How does each of you feel about the situation?

5. Allow feelings to be vented.

5.1. You should encourage group members to express their own views on matters. This enables individuals to relieve their tensions, encourages objectivity, and allows feelings to be evaluated and clarified unemotionally.

In your preparation consider the information above and plan how you can overcome these obstacles.

Lastly, these skills are not easily learned, if you are not immediately successful, don't worry – and continue to practice.

The following Quick Guide will assist you in the future.

1. Guide the meeting through problem-solving

1.1. Often discussions tackle difficult problems or those with far-reaching implications or problems with many alternatives, each having its own ramifications. When approaching such problems ensure the discussion doesn't lose momentum. In such cases recap on the progress made and guide the meeting towards alternatives, proposals or ideas which may have been presented during the meeting.

2. Summarize progress made.

2.1. A summary, used in an objective way will: -

2.1.1. Get discussions back on course and check individual understanding.

      2.1.2. Breakdown a complex problem into its component parts and allows a discussion on each element to be reviewed.

      2.1.3. Review previous ideas and concepts and form a logical progression to the next area for discussion.

      2.1.4. Stimulate further discussion.

   2.2. Remember, a summary may not be used as a means of soliciting acceptance of your own ideas.

3.   Stimulate and collect ideas or solutions.

   3.1. Discussion leaders should not allow solutions to be introduced and discussed too early. This often prevents the free flow of better quality second and alternative solutions from surfacing.

4.   The process of generating and evaluating ideas

   4.1. Idea generation and the evaluation of those ideas should be done separately. You may obtain a better quality evaluation if held separately, allowing time in between a). The collection of alternative solutions and b). The process of evaluating those ideas and solutions. Allowing for a break period at this point separating the two is prudent.

5.   Be careful of quick and easy agreement.

   5.1. When there is quick and easy agreement among members of a group, often called group think, be careful of making hasty decisions. Ask a participant to present both the advantages and the disadvantages of the decision to deliberately consider the negative side of issues.

Section: 3.0. How to Make Confident Group Decisions

You will now cover how you evaluate contributions and move to select a decision.

The following guide will assist: -

1.   Evaluate Contributions

   1.1. Evaluate both the advantages and the disadvantages of the solution objectively, using the contributions and views of the entire group as a team effort and record them for all to see.

   1.2. Be careful not to split the group into two camps on an issue.

1.3. Explore the supporting evidence for the decision and separate facts from opinions and feelings, the more facts you have the easier your decision making process becomes.

1.4. Explore any new problems created by the solutions. It is almost inevitable that new solutions will create their own problems, in fact the more original and creative the solution the more problems may be associated with it. These problems should be thoroughly explored and examined by the group.

Now you are in a position to look at the second half of the process, that of: -

2. Selecting a Solution

2.1. Generally, a thorough job in the evaluation makes this step easy. However, when there are several alternatives to choose from, try one or more of the following:

2.1.1. **Experimentation:** Check out whether there are more than perceived differences between the solutions, if not, select one.

2.1.2. **Integration:** Try to combine alternatives so as to produce an effective solution.

2.3. Treat the failure to agree as a problem requiring discussion.

2.1.1. Failure to reach an agreement should not be perceived by you as a failure. You should allow the group to decide what they want to do about the disagreement.

2.1.2. Do not force your opinions on the group; this includes groups which consist of company employees who report to you.

Plan how you will come to a decision, using the information.

Section: 3.1. Ensuring High Quality Decisions in Groups

When decision-making, the quality of your decision counts and you must evaluate the quality of the group decision.

There are two drawbacks to group decisions, which you have to take cognizance of: -

❏ **Overgeneralizations** based on past experience from within or outside of the company by the group members.

❏ **Reliance on feelings and opinions** instead of using known facts.

Four Procedures

Here are four procedures designed to overcome the above tendencies and increase the quality of your decisions.

By following this procedure, you will have produced a systematic means to evaluate solutions and eliminate those solutions based on: -

- ❏ Personal preference.
- ❏ Controversial solutions.
- ❏ Poor quality decisions.

Procedure to evaluate and eliminate solutions: -

1. **Do not transfer a solution from another situation** without supportive evidence, to eliminate personal preferences.
2. **If the solution rests upon indisputable facts**, ensure this solution is seriously considered.
3. **Where the solution is the result of a disagreement between members of the group**: challenge the facts then test the solution fully.
4. **Before disregarding a solution**: check if the solution has accounted for exceptions or trends in results, if so rather include for further evaluation.

Note: Continually review and analyze your decisions to work on improving the quality.

Section: 3.2. How to Handle Difficult Individuals and the Non-Participant

Unfortunately, meetings are not always comprised of reasonable and rational individuals. The following will show you how to deal with some of the difficult people or awkward situations.

Here are some response technique solutions commonly used with difficult individuals and situations which you may come across from time to time: -

1. **Member appears reluctant to contribute.**
   1.1. Ask the member questions which they would know the answer.
   1.2. Give the member recognition for contributions, however minimal they are.
   1.3. Try to make the member feel their contribution is important.
2. **Member wants to argue.**
   2.1. Do not escalate the argument, stay calm and businesslike.

2.2. Ask the member to restate, clarify or summarize their views.

2.3. Then check your understanding of their views by summarizing.

2.4. Limit the amount of time the member has to discuss their views and thank the member and move on.

3. **Member wants to show dominance through skepticism, sarcasm or disapproval.**

   3.1. Ask the member to explain and clarify any skeptical, sarcastic or disapproving remarks.

   3.2. Be careful of potentially misleading or incorrect reasoning and logic in these explanatory statements and pass them on to the group to answer.

   3.3. Do not condone unprofessional behavior, stay calm and businesslike.

   3.4. Give sincere recognition for the comments and contribution and thank the member and move on.

4. **Member professes authority on a subject.**

   4.1. Ask them to answer the most difficult questions / problems facing the group.

   4.2. Give sincere recognition and thanks to the member for their comments and contribution and move on.

5. **Member talks too much.**

   5.1. Interrupt tactfully; summarize the member's argument and move on to another person.

   5.2. Ask the member a question to bring the member back to the topic in hand.

   5.3. Thank the member for the contribution and move on.

6. **Member pursues own agenda.**

   6.1. Recognize the issue the member has raised and state that you understand their concern with it.

   6.2. If the member raises objections, ask if the member can propose a way of overcoming their own objections.

7. **Member wants to contribute, but what is said is not clear.**

   7.1. Listen carefully to what the member is saying, and summarize what the member has said.

   7.2. Give sincere recognition and thanks for the member's contribution.

8. **There are distractions and/or laughter.**

   8.1. Allow it to continue for a short while to see if it passes.

   8.2. If it persists, ask the reason for the laughter and distraction and then call for the individuals to focus back on the issues of the meeting.

   8.3. Do not condone unprofessional behavior, stay calm and businesslike.

   8.4. Bring the meeting back to the point before the distraction.

   8.5. Summarize the decisions made.

9. **There is arguing among individuals.**

   9.1. Summarize each person's point of view and try to get back to the original point under discussion.

   9.2. Invite other people to contribute.

   9.3. Remind the group of the purpose of the particular item which is under discussion.

10. **Member begins to go into detail.**

    10.1. Give the member recognition for the member's attention to detail and concern for the quality of the decision. Then remind the member of the time limit and move on to the next point.

11. **Member attacks you verbally.**

    11.1. Remain calm.

    11.2. Check your understanding of the member's views by summarizing the member's points.

    11.3. Recognize the member's concern; say you will take the issue up with the member after the meeting and move on to the next point.

12. **Member rambles off the issue**

    12.1. Recognize the member's contribution, and refer the member back to the objective of the meeting.

    12.2. Summarize the member's contribution and move on to the next point.

Remember, it takes a high degree of interpersonal skills to handle meetings and groups with ease and this will come with practice and patience.

Section: 3.3. Taking the Minutes

Don't forget the minutes. However, if you are chairing the meeting – **do not** take the minutes yourself, delegate this to one of the members or even bring in a person to keep record, as your meeting responsibilities will suffer!

After your meeting it is your responsibility to keep a good record of what was discussed during the meeting and what is to happen as a result.

There are four points for better minutes: -

1. **Relate and Reference the Minutes to the Agenda.**

    1.1. Ensure that the minutes relate to the agenda and the objectives of the meeting.

    1.2. The minutes are to note major topics of discussion and particularly decisions which were taken relative to specific agenda items.

2. **Do not record minutes passively.**

    2.1. You should not allow the minute recorder to be excluded from the proceedings of the meeting. The minute taker should have an active role, as the individual who can make pertinent and specific points from these notes.

3. **Ensure the minutes are accurate and factual**

    3.1. As the chairperson, you should check the minutes for accuracy and correct factual record, before distribution.

4. **Keep the minutes future oriented.**

    4.1. A good way of ensuring that the minutes are action oriented is to have a column on the right-hand side of the page for noting who has to take action by when.

    4.2. For example:

Action	Responsibility	Date
Marketing manager to provide competitors' comparative product pricing assessment and report.	DJ	01/04

Alternatively, a special item at the end of the meeting could summarize who is to do what and by when.

Section: 3.4. The Advantages and Disadvantages of Using Groups

Why should you use groups for problem solving?

There are several advantages: -

Advantages

1. **Two or more heads are better than one.**

   1.1. When people pool their knowledge and experience the consequent pooling results in synergy, i.e., the product is greater than the sum of the parts. For this positive effect good group management skills are required.

2. **Understanding - is enhanced by the people who must implement the decisions.**

   2.1. When people have to implement decisions, it is beneficial if they have played a part in considering the alternatives and come to the final decision for themselves.

3. **Different people propose differing solutions.**

   3.1. The greater the number of people participating in a group problem solving, the greater the number and variety of solutions are likely to be generated. This requires the facilitation of a skilled discussion leader

4. **Participating in decision-making enhances acceptability.**

   4.1. When people have played a role in decision-making, even if the decision is not a popular one, their participation leads to greater acceptability. And a skilled discussion leader can overcome resistance in this way.

   4.2. Your employees' commitment or buy in to making a change work will be increased if employees are given the opportunity to be involved in the process.

5. **When the Quality of a decision is important, groups are better than individuals.**

   5.1. With a skilled discussion leader, the group is able to pool experience and knowledge and come to a better-informed and more accurate decision than a single individual.

The disadvantages of using groups for problem solving are essentially, as follows: -

Disadvantages

1. **Social Pressures. (group think)**

1.1. Natural social pressures tend to push individuals towards conformity. The self-disciplining process of working and contributing within group structures and procedures tends to lessen individuality and controversy, sometimes called 'group think'. Unfortunately, this has negative implications for the quality of the decision as a result of the group becoming more cohesive.

2. **An Informal Leader's influence. (leader – follower)**

   2.1. You have spent some time considering how to handle difficult individuals or difficult situations. However, it is a natural tendency of individuals to listen to, respect and often abide by the opinions of those they respect. If the informal group leader advocates a particular course of action other group members may well commit themselves to that action, without logical and careful consideration. Therefore, it is critical that the composition of the group and the inclusion of known informal leaders must be carefully considered and monitored.

3. **The Group Leader requires skills for ensuring quality decisions**

   3.1. You may well have noted previously that almost all the advantages of using groups are based on the group leader being skilled.

Quick Tip: take every opportunity to become an effective group leader by sharpening your discussion skills with regular practice.

In Summary: You have looked at how to manage groups, when to use groups for decision-making and when not to. You have looked at how to handle difficult people in groups, key behaviors for group leaders, agendas, minutes etc.

You will be able to apply the methods you have learned to most meeting situations.

And use the Question Model of Management to assist you throughout these difficult areas and will keep you focused: -

1. **Why** do I need to take action in a particular area?
2. **What** objectives, action plan, shall I set?
3. **Who** will be involved?
4. **When** are my objective and action plan dates?
5. **How** are my objectives and actions, to happen?
6. **What if** a problem develops, what will I do?

7.   **Where** should my objectives and action plan take me?

Your **responsibility** and your **skill** in handling meetings should exceed the **authority** you hold by virtue of your management position, in this way your meetings will always result in a positive outcome.

Remember.........

Management Wisdom

A man who enjoys responsibility usually gets it.
A man who merely likes exercising authority usually loses it.

*Malcolm Forbes

Your systematic preparation of meetings offers many opportunities to improve the efficiency, effectiveness and productivity of your company in terms of time, money and energy saved and better quality decisions.

If you are not happy with the quality of the meetings you are involved in. You now have the power as the meeting leader to influence the quality of the meeting!

Section: 4.0. Quick Guide to Managing Groups Productively

Here is a quick guide which may be useful to ensure you have carried out the necessary planning.

Use the Quick Guide whenever you have to manage a group.

1.   Decide if a group meeting is appropriate for the decision the meeting has to make.
2.   Draw up an agenda.
3.   Determine those who you require to attend.
4.   Draw up a group meeting topics checklist.
5.   Distribute the agenda with any prepared information, if appropriate.
6.   Consider the key behaviors you are going to exhibit as the chairperson.

7. Decide how you will stimulate the discussion.
8. Decide what key behaviors are necessary for each individual.
9. Decide what factors you must consider when handling this particular meeting.
10. Decide if minutes will be necessary and who will take them.
11. Ensure that the decisions made are of the quality you want.
12. Decide what other topics, budget costs and resources need addressing.
13. Turn the decisions into actions.
14. Distribute the minutes immediately after the meeting.

You can use this Quick Guide whenever you are about to hold a meeting, it will give you the comfort of knowing you have prepared well and you have addressed and eliminated none essential meetings from your itinerary.

Effective managers do not live with unsatisfactory or poor quality meetings.

Remember.........

Management Wisdom

Any simple problem can be made insoluble if enough meetings are held to discuss it.

*Mitchell's Law of Committees

Chapter 10: Managing Effective Decisions

---

*The Eighth Rule of Smart Management:
Focus on what makes an effective decision and
put your decisions into action using simple
conventional processes.*

Section: 1.0. How to Make Effective Decisions

Too many reports, too much information or too little information, find out everything you need to know right here to manage information and make effective decisions.

Businesses and markets are changing...

The business world is changing ...are you ready for the future?

We have created a condition of '*Information Overload*', where retrieval of usable information is critical. Most first world countries have left the age of hard copy information behind and are now entrenched in the ever growing problem of handling digital information, along with the development of data information storage and retrieval systems.

It is the managers who are able to train themselves to '*filter and interpret information quickly*' that succeed in this environment. Directors of companies are moving their responsibility and authority for success and revenue to those managers who can *filter* information quickly, *absorb and understand* the information, *package* and *distribute* the information to make *effective decisions* and manage the people and the results of the company.

The key to management success remains, that of making effective decisions!

In the following text, you will think about the decision-making process and in particular look at how you can make effective quality decisions.

As a manager in a company environment you are faced with a wide range of different types of decisions daily. The value and success of a company is influenced largely by the decisions taken by its managers.

Decision making is the primary task of a manager.

Decisions – A Rational or Intuitive Approach

There are managers who take a rational approach to decision making, it is clear they follow a systematic process. They do lots of fact finding, asking others for their ideas and solutions, formulating tentative conclusions and look at the implications of each. And there are managers who appear to be more intuitive. Typically, they get a feel for the problem, they briefly assess the information and a decision is made. These are the two extremes and both work equally well.

Consider for a moment where your own decision-making skills fit currently - perhaps, somewhere between the rational and the intuitive approach. The following sections will take you through a systematic method which supports a more rational approach; however, once learned it will become second nature, more spontaneous and with experience gained it will appear intuitive.

Section: 2.0. Factors in the Decision Making Process

Many managers suffer from the common problem of carrying out so much meticulous analysis of the facts and considering many alternatives, in so much detail that the right decision tends to elude them, this is often called 'Paralysis by Analysis'

Section: 2.1. Obstacles

Consider the following obstacles which may be affecting your decision-making from time to time and getting in the way of your effectiveness: -

1. **The Search for the Right Answer**

    Do you tend to act too quickly towards what appears to be the right answer, without validating or testing the proposed solution? This can be serious if you make the decision based on incorrect information.

2. **Decide in Haste, Repent at Leisure**

This normally happens when there is real time pressure on you, particularly regarding high value, and high quality decisions concerning clients or personnel, where the consequences of making a quick decision can be disastrous.

3. **Filter and Test the Facts**

   The facts can come to you in many forms of opinion, ideas, statistics, trends, rates, figures, graphs, charts, concerns and thoughts, with little time to filter and test for validity.

4. **Old information and Facts**

   Information and facts have aged with time and left too long, so that when you do grasp them, they may have aged to an extent that they may no longer be relevant to the problem at hand.

5. **Personal Feelings and Selective Reasoning**

   Do you allow your personal feelings to cloud your decision, in that you want the result enough that you may subconsciously rearrange or interpret the facts to justify the decision?

These are just a few of the problems with gathering information and data, but these are not unusual and can be overcome with a systematic methods approach.

Quick Tip: good decision makers know that they cannot always gather all the facts; they understand the difficulties in accessing all the information and selecting usable content from the information presented. Personal feelings are replaced by logical reasoning and this is where using systematic methods and processes to arrive at effective decisions become vital.

Section: 2.2. Time Pressure Decisions and the Five Courses of Action

Decision making to tight deadlines can sometimes make you feel as if you are under considerable pressure, however, there are only five courses of action you can choose from: -

	Course of Action	The Effect
1.	Make a positive decision, which turns out right.	This is the choice of the effective manager.
2.	Make a positive decision, which turns out wrong.	This is the choice of the effective manager, who has a recovery plan in place.
3.	Do nothing and hope that the problem goes away.	This can happen sometimes, but there is a greater risk that the problem will get worse.
4.	Postpone the decision and the problem gets worse.	This is what happens most times, when problems are left.
5.	Abdication; get rid of the problem by passing it to your manager or to another division or department and avoiding all personal responsibility.	This is not advisable if you envisage continued employment with your present company.

Of the above courses of action effective managers would only consider 1. & 2.

Decision-making is an integral part of your job as a manager, a part you have to face daily and a part you must do well in order to succeed as an effective manager. If you prepare and welcome the decisions you have to make – then management is for you!

Section: 2.3. Factors to Consider

The decision-making process is a systematic method which acquires, evaluates and generates tentative conclusions and ultimately arrives at a decision. The importance of the decision dictates the extent of analysis and research required. When assessing the importance of a decision you need to evaluate the following factors: -

1. **Factual Information**:

    The main task of a decision maker is to get factual information. Often it may not always be available and therefore you have to rely on your experience, your intuition and a systematic method for obtaining and evaluating the available information. The level of the decision determines the degree of factual information required to finalize a decision e.g. low level decision may need little information, a high level decision may need a lot of information.

2. **Personal Information:**

The greater the information you personally have on the issue the better the quality of the decision.

3. **Experience:**

You gain experience from prior mistakes and failures. Through lessons learned the guideline is not to repeat your prior mistakes. If you do not have experience on a certain problematic issue and no one else has the experience, then you need to experiment and test your decision and remain flexible in actioning your decision with frequent reviews, feedback and alteration of the original decision, if necessary.

4. **Commitment:**

The greater the strategic consequences or impact of a decision on the company the more consideration, input and thought that goes into this decision.

5. **Impact on Personnel:**

When a decision could have a serious impact on people - it is a major decision and should be well thought out.

6. **Future Orientation:**

When current conditions are volatile and circumstances may change in the future, more care is needed with regard to the quality of the decision.

7. **Flexibility:**

In areas of little known or rapidly changing circumstances, it is best to retain as much flexibility in the decision as possible to ensure the course of action developed can be changed easily.

8. **Intuition:**

Finally, you will discover several methods of acquiring facts and analyzing them. Sometimes when factual information is at a minimum good decision makers ensure the decision feels right. Your intuition or gut-feel when a decision has to be made is important, so don't ignore it.

As you progress with the decision making process you may begin to ask yourself whether decision-making is an art or a science? .... *The answer is 'both'.*

Remember.........

Management Wisdom

Discovery often consists of looking at the same thing as everyone else and thinking something different.

*Albert Szent-Gyorgyi

Section: 3.0. Identifying the Types of Decision

You have now covered the factors influencing the decision making process you are now ready to assess the various types of decision.

Section: 3.1. The Five Types of Decision

The Decision Making Process can be used in five types of decision.

Firstly, most decisions can be classified through one of the following questions: -

Type:	Question:	Purpose:
1.	**What is the cause?**	To find out what, where and why matters appear to be problematic.
2.	**Which course of action?**	To choose between several alternatives.
3.	**Yes or no?**	To do it or not to do it.
4.	**What lies ahead?**	Future oriented problem analysis - anticipating problems and proactive problem solving.
5.	**Where do I start?**	When faced with complex problem situations, several of the above decision types may be required to solve a complex problem, which decision types for which problem and in what priority order they should be tackled are questions answered by this type of decision.

It is important: to correctly identify the type of decision you have to make, you can then plan it using the decision making process and then detail the actions you will take under each step.

Section: 3.2. Type: 1. Decision - What is the cause.
Defined as the type of decision needed to discover why things have gone wrong.

Today, we rely heavily on mechanical, electrical, electronic equipment and machines.

Our work environment is becoming more complex and man-machine interface is common. Companies are now more dependent on the use of computer systems and machine interfaces operating within the production and service industry. For this reason, this type of decision is particularly suited to machine or system breakdowns on the production line, in the computer room, for power and water utilities, etc. It is also applicable to addressing some of the human problems, for example, low productivity, low morale, high personnel turnover or absenteeism.

Section: 3.3. Type: 2. Decision – Which Course of Action.
In this section you will follow a similar process discussed previously. This occurs when you are faced with several alternatives and you must choose between them to select a course of action.

For example:
- ❏ Where to situate a branch office when there are three or four possible sites to choose from.
- ❏ A major purchase of capital equipment from your expense budget, with multiple equipment choices.

These are typical when several criteria have to be weighed and considered in order to make the best decision.

Section: 3.4. Type: 3. Decision – Yes or No.
Decisions where you have to decide between two alternatives - a Type 3 decision differs from the previous decisions in that the choice is between two alternatives rather than many alternatives.

- ❏ Typical examples would be when you are faced with a new job offer, or moving to larger premises or not moving.

Section: 3.5. Type: 4. Decision – What Lies ahead.

These require a proactive approach to address future changes and look at the avoidance of potential problems.

Part of a manager's job is to anticipate problems and take steps to minimize the negative impact on the company. It is this type of decision making which is designed to prevent potential and future problems and crisis. For example, changes in technology, economic changes, legislation etc. A good understanding of this type of decision is vital to your success as a manager.

Many of the financial losses incurred by companies are the direct result of a lack of foresight and planning in this decision area.

Section: 3.6. Type: 5. Decision – Where do I start.

You now look to the last in the five types of decisions. It is a combination of all the previous decisions discussed and is important when you are faced with complex situations.

This type of decision is appropriate when there is a deviation, opportunity or threat and the problem is broader than any single one of the four problems described previously.

Examples could be low profits, decreasing turnover, increased competition, low morale, etc., any problem with possibly more than one cause and the need for several different decision types.

Section: 4.0. Quick Guide for Identifying the Types of Decision

When you are making a decision based on one of the five types of decisions there are certain factors which you should ensure you have considered. This Quick Guide can be used with all your decisions to ensure you have left nothing out.

1. Follow the Decision Making Process in Chapter 2. Section: 2.3. Diagram: 03 refer.
2. Review the type of decision initially identified. Do not live with the consequences of an incorrect choice of the decision type and change the decision type if necessary.

3. Decide on the level of factual information required and make use your personal sources of information and knowledge.

4. Use and ensure you have sufficient information available to you. Continue to improve your own personal sources of information areas for future decisions.

5. When there is insufficient experience available to you on the decision, keep it flexible with the ability to change the decision easily.

6. For strategic decisions, ensure commitment and sufficient consideration to the input is applied.

7. When there is an impact on personnel think through the decision carefully. When a decision affects people include them and their contribution, so that they can be part of decision, where appropriate.

8. If you are involving a group in the decision making process, decide on which group decision process is suitable for the decision.

9. When conditions are unpredictable aim for a high level of the quality and credibility in the decision to address future volatility.

10. If circumstances are changing rapidly, build in flexibility and the ability to change easily.

11. Consider the consequences of the decision to minimize the risks in the decision.

12. Establish an adequate management monitoring, control and feedback system from implementation of the decision-making process.

Quick Tip: *you will discover several methods of acquiring facts and analyzing them. Sometimes when factual information is at a minimum good decision makers ensure the decision feels right. Your intuition or gut-feel when a decision has to be made is important, so don't ignore it.*

Section: 5.0. Classical Support Tools and Groups in Decision Making

In the decision making process, one of the areas stressed is the need to get the facts related to the decision. It is important to start with structured systematic methods and analytical processes when solving a problem; however, this can limit creative and imaginative ideas to problem solving. One way of increasing your information knowledge and obtaining broader information and creative solutions is to involve personnel or groups from inside and outside the company in the process.

Advantages of Group Decisions

❏ When the decision maker can merge the many differing points of view and experiences into the decision making process the quality of the decision is improved. This is because the majority of people given the opportunity to discuss problem issues and personally contribute to the decision tend to bring a synergistic effect to the process, where the end result is greater than the sum of its individual contributions.

❏ The second advantage is that people, particularly those closer to the problem tend to focus on the cause rather than the perceived effect/s of the problem. An effective manager would consult with experts in their field and personnel who are directly affected by the problem. It is essential to obtain commitment and support to the final decision, and therefore one should encourage employees to contribute to the solution and decision.

Quick Tip: often people affected by the decision possess vital information which can support the process of breaking down the problem to reveal a course of action, an elegant solution to the problem and a quality decision.

Remember.........

Management Wisdom

Inside every large problem, is a small problem struggling to get out.

*Hoare's Law of Large Problems

Central to decision making is the acquisition of facts, data and information. There are essentially three areas where the facts can come from, as follows: -

❏ Yourself.

❏ Those people who have some interest, stake or knowledge of the problem and/or those employees affected by the decision.

❏ Experts in their field.

Section: 6.0. Characteristics of the Discussion Leader

The discussion leader must pay special attention to the contributions of the group and manage the merging and conflicting ideas and expressions of concern, ultimately guiding the group towards agreement and consensus.

Typical characteristics, which the effective discussion leader will exhibit, are as follows:-

1. **Initiative**: taking proactive steps to introduce, guide and move the discussion forward.

2. **Show Encouragement**: listen carefully to views expressed by individuals and give support and encouragement to less verbal members.

3. **Checking Understanding**: checking the group's understanding of the information or opinions given, what has been suggested and what has been agreed.

4. **Summarizing**: bringing diverse viewpoints together and restating them clearly. By careful sensing of the group's feelings and attitudes the leader can restate views and feelings. This shows the discussion leader understands the views and emotion within the group and defuses sensitive or tense situations.

5. **Restate Positions**: when there are opposing views developing or disagreement within the group, the ability to briefly restate the positions within the group can satisfy the need for individuals to be heard and allow the discussion leader to move the discussion forward.

6. **Asking for Information**: discussion leaders should ask for information more than giving their own information. A discussion leader's information is often perceived as having more

validity or importance than that of the other members of the group which can lead to it being construed by the group as prescriptive and tends to reduce input from the group.

Section: 7.0. Involving Groups in Decision Making

There are several ways of involving groups in the decision making process, which you can use. A series of quick guides of the most popular and effective types are provided.

The first to be considered is Brainstorming.

Section: 7.1. Brainstorming

The concept is simple and frequently succeeds in obtaining imaginative and creative ideas. Brainstorming combines an informal approach to problem solving it opens up possibilities and breaks down assumptions regarding the problem.

The purpose of the discussion leader is to encourage people to come up with thoughts and ideas which may seem a little extreme and outrageous but this helps people to think outside of the box. These ideas even the most extreme, can be combined, modified, changed or improved and built into creative solutions to the problem.

The idea is to: -

❏ Ask a group of people to consider an issue and generate as many solutions as possible.

❏ A large number of solutions are generated.

❏ Each is written up by the discussion leader.

❏ These ideas are evaluated at the end of the session.

❏ Impractical solutions can be eliminated by the group

❏ It is important that an idea however extreme or outrageous is not criticized

Quick Tip: *just prior to the Brainstorming session pose a creative problem to the group to get them into the process e.g. list 100 things you can do with a paperclip and allow free reign to the replies.*

Quick Guide to Brainstorming

A classical group decision making process: -

1. State the problem clearly to the group, and write it up on a white board.
2. Ask for solutions to the problem and encourage creativity - without limitations.
3. Promote as many creative solutions as possible, do not worry about the quality or how ridiculous they may appear at first sight.
4. Write up as many as possible, for all to see.
5. Encourage all participants to contribute fully.
6. Actively support the outrageous and way-out ideas, the more the better.
7. Do not judge the group's contributions as this limits idea generation and creativity.
8. During the session do not allow criticism of any of the ideas by the group members.
9. Ask the group to build on the basic ideas by adding to them or combining, modifying, changing or improving them.
10. All ideas are written down in such a manner that they are clearly visible to the group.
11. Stop when all ideas are exhausted.
12. From the ideas/solutions generated the group then test each idea in terms of feasibility, risk, cost etc. exploring solutions using the more conventional approaches.
13. The best idea / or solutions are then selected by the group.

By following these guidelines you will find enthusiasm and creativity being generated; as most people enjoy giving free reign to their imagination and creativity. Often you will find that an idea from one person will stimulate an idea from another. This building process is invaluable and results in a quantity and variety of ideas.

For larger groups: you could carry out the collection of ideas on paper and anonymously, and then written up for the group to discuss evaluate and select the best idea, this also works well.

Brainstorming improves the quality of the ultimate decision and can be used to break down complex problems into smaller parts for consideration individually. The process is interesting; it works and it can be enjoyable and fun for those taking part.

Section: 7.2. Fish Bowling

The name probably arose as a result of the process of the physical positioning of delegate at the centre of attention whilst presenting their views. The attention of the group remains focused on the central person's views.

Quick Guide to Fish Bowling

There are three variations on this theme: -

1. **Fish-Bowling - Generic Group**

    1.1. The problem is stated clearly by the discussion leader.

    1.2. A central chair is positioned in the middle of a semi-circle of outer chairs.

    1.3. Only the person occupying the centre chair may speak and hence present unopposed and unquestioned. It ensures the presenter is able to present their views without interruption or criticism.

    1.4. The central person then calls for individual discussion and questions from the group.

    1.5. All individuals have an opportunity to sit in the centre chair and present their views.

    1.6. The discussion leader records the views of each presenter and writes them up for all to see.

    1.7. On completion the group discusses and evaluates all views and then agrees on the best course of action from the views or combination of views presented.

2. **Fish-Bowling - Expert Group**

    2.1. A similar approach is to allow 'experts in their field' such as the company's accountants or legal representatives to be called into the group. Each expert can present their view to the group. The group then decides on a course of action with a common information base.

3. **Fish-Bowling - Large Group**

    3.1. The third variation is useful when securing the opinions of large groups and many individuals and to ensure all viewpoints are adequately represented.

3.2. The group is sub-divided into smaller groups to discuss their viewpoints and then a spokesman presents the subgroup's viewpoint to the whole group.

3.3. The Fish-bowling procedure and physical layout is the same and the same rules and procedures for speaking apply.

Section: 7.3. Consensus Thinking

Consensus thinking is a procedure which provides specific steps for a group to follow whilst analyzing a problem and coming to a decision. The big advantage of this technique is that it minimizes group argument.

Quick Guide to Consensus Thinking

1. The discussion leader takes the group through the following specific steps:
2. The problem is stated clearly.
3. All group members share the information they have concerning the problem, with the group. This is an important step to ensure that everyone has the same information.
4. The group then proposes and agrees upon a method of categorizing and dealing with the shared information.
5. The group then generates solutions and when the group arrives at a consensus regarding the most appropriate solution/s, the solutions are prioritized.
6. The best solution or solutions are chosen and the decision and immediate actions are recorded.

A word on the skill of the discussion leader: it is important to keep the group members on track in the above steps and not allow solutions to be selected too early.

In order to facilitate this procedure the following guidelines are suggested: -

1. Stress your confidence in the group's ability to solve the problem.
2. Encourage an open collaborative discussion.
3. Indicate that any statements made should not be personally intended.
4. On complex issues which are not clear summarize and restate a group member's information to clarify their views and understanding for the group.

5. Differences of opinion should be handled sensitively and calmly and generally without argument. Differences of opinion and disagreement can become positive when guided by the discussion leader, as this sometimes makes individuals reassess and adjust their own positions.

6. If tension or argumentative discussion develops, as a result of opposing views on an issue, summarize the opposing views to clarify understanding for the group's good.

7. Don't allow group member's to get into win-lose positions; and encourage an atmosphere of open discussion.

8. Do not push for agreement and consensus too early and let this develop naturally.

9. When the group reaches the point of agreement and consensus on a solution summarize the solution/s proposed and immediate actions.

This method can be tough on the discussion leader; but it can also be enjoyable and improve your discussion and leadership skills.

Section: 7.4. Delphi Technique

The value of the Delphi technique lies in its method of defining the future and is widely used for business and technology forecasting, policy making and research studies. It is aimed at a consensus of the most probable future and has certain advantages over other forecasting methods.

The panel of specialists or experts in their field are normally drawn from both inside and outside the organisation and used to forecast the future.

Typical applications would be to predict the future of marketing in a potentially unstable country or the life cycle predictions and potential sales for a particular product or market trends in a particular industry over forthcoming years.

Overview

❏ Initially, the group does not have any interaction.

❏ Only when individuals have documented and completed their opinions and views with supporting reasons would the discussion leader encourage opinion sharing.

❏ Anonymity allows the panel members to express their opinions freely and avoids publication of errors in the forecast.

❏ The discussion leader is looking for differences in perceptions and consensus trends.

Advantages:

❏ Low cost to administer and evaluate.

❏ Can be carried out on line.

❏ A wide range of expertise.

❏ Individuals are able to interact and express their opinions openly.

❏ Method can be used with limited information available.

❏ Consensus can be achieved in a relatively short time.

Disadvantages:

❏ Time consuming to set up.

❏ Success depends on the quality of the experts.

❏ Widely differing opinions can be difficult to resolve.

❏ High level of evaluation and analysis is required, to avoid misdirection.

Quick Guide to Delphi Technique

The discussion leader takes the group through specific steps. The problem or issue you are seeking to understand is defined for the panel members clearly. The aim is to clarify and expand on issues, identify areas of agreement or disagreement and to arrive at a consensus from the panel of experts.

The process is generally, as follows:-

1. The technique is normally based on three rounds of questionnaires to estimate the likelihood and outcome of future events, by consensus.

2. Each expert is asked to make predictions on the issue through a series of questionnaires. This method can be carried out on-line without the group coming together or alternatively, the experts are gathered together and given questionnaires to complete individually and anonymously. The questionnaires are designed to address the problem and directly relate to the area of expertise of the group. Each expert expresses their opinion and completes an identical questionnaire using a rating scale with supportive comments. There are many variations on this, such as a written forecast or report format which also work equally well.

3. The questions typically relate to a specific time span, trends, effects, consequences, probability, legislation, socio-political and economic implications etc.

4. The rounds are conducted generally as follows:-

    4.1. The first round is to shed light on the broader issues and ensure understanding of the problem or issue.

    4.2. The second round is to clarify any specific issues relating to the problem or issue.

    4.3. The third round to highlight areas of agreement to a decision and a way forward.

5. The experts answer the questions and give support to their answers.

6. The questionnaires are collected and evaluated, aggregated and irrelevant content filtered out.

7. The results are given back showing the whole groups average rating for each question together with the individual's rating for each question.

8. Between rounds the experts have the opportunity to make changes and revisions to their answers and ratings based on the group's average ratings.

9. Should an individual differ dramatically from the group, they are requested to explain or support these major differences.

10. The process is stopped at arriving at a consensus, or when the returning results are stable and a pre-defined point is reached or sufficient information is available for the group to arrive at a consensus.

11. On the basis of the expert consensus a decision and way forward is then taken.

This concludes our discussion on the use of groups and we embark on the decision making process.

Section: 8.0. The Decision Making Process

The decision model is a simple *four-step process with seven actions* to be carried out. It is a systematic and classical method, which is a thorough and logical process to *turn information and ideas into a decision.*

Decision Making Process

The following steps will help you develop and personalize your own systematic decision making methods by considering the factors and responsibilities of the manager when processing and planning the decision, right through to implementation of the action plan.

Step: 1 Generation	Step: 2 Comparison	Step: 3 Selection	Step: 4 Implementation
Process>	Process>	Process>	
Action: (1) Problem Identification	Action: (3) Boundary Conditions	Action: (5) Tentative Decision	Action: (7) Action - Implement Decision
Action: (2) Information Gathering	Action: (4) Appraise Information	Action: (6) Review Decision Against Boundary Conditions	
	<Feedback	<Feedback	<Feedback

The steps of the decision-making model are described, as follows: -

Step: 1. Generation:

Action: (1)

Identify & Define the Problem or Opportunity: The problem / opportunity and reason for making a decision is identified and defined and a solution objective formulated.

Problem Identification

In order to assist you, the following factors would be considered by the effective decision maker when identifying the problem: -

- ❏ Distinguish between problems requiring, urgent corrective action and those not requiring urgent corrective action - and then take the appropriate action.
- ❏ Have monitoring, control and information systems in place which highlight that there is a deviation to the plan and active decision-making is required.
- ❏ Live with the grey areas, lack of information and uncertainty until it reaches the stage of decision-making.

❏ Have an intuitive grasp of the problem/solution, which enables differentiation between small important issues and areas which point to large important issues and particularly those which impact upon the company.

Let's check this with the planning process.

Checklist: Consider the area of identify & define the problem or opportunity and objectively using the statements below, identify areas where you are comfortable and where you may wish to improve the planning of your decision making: -

---

Problem Identification Factors

1. I accept the need to plan proactively.
2. I accept there may be a lack of information available.
3. I anticipate problems and make plans to meet any contingencies.
4. My plans are proactive; action oriented, problem solving and anticipate crisis.
5. I stay in touch with personnel directly involved in the work.
6. I stay in touch with the business which enables me to differentiate between minor deviations and major problems.

If the answer to these statements is yes, well done!

Step: 1. Generation:
Action: (2)
Collect and Collate Information & Data: This process collects all the information at hand and gathers facts & opinions that are thought to be relevant to the problem identified.

Information Gathering
The important consideration in: Step 1. Generation: Action: (2) is the process of sorting and reviewing information which is available and discovering what additional information needs to be considered and then obtaining that information.

The following are factors the effective decision maker would consider when information gathering: -

- ❏ Ask questions which highlight areas where additional information is required.
- ❏ Condense and refine information so that central issues are clear.
- ❏ Do not get stuck in 'paralysis by analysis' mode, by dwelling on too much detailed information.
- ❏ Maintain a balance between the need to gather information and the need to make a decision.

Let's check this with the planning process.

Checklist: Consider the area of information gathering, and objectively using the statements below identify areas where you are comfortable and where you may wish to improve the planning of your decision making: -

---

Information Gathering Factors

1. I simplify complex information and data.
2. I know where to obtain additional information and data.
3. I involve personnel and specialists where and when appropriate.
4. I use formal and informal sources to gather and validate information.
5. I stop gathering information when it only confirms what was already known.

If the answer to these statements is yes, well done!

Step: 2. Comparison:
Action: (3) Boundary Conditions Limitations and Challenges: Boundary conditions refer to the clear definition as to what the decision must accomplish. Specifically, they must state the objectives the decision must reach, the minimum objectives the decision must attain and the conditions the decision must satisfy to resolve the problem identified in Step: 1. Generation: Action: (1). The boundary conditions take into account all the observed events, issues and facts. They must also consider where challenges or limitations exist.

Boundary Conditions

It is important to define the problem correctly or it will be impossible for you to achieve a quality solution which solves the problem. Also realize that one must check to ensure the specifications of a problem and the objectives have not shifted, resulting in a previously correct decision suddenly becoming inappropriate.

To assist you the following, are factors the effective decision maker would consider when reviewing the boundary conditions: -

❏ Do the boundary conditions take into account all the observed events, issues and facts?

❏ Are the boundary conditions clearly stated in terms of the objectives the decision must reach, the minimum objectives it has to obtain, and the conditions it has to satisfy?

❏ Are the boundary conditions static, are they going to change, are they changing or have they changed?

❏ Are all the boundary conditions compatible with the solution?

Let's check this with the planning process.

Checklist: Consider the area of boundary conditions and objectively using the statements below identify areas where you are comfortable and where you may wish to improve the planning of your decision making: -

---

Boundary Condition Factors

1. I determine what results must be achieved.
2. I determine what obstacles must be overcome.
3. I consider what time restrictions and other pressures exist.
4. I decide what resource limitations exist within the company.
5. I assess any penalties which may exist.
6. I evaluate the risk.
7. I explore all issues that may affect the plan.

If the answer to these statements is yes, well done!

Step: 2. Comparison:

Action: (4) Compare Alternative Solutions: Make a list of alternative solutions from the information collected, collated and evaluate and compare them in relation to the boundary conditions in Step 2. Comparison: Action: (3).

Appraise Information

So far, you have found you have a problem which requires some action. You gathered the relevant information and from that you decided what objectives the decision had to meet in the boundary conditions.

One needs comparative information for each of the solutions selected to ensure it fits in with your boundary conditions.

You can now evaluate and appraise information and make sense of the information you have obtained. Processing, sorting, prioritizing and evaluating the information against the boundary conditions to satisfy the requirements of the problem.

Effective decision makers would consider the following factors when evaluating information:-

- ❏ Use a systematic approach to consider and compare all of the information.
- ❏ Be able to identify and deal with trends and broad issues.
- ❏ Take cognizance of exceptions, anomalies and ambiguities.
- ❏ Apply past experience or lessons learned.

Let's check this with the planning process.

Checklist: Consider the area of appraise information - It is in this step that you collate, evaluate, order and assess the information in relation to the boundary conditions and objectively using the statements below identify areas where you are comfortable and where you may wish to improve the planning of your decision making: -

Appraise Information Factors

1. All relevant information has been gathered and I decide what boundary conditions the solution has to meet.
2. I collate and evaluate the information and solutions proposed.
3. I detail internal and external relationships for each solution.
4. I consider how much time each solution will take.
5. I assess resources available internally and externally.
6. I assess the impact on personnel and clients and who needs to be notified, by when and how.
7. I consider training issues.
8. I know the final cost of each solution.

If the answer to these statements is yes, well done!

Step: 3. Selection:

Action: (5) Rank & Prioritize the Best Tentative Solutions: Rank and prioritize a short list of the best solutions from the alternatives and flexible enough to be changed or modified later, if necessary.

Tentative Decision

To continue the process you will now look at the tentative decision. In this step you: -

1. Generate several alternatives
2. Analyze these alternatives
3. Choose the best alternative and then go on to check and review the decision against the boundary conditions.

Quick Tip*: one of the problems you are faced with in management is that you are constantly under pressure to take action. Sometimes the need to think and check is often seen as a lesser priority to taking action, sometimes any action - it is not!*

The effective decision maker would consider the following when arriving at a tentative decision

❏ Tentative decisions take into account all the issues observed events and facts.

❏ The tentative decision must clearly demonstrate a link between the information obtained and the decision.

❏ Acceptance and/or resistance to the tentative decision are not considered, at this point.

You have made a tentative decision and you have considered in detail its implementation. The sequence of events, how long it will take, people, time and money allocated to each of the events and the necessary resources and support personnel in case problems materialize.

Let's check this with the planning process.

Checklist: Consider the area of tentative decisions and objectively using the statements below identify areas where you are comfortable and where you may wish to improve the planning of your decision making: -

---

Tentative Decision Factors

1. I ensure all actions are listed in sequence with start and completion dates.
2. I assess resources available to each action.
3. The timing for completion is realistic and flexible.
4. I identify threats and opportunities.
5. I consider a contingency plan and standby resources, in case problems may develop.

If the answer to these statements is yes, well done!

Step: 3. Selection:
Action: (6) Select the Best Solution: Review the shortlist of best solutions and select the best solution/ decision and eliminate the alternatives before moving to implementation.

Review Decision, Against the Boundary Conditions
The boundary conditions in Step 2 Comparison, Action (3) saw how the decision took place within a particular environment; and to be effective you must take cognizance of the objectives the decision has to satisfy. Consideration of the reality in which the decision must operate is similar; it has to deal with opinions, reactions, resistance to the decision, limitations and sometimes compromise.

The following are factors the effective decision maker would consider when reviewing the best decision against the boundary conditions

❏ Does the decision take cognizance of all the boundary conditions?

❏ Will the decision resolve or ignore any history associated with the problem?

❏ Are there any real issues that preclude the boundary conditions from being met?

❏ Are there any compromises that have to be considered?

Let's check this with the planning process.

Checklist: Consider the area of review decision against the boundary conditions and select the best solution, and objectively using the statements below identify areas where you are comfortable and where you may wish to improve the planning of your decision making: -

---

Review Decision against the Boundary Conditions and Select the Best Solution:

1. The solution/decision satisfies all the boundary conditions.
2. I consider reactions to the solution.
3. I decide how restrictions and limitations will be overcome within the plan.
4. I determine what potential threats or opportunities which may emanate from the solution.
5. I account for internal and external timing limitations.
6. I check resource support and materials availability.
7. I have alternative personnel on standby, in case of problems.
8. If problems occur, I have the authorization for additional overtime or resources and have discussed this with the relevant personnel.
9. I consider all issues which may affect the plan.

If the answer to these statements is yes, well done!

Rational vs. Creative

You have followed a rational, systematic and sequential process in making decisions, dealing with the analytical, controlled, technical and administrative aspects of the decision. Research has shown that our intuitive, creative, emotional, artistic and conceptual side also plays an important role in the decision-making process and sometimes surfaces in the feeling you may have about a decision. The decision should feel right, if it doesn't try to identify the area where you feel uneasy and correct or minimize it.

Quick Tip: *when you review the decision against the boundary conditions reflect on how you feel about your decision and if you feel uneasy about the decision, sleep on it, this works wonders for resolving any issues which you may feel uneasy about.*

No doubt, decision-making can be tough, but what you have covered is a worthwhile systematic approach which will make the experience for you easier and enjoyable.

Step: 4. Implementation:
Action: (7) Implement the Decision though an Action Plan: Break down the decision into its component parts or tasks and incorporate them into an action plan.

Action - Implement Decision
And now the final step in the decision-making process: -

Required ACTION? - implement the decision!
This step of detailing the action and implementing the decision it is critically important to answer the following questions: -

- ❏ What has to be done?
- ❏ Why is it necessary?
- ❏ Who carries out the action and must be notified?
- ❏ When is the action to be carried out?
- ❏ Where is the action carried out?
- ❏ How is the action to be carried out?
- ❏ What if a problem occurs... is there a contingency planning in place?
- ❏ Where to.... feedback and comparison on where the solution is with regard to the problem identified in Step 1.

Management feedback is necessary; this may be in the form of a feedback report or a simple evaluation to be carried out by the decision maker. The decision ultimately has to be monitored and feedback compared to Step 1: Problem Identification.

The effective decision maker would consider the following factors when implementing the decision.

❏ All the steps of the decision making process have been considered and are in the correct sequence.

❏ Putting the decision into action takes cognizance of the what/ why, how, when, etc., factors listed above.

❏ Sufficient action is to be taken for the decision to be fully effective.

❏ A feedback system is in place to monitor the effects and/or deviations to the decision.

You have looked at one of the most important and critical jobs of a manager; that of making decisions and the process by which it is accomplished. By carrying out these systematic methods and processes you are clearly defining your objectives and action plans and firming up and fixing your target dates to ensure achievement.

Section: 9.0. Quick Guide to Making Effective Decisions

The following guide will ensure you don't miss anything and that you have considered all the factors when making a decision.

The Purpose of the Decision Model is fourfold: -

Step: 1. Generation:

Action: (1) To define the Problem/ Opportunity

Action: (2) To Collect and Collate Information & Data

Step: 2. Comparison:

Action: (3) Specify the Boundary Conditions, Limitations and Challenges

Action: (4) Compare Alternative Solutions from the Information & Data

Step: 3. Selection:

Action: (5) Rank & Prioritize the Best Tentative Solutions

Action: (6) Select the Best Solution

Step: 4. Implementation:

Action: (7) Implement the Decision though an Action plan

The Decision Model is a logical procedure to define the problem/opportunity, process the information and data, specify the boundary conditions, select the best solution, implement an action plan and determine the end result/s required.

There are also several other factors to consider: -

- ❏ Use the decision-making process.
- ❏ Groups could be used in decision making to improve the quality.
- ❏ Expert group information and judgment can increase the reliability of the information.
- ❏ The more reliable your information, the sooner you can cease the collection and evaluation.
- ❏ There comes a time when information collection and evaluation must cease and decision/s implemented.
- ❏ The feedback of your decision to the original problem (Step 1) is vital for consistent quality of the decision.

Remember.........

A successful decision-making ability is the primary skill of an effec tive manager.

These factors will enable you to move towards excellent quality decisions. You are now ready for effective decision making and the next step is to implement your decision using an action plan!

Section: 10.0. How to Implement a Decision and Action Plan

You have now arrived at a decision and need to implement an action plan.

Your written and detailed action plan outlines actions, coordinates resource allocation and timing needed to reach one or more of the decision objectives. An action plan allows managers and personnel to monitor their progress and handle the decision efficiently for the benefit of the company; it aids monitoring, control and feedback on the decision.

Section: 10.1. How to Start Action Planning

Typically, the managers who know that time has to be made for planning, prioritize their actions and achieve the important and urgent tasks which contribute to their key performance areas and take control of their own time.

Section: 10.2. The Action Planning Process

You have looked at the Action Plan Model (Chapter 2. Diagram: 04 refer). By applying the action planning model the process is a relatively quick, simple, rational and systematic method which you can use successfully.

To recap, the purpose of each of the following models is as follows: -
(1). **The Question Model**: *generates information and ideas.*

(2). **The Decision Model**: *processes information and ideas towards a decision.*

(3). **The Action Plan**: *turns the decision/s into action.*

Section: 10.3. Levels of Complexity

Depending on the complexity of the decision, you can use the following models to suit your circumstances. The following diagrams 05 and 06 present an overview of the action planning processes that can be used for non-complex and complex decisions.

Diagram: 05. Action Planning for Simple Non-Complex Decisions

The Question Model Chapter 2. Diagram: 02 refers	*The Action Plan* Chapter 2. Diagram: 04 refers
Generates information and ideas	*Turns information and decision/s into action.*
A four step process 1: Focus on the Objective. 2: Focus on Action Plan & Resources. 3: Focus on the Method/s to achieve the Action Plan. 4: Focus on monitoring and measuring the current feedback to the original Objective & The Contingency plan.	*A three step process* 1:Headline Information 2:Task Information 3:Monitoring Progress & Completion Information

Diagram: 05. Action Planning for Non-Complex Decisions: For simple non-complex problem or opportunity decisions, you could use the Question Model (Chapter 2. Diagram: 02 refers) as a stand-alone model for problems and opportunities towards reaching a decision and implementation through a simple action plan.

Diagram: 06. Action Planning for Complex Decisions

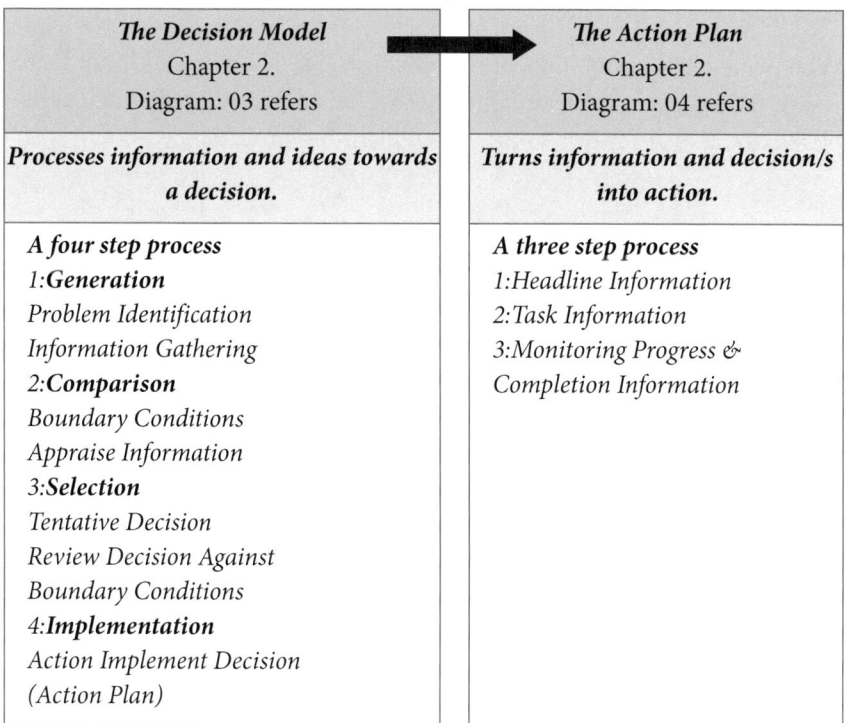

The Decision Model Chapter 2. Diagram: 03 refers	*The Action Plan* Chapter 2. Diagram: 04 refers
Processes information and ideas towards a decision.	***Turns information and decision/s into action.***
A four step process 1:**Generation** *Problem Identification* *Information Gathering* 2:**Comparison** *Boundary Conditions* *Appraise Information* 3:**Selection** *Tentative Decision* *Review Decision Against* *Boundary Conditions* 4:**Implementation** *Action Implement Decision* *(Action Plan)*	*A three step process* 1:*Headline Information* 2:*Task Information* 3:*Monitoring Progress &* *Completion Information*

Diagram: 06. Action Planning for Complex Decisions: As the decisions, problems and opportunities increase in complexity and strategic importance to the company, you can add the Decision Model (Chapter 2. Diagram: 03 refers) and the Action Plan Model (Chapter 2. Diagram: 04 refers), as required.

For the purposes of this exercise; the Implementation or Action Plan is the end result of the Decision Model (and / or the Question Model) which processes information and ideas towards a decision and the Action Plan turns the information and decision/s into action.

Quick Tip: *start the process with the Question Model first, if the decision develops into a complex and/or more strategic decision, you can add the Decision Model to accommodate more detailed information towards the decision.*

Implementation of the Action Plan –
Implement the decision with a monitoring and control feedback system using the action planning process for reviewing current status and

comparing results and with the original problem identification to ensure satisfactory progress.

When you use this systematic process you will see how useful it can be for you in rationalizing your thoughts towards an effective decision and action plan. Now, let's apply this to the action planning process.

Section: 11.0. Summary Review: Action Planning

To recap from the previous sections, you have been through the decision making process and you have compared your current decision making skills in the decision making and planning process. Now you need to consolidate all the information and look ahead.

Section: 12.0. Description of the Action Plan Model

You now bring all the information, tasks, resources and timeframes together in the action plan. The purpose of the action plan is to turn the decision into action which leads to a positive result.

1. **Developing an Action Plan**

Action plans specify *what* the actions or tasks will be and *who* will complete each task in a certain time to reach each of the *target dates* (*when*) each task is carried out over a specific time period to meet the overall timeframe of the plan and accomplish the company's problem or opportunity objective. Ideally, the manager and personnel directly involved in their area would contribute to the action plan and address the task/s that are to be carried out, generally as follows: -

- ❏ What tasks need to be carried out?
- ❏ When will the results be achieved for each task to meet the overall timeframe of the problem or opportunity objective?
- ❏ How will each task contribute to the company's problem or opportunity objective?
- ❏ What specific results must be achieved to reach the company's problem or opportunity objective?
- ❏ How will those results be achieved?

2. **Developing the Company's Problem or Opportunity Objective and Timeframes**

   ❏ The company's problem or opportunity objective should contain quantifiable and measurable results which are produced when tasks are implemented and completed (e.g. '*x*' increase / or decrease by '*y*' time).

   ❏ Ensure the tasks contained in the action plan are monitored, compared and reviewed.

   ❏ Remember the task start and end dates are guidelines for completion and these where possible should be flexible with the ability to move these dates, if necessary rather than being rigidly structured.

   ❏ Alternatively, if the company's problem or opportunity objective *is not flexible*; due to circumstances outside the control of the company; you may need to build in contingencies or have additional resources available to meet the company's overall objective timeframe e.g. overtime, additional resources, etc.

   ❏ Any delays or deviations to the company's overall objective timeframe contained in the action plan should be reported by the manager and personnel involved so that alternative action can be taken in good time.

3. **Developing Tasks and Timeframes**

The manager and ideally each employee directly involved in his/her area should contribute to the development of the action plan tasks and the company's overall objective. The action plan should illustrate how <u>all</u> the tasks will be implemented.

   ❏ Firstly, break down the solution / decision into its component parts for each independent task.

   ❏ The action plan should reflect in specific detail how each of the tasks will be accomplished, from start through to completion.

   ❏ Any possible 'known' delays or deviations to the tasks contained in the action plan should be fully understood by the manager and the manager's personnel so that alternative action can be built into the action plan or action taken prior to commencement.

   ❏ Each task should relate to the company's overall problem or opportunity objective.

❏ The format of the action plan depends very much on the nature and needs of the company and can be modified to suit the situation.

Section: 13.0. A Simple Action Plan Model Overview

You could use the action plan model in Chapter 2: Section: 2.4. Diagram: 04. The Action Plan Model as a template, to develop an action plan for the problem/opportunity objective identified; make sure you break down the overall objective into simple specific tasks or action steps. Place each of these tasks into the action plan in sequential date order and fill out the fields, across the form.

SIMPLE ACTION PLAN						
1. Headline Information:						
*Refer to Chapter 2: Systematic Methods and Response Techniques, Section: 2.4. Description of the Action Planning Model Diagram: 04. The Action Plan Model for details.						
2. Task Information:						
1.	**2.**	**3.**	**4.**	**5.**	**6.**	**7.**
Tasks	Responsible Person	Estimated Start & End Date	Resources [The 5xMs]	Additional Resources [Internal/ external]	Date the Task is Completed	Comments on the Task Result
3. Monitoring Progress and Completion Information:						
*Refer to Chapter 2: Systematic Methods and Response Techniques, Section: 2.4. Description of the Action Planning Model Diagram: 04. The Action Plan Model for details.						

Notes to the Action Plan:
1.0   Headline Information

*With reference to the action plan model in Chapter 2: Section: 2.4. Diagram: 04. The Action Plan Model.

This area normally contains the name of the originator of the action plan and commencement date, a brief description of the problem or opportunity. The aim of the problem or opportunity and the barriers, limitations or challenges anticipated and how these will be overcome and the progress review dates. The target date the plan commences the target date the plan finishes and the overall deadline date and the reporting structure.

2.0 Task Information

1. **Task No:** Firstly, give each task an Identifying number #1. #2. #3. etc.etc.

2. **Column (1) Tasks:** Identify specifically what will be done to take each task to completion and enter task to be carried out.

3. **Column (2) Responsible Person:** Enter the name of the Person Responsible or team leader responsible for each task.

4. **Column (3) Estimated Start & End Date:** Enter the 'Estimated' Start and End Date for each task and build in some flexibility, if possible.

5. **Column (4) Resources – 5xMs:** Consider and allocate resources in terms of the '5 Ms', required to complete each task.

    5.1.1. **MEN:** Personnel

    5.1.2. **MONEY:** Cost / Funding

    5.1.3. **MACHINES:** Equipment

    5.1.4. **METHODS:** Procedure

    5.1.5. **MATERIALS:** Raw and other materials

6. **Column (5) Additional Resources:** [internal/external] Detail the additional support resources, (who/what?). Additional resources that the responsible person would require to complete the task/s and where these internal or external sources will come from.

7. **Column (6) Date the Task is Completed:** Enter the 'actual' date the Person Responsible (or team leader) completes the task.

8. **Column (7) Comments on the Task Result:** On completion of a task – ask, what will the task accomplish towards the overall objective? Is it on time? Are there any delays? Is this a movable date or critical?

Note: *On completion and allocation of all resources and time frames, the action plan is now ready for implementation.*

3.0 Monitoring Progress and Completion Information

*Refer to Chapter 2: Section: 2.4. Diagram: 04. The Action Plan Model.

The action plan provides a means to monitor progress and give feedback to management and personnel and at completion of the action plan provides a means of evaluating the extent of accomplishment and success of the overall objective.

Quick Tip: modify the form to fit your specific requirements. Encourage personnel to get involved in contributing to the solution /decision. Make sure you break down the objective into simple specific action steps. Ensure any additional resources / high cost items are budgeted into the plan. Keep copies handy for use in meetings for progress reviews and ensure all personnel involved have a copy of the up to date action plan and programme.

Implementation of the Action Plan Decision:

You should note at this point, the importance of ensuring that all aspects of the what, why, when, etc. part of the plan have been adequately defined and confirmed. Time spent here will save time changing and modifying the plan later.

Let's check this with the planning process.

Checklist: Consider action planning in implement the decision, and objectively using the statements below identify areas in planning where you are comfortable and where you may wish to improve the action planning of your decision: -

---

Action Planning – Implement the Decision

1. I know why the plan is necessary.
2. I know what has to be done.
3. I know how the action is to be carried out.
4. I know who carries out the plan.
5. I know where the plan is to be implemented.
6. I know when the plan is to be carried out.
7. I have taken sufficient action to ensure the plan is agreed and executed by all those who must be involved in its completion.
8. I know 'what if' a problem develops – I have a contingency plan.
9. I have checked that all the steps and sequences in the planning process are correct.
10. I have a management feedback system in place.
11. I know where we want to be on completion.

If the answer to these statements is yes, well done!

Section: 14.0. Quick Guide to Conventional Action Planning

You can ensure your planning remains at a professional level by reviewing your planning periodically, perhaps every three to six months to check how you are doing.

The following Quick Guide will assist you with planning in the future: -

1. Build the question, decision and planning models into your decision making and action planning.
2. Ensure sufficient time for you to plan and take control of your own time.
3. Assemble sufficient data, facts and resource information.
4. Identify what will be done to take each task to completion.
5. Select a person responsible or team leader responsible for each task.
6. Estimate the start and end date for each task and build in flexibility.
7. Allocate resources in terms of the '5 Ms' required to complete each task.
8. Consider the additional support resources that the responsible person may require to complete the task/s and where these internal or external sources will come from.
9. Realistically consider the end completion date for all tasks.
10. Decide if the tasks and action plan will accomplish the overall objective.
11. Provide adequate feedback to the original problem identification.

And use the Question Model of Management to assist you through the Control of the Action Planning process and help you to stay on track, during the implementation stages of the Action Plan: -

1. **Why** do I need to take action in a particular area?
2. **What** objectives, action plan, shall I set?
3. **Who** will be involved?
4. **When** are my objective and action plan dates?
5. **How** are my objectives and actions, to happen?
6. **What if** a problem develops, what will I do?

7. **Where** should my objectives and action plan take me?

Remember.........

Management Wisdom

It always takes longer than you expect, even when you take into account, it will take longer.

*Hofstadter's Law

Chapter 11: Ideal Monitoring and Control Methods

The Ninth Rule of Smart Management:
Learn what makes focused managers develop
ideal and appropriate monitoring and control
methods that work.

Section: 1.0. How to Use Appropriate Monitoring and Control Methods

You are surrounded by controls in your everyday life. Controls help you to organize and manage your life with a certain amount of predictability. For example, you receive the weather report, traffic report etc. and act accordingly.

There are many performance controls in the company environment, which range from aiding work tasks to monitoring financial performance. Never the less, controls are generally divided into two categories: -

- ❏ Preventive.
- ❏ Corrective.

Both preventative and corrective controls can be applied to all resources within the business, when considering resources in terms of the '5 Ms', controls can be applied to the following resources: -

- ❏ Men: personnel, services and performance
- ❏ Money: costs, funding and financials, profit and loss
- ❏ Machines: plant & equipment, tools and transport
- ❏ Methods: procedures and systems
- ❏ Materials: raw materials input and production output

Preventive controls: The most typical example is that of planned maintenance to prevent major machine failures and breakdowns of plant and equipment. Preventative controls are also required for personnel, services and performance, within companies and businesses in general.

Corrective controls: these are typically instituted when there is a deviation to the planned performance result, annual profits, services where a failure or a complete breakdown has occurred and corrective action is required to get performance back to the planned result or level and prevent a recurrence.

Over Controlling and Under Controlling

Both types of control are necessary; however there must be a balance between both corrective and preventive controls to avoid over controlling and under controlling: -

For example, over control: in terms of personnel teams can lead to stifled initiative and low motivation.

Remember.........

Management Wisdom

Push something hard enough and it will fall over.

*Fudd's First Law of Opposition

And under control: in terms of personnel teams can lead to personnel becoming confused without sufficient direction and leadership.

Therefore a perfect balance is sought............

Self Assessment:

The following will test your current monitoring and control standards and help you to asses where you need to work on specific areas: -

Your Current Monitoring and Control Situation

Answer yes or no to the following:

1. My control systems help guide my personnel and myself in operational tasks.
2. My personnel fully understand the monitoring and control systems and why they are necessary.
3. The information I receive is simple, relevant and timely.
4. My monitoring and control systems enable me to anticipate problems in my major result areas.
5. My monitoring and control systems produce positive results.
6. My control systems are reviewed and updated regularly.
7. I have achieved a balance between under and over control.
8. I receive information from both internal and external sources which may affect my major result areas.
9. All my personnel are fully involved in the process.

If the answer to any of these statements is yes, well done!

If the answer to any of these statements is no, take note and work on them.

Section: 1.1. Using the Monitoring and Control Process

You have tested your level of satisfaction with your current monitoring and control situation. You can now address the process of control.

The monitoring and control process consists of six steps: -

The Six Step Control Process		Purpose
1.	Set Objectives	For those areas, which you need to control.
2.	Establish Standards	To be measurable and quantifiable.
3.	Establish Accountability	To specifying whom, what, and when.
4.	Measure and Compare	Record actual results with the planned results.
5.	Take Corrective Action	To deal with the variances.
6.	Commitment to Controls	To encourage personnel to use process.

Quick Tip: *These six steps in the monitoring and control process will ensure you arrive where you plan to be.*

Section: 1.2. The Six Step Control Process

The six steps in the monitoring and control process are explained as follows: -

Step: 1. Set Objectives.

In production-type work it is usually relatively easy, objectives relate to output which is often visible both in terms of quality and quantity. In service type work objective setting can be a little more difficult, but it is also essential to correctly quantify and measure output of a service operation.

Let's look at your objectives: -

❏ What is your department measured against – production / sales / service / support?

❏ What does your department contribute to overall company effectiveness or profit?

❏ What must your department do consistently to keep your company in business?

❏ What objectives do you want to achieve for your department?

The answers will enable you to see what your department's objectives are and these should coincide with your major result areas.

For example, if you are in charge of the sales department of your company, you will probably set objectives in the following areas: -

- ❏ Turnover.
- ❏ New product introductions.
- ❏ New accounts opened.
- ❏ New business areas developed.
- ❏ Profitability, in terms of the efficiency of your department against budget.

Step: 2. Establish Standards

Now let's look further into your objectives with the intention of firming them up, so that you can compare actual results against your planned results.

To do this you need to set standards and benchmarks.

1. The reason to set standards and benchmarks is to establish planned performance levels which are realistic.
2. To enable you to compare actual departmental performance against what was planned.
3. To enable you to measure your overall objectives and performance towards achieving them.
4. Standards and benchmarks are measurable, flexible and realistic and fact based therefore personal opinion, likes, dislikes prejudices and assumptions are eliminated where possible.

Controls have four characteristics: -

- ❏ Measurable
- ❏ Flexible
- ❏ Realistic
- ❏ Fact based

As follows: -

1. **Measurable**: This is perhaps the most important characteristic when considering standards.
    1.1. There are many ways of measuring, for example: -
        1.1.1. Numerical measure: quantity and quality are used.
        1.1.2. Monetary measure: through budgets, income, expenditure and sales.

      1.1.3. Time measure: where competing against deadlines or within parameters are important.

      1.1.4. Descriptive measure: in difficult-to-quantify areas where impressions and sensory information are used.

2. **Flexible**: When setting controls and expecting personnel to use their initiative, flexibility is essential.

    2.1. Flexibility is necessary when you want commitment.

    2.2. For example: You may require production personnel to keep to their working times, during normal production, but when a production deadline or specific output is imminent, you may give production personnel some flexibility over their specific working times, due to the requirements of the deadline or output.

3. **Realistic**: Your standards must be based on the real work environment of your personnel. In an environment which may be ever changing and demanding, standards can be updated and changed. For example controlling the lunch hours of your external service personnel may be of much less value than their daily service calls and reports being completed on time.

    Quick Tip: *sometimes it is more productive to focus on what is being achieved, rather than focusing on attendance.*

4. **Fact Based**: Standards and benchmarks are fact based therefore personal opinion; likes, dislikes, prejudices and assumptions are eliminated where possible from the standards and benchmarks that you set.

Step: 3. Establish Accountability

Accountability counts, when looking into the monitoring and control process, giving authority to individuals and assigning accountability is an important and integral part of the process. When a manager assigns authority and accountability to personnel there must be a clear directive of what is expected from those personnel.

Assigning accountability is based on the fact that you have delegated sufficient authority to your employee to carry out the task; this delegated authority ensures that your personnel are accountable for the results, but remember......... **you** still carry the overall responsibility and accountability!

Quick Tip: *when applying monitoring and control techniques it is important that you check for understanding, at every stage with those directly involved.*

An important distinction when considering accountability is that of comparative controls:

Comparative controls can be historical or present day, as follows: -

❏ **Historical Past Performance versus Present Day Performance**.

Refers to the method of comparative controlling for deciding what the past performance standard compared with the present performance.

For example, comparing present costs with historical cost trends; present sales with past sales records, present personnel turnover with previous year's personnel turnover.

❏ **Present Day Performance versus Future Planned Performance**.

Typically refers to comparative controls, which provide a basis for deciding what present standards should be and then monitoring and comparing future performance.

For example, studying present day business with a planned new business introduction and then instituting appropriate turnover, cost budgets, and work standards to aim for the new business objective.

Step: 4. Monitor and Compare

To manage the process you need look at measurement and variances, specifically what you want to achieve against what has been achieved.

This is not new in production; target figures, budgets and output quotas are readily available to continually measure performance.

Carefully designed standards in your measurable and tangible major-result areas can be monitored to reduce problems in your work areas and contribute to solving problems in your less-measurable and intangible work areas.

There are three ways of measuring actual performance against the planned performance, as follows: -

1. **Verbal Reports** are control methods of assessing performance and are particularly useful when there is no need for back up records, and when the measurement is not complex.

2. **Written Reports:** The second control method of acquiring measurement of performance against the plan is that of a written report.

These can be through digital or electronic readings, measurement and analyzed. These written methods are best when the information is complex and when a snapshot is required per day, per week or per month and a record is necessary.

3. **Personal Observation**, when it directly involves your own work area and personnel this method is particularly valuable when urgency and first hand information is important, and you can access a work area and make a personal assessment of the situation or performance.

Step: 5. Take Corrective Action

Through the monitoring and controls you have implemented, you may come across areas indicating differing performance variance. You need to manage these variances and take corrective action using the following response techniques.

A Major Negative Deviation

For example, if you find that sales have decreased drastically for the period being measured. You would take the necessary corrective action. This may involve getting together with your relevant sales personnel to obtain the relevant facts and to ascertain why things are going wrong and what can be done to correct the situation. Perhaps more detailed and more frequent reporting will be required over the next period to ensure that the area responds to the corrective action you and your sales personnel have implemented.

A Minor Negative Deviation

If you discover a minor negative trend in performance you need to take action, but perhaps with less urgency than in the previous case. The initial preventive action would be a discussion with the relevant personnel to ascertain what is going wrong and what actions are required to reverse the trend and whether it is necessary to institute corrective action and tighter and more frequent controls.

A Positive Deviation

When the monitoring and controls indicate you are ahead of your planned performance, and you are outperforming the sales budget. Assuming that the sales standards are set to reflect realistic performance for the area under consideration and not set too low, congratulate your sales personnel for an excellent job - well done.

Secondly, perhaps an investigative meeting with your personnel to ascertain from their suggestions what can be done to maintain the positive performance results.

Step: 6. Commitment to Controls

There are several general issues concerning monitoring and controls where commitment from personnel to your monitoring and control system is an important part of the process.

1. **Why Controls can be ignored**

   First, let us look at why monitoring and controls are sometimes ignored by personnel: -

   The monitoring and control systems and the reason for the controls are not fully explained to personnel, as a result it is not fully understood by personnel why the controls are necessary.

   It can appear incorrectly, that controls only affect personnel and not the manager.

2. **Management by Exception**

   Management by exception is that a manager should only take action when controls indicate that things are going wrong. The problem with this approach is that it can have a negative effect on personnel if the manager limits personnel interaction to only getting involved with personnel when things are going wrong, this approach has to be handled carefully by the manager and needs to be balanced with informal reviews and feedback.

3. **Regular Informal and Formal Reviews**

   Personnel generally prefer regular informal progress reviews and feedback to facilitate communication and good management.

   Regular informal and formal reviews gain commitment to your monitoring and control systems and also:
   - ❏ Facilitate good communication between the manager and personnel.
   - ❏ Enable the manager to check performance against set and agreed standards.
   - ❏ Establish the manager's interest in the employees' objectives.

Another aspect which is important to gain commitment to your monitoring and control techniques is to explain why it is necessary to monitor and compare performance and particularly when modifying or changing the system.

4. **How to gain commitment to monitoring and controlling systems**

Here you have to encourage a buy-in approach from personnel; they need to see the benefits from monitoring and controlling the process to improve their work environment, by making their work more streamlined, more efficient and effective and as a result achieves improvements in the overall resources and performance of the company.

❏ Explain in detail the need for the controls and their objective.

❏ Give feedback to the people who operate under performance controls by providing them with a consolidated and summarized version so that it helps them see how they contribute to company performance and provide recognition for positive results, this will ensure commitment.

❏ People from the work area can normally understand how performance controls may work better; therefore encourage open discussion, comment and suggestions regarding performance controls from them.

❏ Review the performance controls to improve or alter them with changing circumstances and scrap them once they are no longer relevant.

Finally, controls must be cost effective. They must give a return on the time and effort investment on the part of the personnel who operate under them and this must be seen as quantifiable and measurable.

Section: 2.0. Summary Review: Perfect Monitoring and Control Methods

Now let's summarize and review what you have covered: -

1. You assessed your controls and your satisfaction with the controls you presently have and you noted any areas which were of concern to you.

2. You checked if your objectives and major result areas were a little vague or difficult to quantify and measure.

3. Good standards are measurable, flexible and realistic.

4. You addressed assigning accountability and you saw the need for historical comparative controls and present comparative controls, delegation of authority and the amount of detail needed in a monitoring and control system.

5. You looked at measurement of actual performance against planned performance and found that the three ways of measuring were verbally, in a written report and by observation.

6. How to manage variances and corrective action, preventive action and over performance were discussed.

7. You looked at management by exception, together with how to gain commitment to monitoring and control methods and the need for the controls to be cost-effective and regularly reviewed.

Section: 3.0. Quick Guide to Perfect Monitoring and Control Methods

Below is a quick guide, which you can use to review your perfect monitoring and control methods. Perhaps you may want to schedule a controls review on a regular basis to fine tune them with your team

A Quick Guide to Perfect Monitoring and Control Methods:

1. **Do you get enough information from your personnel about their problems, frustrations and progress?**

    1.1. Is it timely?

    1.2. If not, what can you do about this to improve it?

2. **Are you able to anticipate a crisis?**

    2.1. Are there controls and feedback procedures in place which could assist you

3. **Do you have adequate objectives for the areas you need to monitor and control?**

3.1.   Are they known and accepted by those company employees who work with them?

4. **Do you have standards, which are reasonable and stated in measurable terms?**

   4.1. Are they being achieved?

   4.2. If not, what can you do about this to improve it?

5. **Have you established clear accountability for the attainment of the objectives?**

   5.1. Does the accountability specify who is responsible for completion?

   5.2. What?

   5.3. When?

   5.4. If not, what can you do about this to improve it?

6. **How are you measuring the results against the planned objective?**

   6.1. Are you getting the results in time?

7. **What action is necessary to deal with any variance?**

   7.1. Who needs to be involved in the decision process?

Use the Quick Guide frequently; it will keep you on track to your own and your company's objectives.

And use the Question Model of Management to assist you through the monitoring and control methods: -

   1. **Why** do I need to take action in a particular area?

   2. **What** objectives, action plan, shall I set?

   3. **Who** will be involved?

   4. **When** are my objective and action plan dates?

   5. **How** are my objectives and actions, to happen?

   6. **What if** a problem develops, what will I do?

   7. **Where** should my objectives and action plan take me?

Perfect monitoring and control methods do not come easily, they take time and practice to get them right. The previous sections will help you determine the correct monitoring and control systems for your business, which will reduce problems in your work areas.

Remember.........

Management Wisdom

It is common sense to take a method and try it. If it fails, admit it frankly and try another. But above all, try something.

*Franklin D. Roosevelt

Chapter 12: The Complete Negotiation

The Tenth Rule of Smart Management: Understand how negotiation is a skill which requires you to be aware of issues, positions and strategy to ensure all the parties reach agreement.

Section: 1.0. An Introduction to Negotiation

Negotiation is not just communication; negotiation can come in many forms and be one of management's most interesting and enjoyable interactions. Feedback is immediate and you know when you have handled an issue well or badly by the reaction of the person you are negotiating with.

The Key Areas to Negotiation are: -

❏ **Preparation**
❏ **Negotiation**
❏ **Feedback**.

Negotiations come in all shapes and sizes, supply contracts, export orders, legal contracts, service and maintenance contracts, etc.

There are certain rules and skills involved. The effective use of these skills and a thorough knowledge of the rules, methods and skills will result in a winning agreement.

Remember.........

Management Wisdom

Hope for the best, prepare for the worst.

*Unknown

First let us define a negotiation, in simple words; negotiation comes about through an identified need, when there is a supply and demand situation. When one party has something the other party wants and vice versa. These needs can be tangible or intangible.

The main objective of most negotiations is to reach an agreement. It is a process of moving toward an outcome and an agreement which satisfies both parties.

It is the process, which contains many facets, rules and skills with various areas of exploration, bargaining and bidding towards reaching the agreement.

These are the necessary skills involved: -
- ❏ Set the right climate.
- ❏ Develop trust.
- ❏ Control the agenda.
- ❏ Prevent deadlocks.
- ❏ Make opening bids.
- ❏ Move towards agreement and closure.

The Tactics involved: -
- ❏ Revealing your mandate.
- ❏ Revealing your information.
- ❏ Recess timing.
- ❏ Incentives.
- ❏ Inducement.

Much has been written on negotiation and the process. You have been using these skills at different levels most of your life; you may have developed them from your experience and learned from your successes and mistakes of bargaining or from being taught about the negotiation process.

The following will introduce you to the systematic methods and take you through the response techniques and formal process to strengthen your present knowledge.

Section: 1.1. The Prerequisites
All winning negotiations have a few very clear prerequisites, without which the process can become very frustrating.

If you are the negotiating party you have to ensure the following prerequisites are in place.

1. **Understanding of the overall company objective and policies**

   1.1. When negotiating for the company ensure you know the overall company objective that you are to achieve in the negotiation and ask: -

   1.1.1. Is it to reduce costs?

   1.1.2. Is it to add value?

   1.1.3. Is it to improve quality?

   1.1.4. Is it to increase market share?

   1.1.5. Is it to increase turnover?

   1.1.6. Is it to obtain a short-term profit?

   1.1.7. Is it to grow the company?

You know that when you negotiate it is normally to buy or to sell something, perhaps a joint venture or even a merger, however the questions remain the same: -

❏ Why are you negotiating, what is the objective?

❏ What is the company getting out of it?

❏ What does your managing director or directors want for the company?

❏ What is the long term effect of the negotiated agreement?

You can explore more options in a negotiation if you understand the broad overall objectives of your company and these questions are important because the answers set your target objective and give you the flexibility you may need during the negotiation.

Quick Tip: *the more alternative solutions you have in the negotiation, the more power you have.*

2. **A clear mandate and objectives for negotiation are important**

   2.1. You require a clear mandate, your authorization levels and detail of the company's objective during the negotiation; you can then develop specific negotiation objectives as a clear mandate, your authorization levels and detail of the company's objective lays down the boundaries which you may not exceed:-

   2.1.1. Sell for no less than....

      2.1.2. Buy for no more than....

      2.1.3. Buy for delivery by....

      2.1.4. Buy at this quality level/standard....

      2.1.5. Etc.

Effective managers make sure that they have a clear mandate which will allow flexibility, providing the company objectives are met. It is prudent to clarify, in writing, what your company's objectives are in relation to any major negotiation you undertake.

3. Thorough preparation

    3.1. Your preparation for negotiations is important, effective negotiators focus most of their effort on the preparation stage and this planning includes: -

      3.1.1. Establishing the mandate.

      3.1.2. Identifying the other party's requirements.

      3.1.3. Analyzing the issues.

      3.1.4. Establishing target objectives for each issue.

      3.1.5. Planning the agenda.

      3.1.6. Tactical plans and timing.

Preparation for a negotiation is essential; it is a complex management task. You must prepare both physically and mentally particularly if the negotiation may be prolonged. Negotiation can be stressful at times and it is important to stay on-track and deal with the major issues and not get sidetracked or caught up on smaller non important issues.

Good preparation and planning tactics well in advance will add to your flexibility and skill.

Section: 1.2. Preparation

Negotiations are won and lost on the quality of preparation, rather than on the interactive skill of the parties and this is where you will place your emphasis.

Preparation in negotiating is vital to a successful outcome.

The first step in an effective negotiation is to identify all the issues that must be settled.

Let's use the example of a house purchase where the issues might include some of the following: -

House Purchase
- ❏ Price
- ❏ Occupation date
- ❏ Repairs
- ❏ Other extras

As the purchaser, you would have specific dates, prices and requirements.

The next step is to break down each issue into its smaller components. This way you create flexibility for yourself that allows you to give concessions and make trade-offs.

In the house example; you could have very specific requirements, some more important to you than others. The point is, to list them all however small and trivial they may seem, as the other party may have a different view of assessing what is important, small and trivial.

This leads us to a rating of each issue or element.

- ❏ Which are important to you?
- ❏ Which are you indifferent about?
- ❏ Which do you not care about!

In other words, your rating may be something like the following example: -

- ❏ 1 = must win
- ❏ 2 = nice to win
- ❏ 3 = throw a way
- ❏ 0 = deal breaker (not negotiable)

House Purchase Example			
Issue	**Elements**	**Rating**	**Comments**
Price	Above Maximum 'x' price	0	Deal breaker
	Maximum is 'x' price I can pay	1	Must win
	Minimum is 'y' price	2	Nice to win
	10% Deposit	1	Must win
	Discount	2	Nice to win
	Lowest Interest rate	2	Nice to win
	Loan/mortgage/bond with Co. X	3	Throw a way
Occupation	No occupational rental	1	Must win
	Immediately	2	Nice to win
	On payment of deposit	2	Nice to win
	On payment by building society	3	Throw a way
Repairs	Building work	1	Must win
	Paintwork	2	Nice to win
	Electrical	2	Nice to win
	Plumbing	2	Nice to win
	Swimming pool equipment	3	Throw a way
Extras	Carports	1	Must win
	Paving	1	Must win
	Fencing	2	Nice to win
	Security	2	Nice to win
	Awnings	3	Throw a way

By splitting up issues and rating the elements, you are increasing your flexibility and power in the negotiation because you are converting a **win issue** into **elements which will include 'must win', 'nice-to-win' and 'throw-away'**.

You can use the example above to practice on your preparation for a work related negotiation by defining the issues, breaking them down and rating each element.

Section: 1.3. The Opponent

When working on the preparation you would study and assess your opponent. However, because you do not want to think of the negotiation as personal, emotional, confrontational or as a win-lose situation, rather see your negotiation as two parties seeking a solution to a problem. With this approach in mind, you should avoid using the word 'opponent', 'adversary' or 'them' in relation to 'us - them' and refer to your opponent as the 'other party' in the negotiation, at all times.

Let's start identifying the other party's requirements; there are two types of requirements:

- ❏ Priority Issues
- ❏ Self-image

The Priority Issues; are relatively tangible and would probably be somewhere close to your own range of issues. Nevertheless, the point is to anticipate these issues and to estimate what the other party's priorities are, and why. This is where research and good questioning at any meetings prior to the negotiation may pay off.

The following example is for a simple project negotiation where you are the buyer and the other party is the seller.

You may want to use the following key: -

- ❏ 0 = not negotiable (or deal breaker)
- ❏ 1 = must win
- ❏ 2 = nice to win
- ❏ 3 = throw a way

Project 'X'							
Issue	**Elements**	**Rating**	**Own best position**	**Own worst position**	**Other party's best position**	**Other party's worst position**	**Comments**
A. **Price** **Proposals**	**Highest**	0		*	*		Could offer early payment?
	Medium	1		[Common	Ground]		
	Lowest	2	*			*	
B. **Delivery**	**Shortest**	2	*			*	Could live with medium delivery?
	Medium	1		[Common	Ground]		
	Longest	0		*	*		
C. **Penalty** **Payments**	**5%**	3	*			*	Could trade penalty for lower price?
	10%	1		[Common	Ground]		
	15%	0		*	*		
D. **Transportation**	**Their cost**	1	*			*	Could trade transport for lower price?
	Split cost	2		[Common	Ground]		
	Our cost	0		*	*		
E. **Off Loading**	**Their cost**	1	*			*	Could offer use of our offloading?
	Split cost	2		[Common	Ground]		
	Our cost	0		*	*		
F. **Accommodation**	**Their cost**	1	*			*	Could split costs?
	Split cost	2		[Common	Ground]		
	Our cost	0		*	*		

The other party's perspective

When assessing the other party always put yourself in the other party's shoes and you may come up with additional issues. The best way of trying to establish the other party's requirements is by looking at each issue from the other party's perspective, but do not assume that their viewpoint will be the same as yours.

When you do your planning on the other party's requirements and their best and worst position, remember that the worst position – is the least the other party will accept and the best position – is the highest objective they could aim for. This will assist you in reassessing things you may not have thought of but may be on their agenda.

Self Image; self esteem, self-worth, self respect, ego, status all play a part in negotiation. It is sometimes less evident, but it is present in all people and is perceptible at different levels. All negotiators enjoy winning, they want to look and feel in control even when they have to concede. Self image and ego can drive the other party's demands and these may be high or increases in importance purely because of the negotiators own self image and their need to win.

When assessing the other party's position on the issues take cognizance of the level of the other party's self image. If the other party has a high self image; money, financial reward, status and winning may hold important economic and ego value.

Assess the other party's company objectives and values it may assist you in ascertaining their objective, commitment, requirements and behavior in the negotiation. You will be able to relate to their company objectives and values when you make offers and concessions.

Summary
Question and establish what the issues are, what drives the other party's best and worst positions, the other party's self image and how all of this relates to their company objectives and values. Put yourself into the other party's shoes.

Section: 1.4. The Issues
If you understand the other party, their company and the core issues, you will strengthen your position in the discussion, particularly if the other party has not assessed you and your company.

By now each of your negotiable issues should look something like this: -

Your worst position & The Other Party's best position	Common Ground Area for Agreement	Your best position & The Other Party's worst position

Quick Tip: *it is not only the common ground on a particular issue which leads to agreement; it is also the company to company relationships or the* *degree of dependence on each other for future business and survival long term. Developing personal relationships during discussions and negotiations can be used to cement this understanding.*

Important note: Sometimes, negotiators may fail to consider the longer-term aspects when making their demands in a negotiation.

For example a worker's union, may make demands which are too high and could eventually result in putting the company in difficulty or even out of business, with union members being relocated or redundant. The point is that when there is a longer-term relationship between two parties, it must be a sustainable.

It is important to identify early in the preparation for the negotiation the relationship your company wants; with a clear view of the extent of interdependence you can then consider tactics. In the longer term relationship, ultimately both parties should come out of the negotiation with a win-win and a positive agreement which satisfies this relationship. This area of understanding would form part of the introduction opening and setting the climate for the meeting.

If you sell regularly to a major client and you are depend mainly on their purchases for your revenue and survival you would not use harsh and 'take it or leave it' inflexible tactics. The same applies if you are in a highly competitive market.

On the other hand, if you are selling a house in a market with a high demand and short supply you may be able to command a higher price and terms very much in your favor.

Let's consider a few negotiations and their type of relationship: -

1. **Selling a house in a buyer's market.**
   1.1. This is a short-term relationship and the seller has less influence on the terms than the buyer.
2. **A union-management negotiation.**
   2.1. A long-term relationship with a fair degree of interdependence. Good relationships should be maintained.
3. **A renewable contract to supply a large company of stores.**
   3.1. A long-term relationship with a high degree of interdependence. A fair and reasonable agreement is a priority.
4. **An installation project for major capital equipment.**

4.1. Relatively short-term relationship with not much interdependence. Care should to be exercised on contract terms if there is potential for longer term relationship.

5. **Having a swimming pool installation.**

   5.1. Short-term relationship with not much interdependence. Care should to be exercised on the contract terms.

Assess a negotiation from your current workload or one of those negotiations you regularly address and consider if the relationships would be short or long-term and the degree of interdependence.

Section: 1.5. Types of Power

Personal power is a matter of perception and self confidence, for example; a person negotiating on behalf of a large company with strong purchasing power may feel at a disadvantage purely because the person has a poor perception of their own self image and personal power. On the other hand, a confident salesperson with a positive self image from a small new company, with no company power, may negotiate and close many sales agreements purely on their perception of their own personal power and self-confidence.

Consider the following in helping you to assess your own power base in relation to the other party: -

1. **The Buying Power of Your Company - Coercive Power**: large corporations can pick and choose between various suppliers for best prices, discounts, terms and conditions. Because their purchase order represents large sums of money to the supplier. Competition among suppliers can be severe and they will be compliant to get the order, therefore large companies and corporations have negotiating power. Even in subsequent negotiations the larger companies still have a great deal of power, often called **coercive power** through the threat of discontinuing the contract or relationship.

2. **Supplying and Buying in Short Supply and Over Supply markets:**

   2.1. **Short Supply:** If you are selling a commodity which is in short supply, you hold **supply power**. And if you are buying in a short supply market and you need the commodity, you have less negotiating power and may have to concede to the seller's terms and you have little **buying power**.

2.2. **Over Supply:** If you are selling a commodity which is in an over supplied market you have little **supply power.** On the other hand, if you are buying in an over supplied market and you have many sellers, you hold **buying power.**

3. **Knowledge and Skill - Expert power:** The skilled negotiator who knows the company's requirements, the company's products and services well and who has prepared meticulously has the knowledge and skill to match the specific requirements of both parties, this is **expert power.**

4. **Balance of Power:** If both parties hold equal power and are well prepared and skilled there is a **balance of power.**

The principle is to move the balance of power in your favor. Prepare well, find the core reasons why the other party wants to do business with you, and ask – what is in it for this company?

The objective is to know more about the other party than they know about you, so that your negotiating power is increased.

Consider the power you will have for your next negotiation in relation to the other party.

Section: 1.6 Formulating the Strategy

The negotiation strategy is essentially dependent on how you need the relationship to develop during and after the session.

In order to formulate a strategy for the negotiation you need to put together all the facts you have prepared.

Long Term

If you require a long-term relationship you need a win-win negotiation. A win-win negotiation requires you to give and take to allow the other party to win on some of your minor issues, in short, a cooperative discussion to mutual benefit.

Short Term

On the other hand, when you do not have a long-term relationship strategy you could initiate the discussion with high demands and remain relatively inflexible, justifying what you want and allowing the other party the opportunity to state their case, but remaining insistent on your demands and substantiating your position.

The effective manager will plan so that the issues are independent of each other, in other words, discussing price is not dependant on the occupation date in the house purchase example.

Skilful negotiators will plan so flexibly that when presented with an agenda they could agree completely to the other party's agenda. This agreeable attitude from the start sets an amicable climate.

Some guidelines on the order of agenda in a negotiation: -
These are the five categories of the negotiation agenda; within each of these you should retain flexibility on which issue is discussed first.

Whilst this is the suggested order of the agenda, you should plan a flexible agenda which you can easily switch from one issue to another. So when an issue looks like it may be locking up, you can switch to another issue and switch back to the problem issue later in the discussion, the purpose of this is to allow you time to consider the potential unlocking and resolving the problematic issue and keep the discussion moving forward.

The order of agenda in a negotiation
1. **Clarify any assumptions** as early as possible. This is of primary importance, if not done early it could cause misunderstanding later which could end in a prolonged negotiation or no agreement.
2. **Discuss problem issues, which need creative solutions early** in the negotiation when the climate is warm and congenial. Solutions are difficult to find in a competitive atmosphere.
3. **Settle win-win issues first**, it keeps the climate congenial longer and this contributes towards a mutual agreement.
4. **Discuss the low priority win-lose issues.** The throw away issues are next, but only use them if appropriate at the time.
5. **Negotiate the high-priority difficult issues**. If the preceding issues have been carefully selected and the atmosphere remains amicable it will make the high-priority issues slightly easier to handle.

Section: 1.7. Concessions and How to Make Them
You will try to encourage the other party to state their opening demand on the issue first. This will tell you what the other party's extreme expectation is, as most people start off with very high demands. As you probe further on the demand presented, you will have time to align your thoughts on your own expectations.

Skilled negotiators believe that the opening demand could make or break a negotiation simply because it affects the other party's expectations. If the other party comes with an exceptionally high demand it would tend to reduce your expectation of the negotiation and causes some conflict if you are not prepared for it.

The strategy used in many negotiations is bid or demand high – expect lower, find and settle for middle ground.

Therefore, rather go in at a higher demand than you expect at settlement, it will reduce the other party's expectations. An opening moderate or low demand from you may put you at a disadvantage in the final settlement agreement.

A comprehensive list of low level concessions in a negotiation will prevent you from feeling pressurized when making them and prevent you from making concessions that you have not accounted for.

Making concessions should not cause you discomfort and you can make concessions agreeably, because you have prepared well. Many of the concessions would be small on large and less important issues, and some throw away concessions which will cost you little in the negotiation.

People like to win and a skillfully worded concession boosts the self image of the other party. Concessions have value in breaking a deadlock. Making a concession helps keep the discussion going and re-opens the negotiation on sensitive issues.

To make a concession during the negotiation: -
1. Do not rush to make them.
2. By making many small ones rather than a few large ones.
3. Getting one back for every one you give.
4. Trading them, by giving a small one to get a bigger one back.
5. Do not make concessions, if they are not required or requested by the other party.

Section: 2.0. The Preparation Summary

The summary below will help you cover all the critical aspects of future preparation and planning for negotiation.

1. What exactly is my mandate and objective/s for the negotiation?
2. What is my level of authority in the negotiation?
3. Which company objectives must my negotiation achieve?
4. Are there any specific company values or policy I must be aware of when negotiating towards settlement?
5. Which are the main issues on which agreement must be reached?
6. What do I want from this negotiation in terms of a future relationship?
7. What are the other party's company objectives?
8. What is the other party's self image?
9. What is the other party's power position?
10. What do I anticipate the other party's best and worst position to be on each sub issue?
11. What is the settlement range for each issue?
12. What assumptions need clarification?
13. What is my own power position in terms of skills, supply and demand, and company strength?
14. How can I break down each issue into smaller elements on which to negotiate?
15. How is each sub-issue rated in terms of the objectives, must win, nice to win, and throw a ways?
16. Which concessions can I make without losing on main issues?
17. What is my own best or worst position for each element of an issue?
18. What follow up is required?

You are now ready to negotiate and remember; flexibility is the key.

Quick Tip: keep the Question Model of Management in mind as a checklist.

1. **Why** do I need to take action in a particular area?
2. **What** objectives, action plan, shall I set?
3. **Who** will be involved?
4. **When** are my objective and action plan dates?
5. **How** are my objectives and actions to happen?

6. **What if** a problem develops what will I do?
7. **Where** should my objectives and action plan take me?

Section: 3.0. Creating the Climate

Interactive skills used in negotiations are nothing new; you have been negotiating most of your life in one form or another and you have been using these skills.

Within the negotiation there are definite areas each requiring particular skills. If you think back to the sections on discussion skills and problem solving, the areas are: -

- ❏ **Creating the climate**
- ❏ **Negotiating**
- ❏ **Agreement**

The Climate: is created in a very short space of time and it could be an uncompromising and tense climate or a warm friendly climate or even a formal climate. The opening moments of the negotiation are therefore of critical importance if you want to ensure that the climate is businesslike yet collaborative and cordial.

First Impressions: are important as most personal impressions are formed in less than a minute of meeting someone. Skilled negotiators spend up to five percent of the negotiating time on setting the climate.

Prior to the meeting: a skilled negotiator will seek out informal groups and discuss neutral subjects in a cordial, but businesslike manner with the other parties. When the tea and coffee is finished the negotiators move to their seats to start exploring the terms and agenda for the negotiation and by then the climate may already be set.

Businesslike: in that you should dress and behave accordingly. You should be sure of things like a handshake, eye contact, movement and speech as they all contribute to a businesslike atmosphere.

Collaborative: in that you should spend some of the initial time on discussing neutral subjects like current news items or sport. This type of tactic gives both parties time to adjust to each other.

The Agenda

1. You now need to reach agreement on the agenda – if not agreed prior to the meeting.
2. The **range** of issues to be settled.
3. The **order** in which they are to be discussed.
4. The **timing** for the negotiation.

The **next meeting**, a date agreed, if the negotiation is not concluded.

It is important to discuss the above points early on or prior to the meeting, so that there are no surprises later in the negotiation when someone could suddenly raise an issue you are not expecting. An early explanation period clearly tells you where the interest of the other party lies without you having to request it. It gives you time to restructure your thoughts and plans, if necessary.

Timing: is important to get an idea of the pace you need to move forward. Agreement on total time prevents negotiators from using excuses to leave and attend another meeting to buy time when you are close to closing the agreement. It is also important to set a date for the next meeting, if the meeting is not concluded.

This covers three important areas: -
- ❏ Fixes the total time for meeting
- ❏ Prevent delaying tactics
- ❏ Sets a subsequent meeting, if the negotiation is not concluded.

Quick Tip: approach all negotiations, as if you have infinite time to reach an agreement, this will remind you that you will not be pressured into making a decision in haste and will reduce the power of the other party, particularly if they are under pressure to reach agreement.

Section: 4.0. Negotiating & Agreement

You will conduct yourself confidently and sincerely but with assertiveness.

The remaining two areas of the negotiation process are: -
- ❏ **Negotiating**
- ❏ **Agreement**

Within each issue that is discussed, there are a few sub-areas or elements, exploring each other's requirements, bargaining towards advantages and settling agreement, in writing, where possible and appropriate.

Consider a negotiation which includes four main issues **price, quality, delivery and terms**.

Initial Exploration

During the initial exploration each party would have indicated their priorities. Issues are discussed and explored. Each party would make opening demands. The questioning and justification which follows on the opening demands would be the negotiation of each issue, and generally involves more discussion, bidding and bargaining from both parties, to justify their position.

Preparation Papers, and Concessions

It is important to have your preparation papers at hand, especially your list of possible concessions, your rating for each issue e.g. must win, nice to win, throw a ways and your minimum/maximum expectations for each issue and sub-issue. Keep these pre-planned expectations in mind as this will ensure you move forward and make gains and avoid becoming too competitive or inflexible on issues towards an agreement.

Creativity

When carried out in a creative problem-solving manner negotiation is particularly satisfying. Each party makes suggestions and proposals for reaching a good solution or decision; they discuss alternative proposals and combinations and then measure tentative solutions or proposals compatible with the companies' objectives and policies.

Settlement Area

During the settlement area of the discussion; both parties commence signifying their agreement on a particular outcome or a combination of issues and a proposed agreement solution.

Check

Check the agreement against your mandate, your company objectives and policies and remember to record all the details - preferably in writing and signed by both parties.

Quick Tip: a negotiated agreement is only as good as its implementation within your company in its intended form.

Section: 5.0. Quick Guide to Negotiation

Negotiation is a fascinating subject on which much has been written. The objective of most negotiations is to reach an agreement. It is a process of moving towards an outcome and agreement which satisfies both parties.

The same skills important for all other interactive situations as in discussion and conflict resolution are used in negotiation. Let's look at the skills used in negotiating.

- ❏ **Looking for facts and solutions**
- ❏ **Listening**
- ❏ **Summarizing**
- ❏ **Preventing Misunderstanding**
- ❏ **Suggesting procedures and solutions**
- ❏ **Sharing feelings.**

These same skills can be applied in different situations.

Apply these skills to the four main areas of negotiation.

1. **Creating a climate** – involves providing and asking for information in a sociable, collaborative and professional manner.

2. **Exploring** the terms and agenda involves a larger range of discussion skills; looking for suggestions from the other party and listening to find out what the other party's expectations are, suggesting your own issues, and agreement of the discussion order and timing. And finally, preventing misunderstanding by summarizing what has been agreed.

3. **The Negotiation** area contains the whole spectrum of discussion skills, exploring the other party's position on your solutions/proposals, asking about their justification, counter suggesting, suggesting your solution/proposal providing information about your own position and rationale; all the time preventing misunderstanding through summarizing at various key points in the discussion.

   You would also have to disagree when the other party makes a suggestion, which your company cannot accommodate or you are not authorized to agree on.

   3.1. **Disagreement**

      Disagreement is normally softened, by coupling it with a shared feeling comment and explaining and justifying why the proposal cannot be accommodated by your company.

3.2. **Extra Time**

    If you need extra time to consider the proposal you can explain the proposal exceeds your authorization level you have to refer it up a level and come back on the issue.

3.3. **Bidding and bargaining** essentially means suggesting and counter suggesting various ways to get to a settlement.

3.4. **Remember:** the objective is to get to an acceptable settlement for both parties, preferably, in an amicable way and without either party losing face.

4. **The Settlement** area should also prevent misunderstanding using comments and summaries which will ensure that you have an agreement which is of value to your company.

    At this stage courtesy, good manners and respect for the other party are important and will ensure an amicable closure to the meeting. The settlement area would also include supporting statements pertaining to the other party's positive attitude, cooperation and contribution during the meeting towards an acceptable agreement for both parties.

Remember.........

Management Wisdom

If you know the enemy and know yourself you need not fear the results of a hundred battles.

*Sun Tzu

Now you can go ahead and make negotiation appointments with a new increased confidence.

Chapter 13: Making Powerful Presentations

The Eleventh Rule of Smart Management:
Build confidence and professional presentation
skills at every opportunity.

Section: 1.0. How to Make Presentations Work for You

So you have to make a presentation, don't worry, you can build confidence and professional presentation skills with the following: -

Presentations scare me…

You are not alone, many businessmen and executives would rather bungee jump, than make a presentation - without the cord! This chapter will show you how to harnesses the amazing power of presentations simply, and equip you with good presentation skills to make your job more interesting and enjoyable.

Until the advent of electronics the tools to create and present information were time consuming and so expensive that they were reserved only for the most senior executives.

However, computers, Microsoft PowerPoint type applications and the internet have changed all that. Now anyone with a little know-how and creativity can present professionally and take advantage of the presentation arena.

You are going to start looking at a skill which is becoming more and more important to managers. Mangers must use plans, analysis, meetings and presentations to inspire action and gain support. As a manager and leader you will certainly be called upon to make a presentation from time to time. These sections will help you make professional presentations with ease!

Remember.........

> ## *Management Wisdom*
>
> *Leaders must march ahead of the movement, not lag behind it.*
>
> ***Mao Tse Tung**

As we enter the age of information making presentations becomes critical for selling ideas and concepts, increasing the knowledge of others, communicating new methods and research, sharing experiences and most importantly, selling yourself, your personality, attitude and knowledge. Each time you say something you are presenting yourself and your ideas - to your environment and the people around you.

Presentations are used at social and political gatherings, company meetings and business seminars.

But our purpose here is mainly that of business presentations, so you need to consider the types of presentations you have to make currently or in the future and think about how you may appear or sound to others.

Self Assessment:

To help you focus on some of the important aspects of your presentations answer yes or no to the following statements:

> ### Presentation Skills
>
> 1. I start off my presentation showing my own commitment and I get attention.
> 2. I link my presentation to my audience's knowledge and experience.
> 3. My explanations and examples are relevant.
> 4. My audience understands the content of my presentation.
> 5. I have facts available to overcome objections.
> 6. I always complete the presentation with a good summary.
> 7. The audience knows what action is required.
> 8. I always achieve commitment to the content of my presentation.
> 9. I follow up on any actions emanating from my presentation right away.

If the answer to any of these statements is yes, well done!

If the answer to these statements is no, take note and work on them.

Be assured that it is natural for you to be nervous, but you now have help to take that nervous energy, control it and redirect it into powerful presentations.

Section: 1.1. Determine Your Objective

It would be appropriate at this point to note that the main reason, the objective for making most presentations is to shift the audience's way of thinking, be it a person or a group to your way of thinking through a logical process.

When making a presentation, you are the 'leader'. The group gives you leader status and authority by listening to you. Your presentation should therefore motivate, inform, persuade or inspire your audience.

Many leadership studies indicate that the characteristics of good leaders are driven towards achievement, emotional control and fluency of speech, knowledge, creativity, self-confidence and good interpersonal skills. And for sure, not all good managers and leaders are born with these skills or possess all of these traits; however, you can learn these skills and by carefully watching and listening to good speakers and presenters you can develop your own personal style.

At the same time, your job as a presenter can also be likened to that of a salesperson and you need to sell your presentation to your audience in terms of benefits, advantages, disadvantages, cost, time involvement, examples and samples etc.

Quick Tip: *In essence you need to become passionate about your presentation and pass that passion to your audience.*

Many successful directors, engineers and accountants have donned their sales hat to become engaging and powerful presenters who prepare thoroughly and present professionally; they know their company, their products and the products of competitors, their customers and the full content and purpose of the presentation.

People respect and follow a good leader and they enjoy a good presentation.

In summary: -

a) The presenter's leadership function is to adjust or even shift the audience's way of thinking.

b) The presenter's role as the 'group leader' is to convince the audience, on the benefits, advantages, disadvantages, cost, time involvement, examples, and samples etc.

Quick Tip: *changing opinions, ways of thinking, methods and attitudes is achieved through a logical and systematic process and with an almost passive or reflective, but enthusiastic acceptance by your audience. It is rarely achieved through argumentative pressure or a force of will.*

Section: 1.2. Consider Your Audience

There are two ways of ending up in front of an audience.

1. **The audience selects you:** to make a presentation on a topic they would like you to present your views on.

2. **You select the audience:** when you have something to present and need to share with your audience or require support or action on.

Either way, you need to analyze your audience as part of the planning process. For example, you need to know who you're presenting to before deciding on format, content and what visuals and examples to use and the summary and follow up required.

If you decide to hand out information, carefully consider the extent of information to be circulated, this is normally only relevant to graphs or tables which are too detailed or voluminous to be presented and these should be circulated **after** the presentation, as appropriate.

Words of warning:

1. Do not hand out copies of your presentation either prior to or during your presentation.

2. Do not hand out general background information and supporting documentation, during your presentation.

An audience description should specify: -

1. **Interests**

1.1. What does the majority of your audience specialize in?

1.2. What are their priorities?

1.3. What attracts their interest, profit, savings, quality, time or knowledge etc?

2. **Motivators**
    2.1. What do they get out of the presentation?
    2.2. What are their problem areas?
    2.3. What is the benefit to them?

Note: Interests or motivating factors may change over time, but you should make sure that your presentation will help your audience towards a perceived benefit – such as, time saving, lower costs, less effort or increased knowledge etc.

3. **Attitudes**
    3.1. What positive and negative attitudes are you aware of from members of the audience?
    3.2. What prejudices are there?
    3.3. Are there any personal agendas that you are aware of?
    3.4. What do they think of your company?
    3.5. What do they think of your subject matter?

This will help you plan to overcome negative attitudes.

4   **Education**
    What kind of education has your audience had?
    4.1. Informal?
    4.2. Formal?
    4.3. Commercial?
    4.4. Engineering?
    4.5. Scientific?

This type of assessment will help you decide on your level of vocabulary and visual aids. However, typically the answer would be KIS = 'Keep It Simple'.

Section: 1.3. Planning and Preparation

Think of an issue which you feel really strongly, even passionate about in your work environment something which you feel you really must convince others about, and then go through the planning and preparation of a presentation.

Your first concern in the preparation is to decide the purpose of the presentation: -

1. What is the main point of your presentation?
2. Do you want to impart knowledge, sell an idea or motivate your audience to a specific action?

The purpose of the presentation should be clear and run right through your presentation in a logical systematic order from the opening to the summary and closing.

A good presentation is always organized into three parts: -

1. An opening.
2. A body.
3. A closing summary.

You will be handling each of these aspects below. Organize some of your thoughts for the presentation, as follows: -

❏ Write down your purpose for giving a presentation.
❏ What do you want out of the presentation?
❏ What change or action do you want?

Arrange your thoughts into a logical sequence and place them into an introduction, a body of facts and a logical conclusion.

❏ One of your presentation objectives is to impart your enthusiasm to your audience, for the subject matter being presented.
❏ Remember, enthusiasm for the subject matter must come from you first – so don't hold back!

Part of your preparation is focusing on your enthusiasm so that you can transfer it to your audience, use some of the energy from your nerves to maintain your enthusiasm and put across your genuine commitment to the subject matter.

Now the introduction, body and summary in more detail:

Introduction:
Consider for a moment the most dynamic presentation you have ever heard. How did the presenter catch your attention and your interest from the start?

Did the presenter start with: -

❏ An unexpected question

❏ An amazing and interesting fact

❏ An impossible challenge

❏ A shocking story or statement

❏ A surprising and interesting picture

❏ An attention-grabbing sample or object

The prime purpose of planning the introduction of your presentation is to: -

- *Get and hold your audience's attention immediately!*

Don't commence your introduction with: -

❏ An apology.

❏ A slow lethargic monotone.

❏ A joke, even if it is appropriate to your subject.

The Body of the Presentation:
The purpose of planning the body of your presentation is to: -

- *Keep your audience sat-up and listening!*

The body of your presentation should cover the specific aspects and develop those ideas by using supporting facts and examples.

Make an outline of the body of your presentation. Write down four or five specific aspects you want to cover in the body of your presentation - just the headings for now. Break your topic up into manageable sections so that you can be sure to cover the highlights of your idea.

Consider the logical progression of issues you want to present.

	Question	In your presentation
1.	What is the problem?	Be specific.
2.	What are the root causes and effects?	Be factual.
3.	How can things be corrected?	Detail your proposed solutions.
4.	What should your audience do?	Detail a specific action or plan.

This part of your presentation should lead your audience to your conclusion in a logical step-by-step approach.

Remember on technical issues people like to hear facts and figures and supporting examples. So, if you were presenting the company's budget, high level or bottom line figures and simple tables and graphs in a summary format only, will enhance your presentation, as a general rule keep detailed figures and vast amounts of data out of your presentation – unless, the purpose of the presentation is to discuss figures down to a detailed level.

Never the less, have your detailed supporting data and information to hand and available for discussion, if required, this approach will also give credibility to your presentation, but again avoid getting bogged down in the infinite detail at a presentation; as this can lead to extreme boredom and the loss of the will to live for your audience, detailed figures should be circulated later, if required and appropriate.

Summary

Summaries and conclusions are important as they contain the final thoughts with which you leave your audience. Depending on your objective, your summary should include the main points you are making and what action you would like your audience to take.

Outline for Presentation

The following outline will assist you in planning your presentation: -

Detail your introductory key points and list the key aspects of the body, and your summary. Write out your presentation using the information you have on planning and audience analysis and the notes you have made. Write in outline or short notes on all the points you need to make.

Draft - Outline for Presentation		
Introduction	**Body**	**Summary**
Presented to get attention and make your audience sit up and take note: ❑ Purpose of Presentation. ❑ Background to the apparent problem or situation. ❑ Current status.	Presented factually and supported by evidence: ❑ Background solution one. ❑ Supporting information. ❑ Background solution two. ❑ Supporting information. ❑ Proposed solution/ Recommendation. ❑ Supporting Information. ❑ Costs to Company. ❑ Approvals & the Action Required.	Presented briefly to reinforce the situation and get action / commitment: ❑ 1.0. Purpose of Presentation. ❑ 2.0. Background. ❑ 3.0. Current status. ❑ 4.0. Proposed solutions or Recommendations ❑ 5.0. Alternative Solutions or Recommendations ❑ 6.0. Approvals & Action Required ❑ 7.0. Close

To Recap:

Your presentations need to consider: -

- ❏ The types of presentations you need to make.
- ❏ Leadership and salesmanship in presentation work.
- ❏ Audience analysis.
- ❏ Preparation of your presentation.

Once you have the audience analysis and your basic presentation outline bring the two together and then assess and evaluate your presentation work.

Qualify your Audience

To qualify your audience, you need to detail the people you should ask to attend the presentation and why they are attending and then remove non essential participants

Ask:

- ❏ Who is critical to implementation and should be present?
- ❏ Who is missing?
- ❏ Who cannot make a contribution?
- ❏ Do you need some supporters in the audience?
- ❏ Who will be offended if not invited?

First look at your draft presentation in relation to the people attending. Look at each of the critical points you will be making: -

- ❏ Who in your audience will support the subject matter and why?
- ❏ Who in your audience will be against the subject matter and why?

For example: for the installation of new computer system, a sample of your audience assessment may look something like the following: -

Proposal: Installation of a New Computer System		
Members for proposal and reasons		**Audience Focus**
A. members	Been involved in the installation of similar computer systems before without problems.	Reinforce assistance during / after installation.
B. members	For anything that will get the job done quicker.	Reinforce speed of system installation with examples.
Members against proposal and reasons		
C. members	Had training problems with installation on a similar computer system.	Highlight assistance and training on the system with examples.
D. members	Finds system difficult to use.	Highlight assistance and training on system prior to / after installation, with examples.

When you have completed your audience assessment revert back to your draft presentation and see how you could make better use of the audience focus and what reinforcement you could provide for your supporters, and which would reduce any negative views.

Always start by assessing your proposals and recommendations and considering: -

❏ An argument which supports your proposal and detail how you will support this.

❏ An argument against your concept and how you will counteract it.

If possible, try to obtain the views of attendees who are against your proposals ahead of time, in order that you may address and counteract these views within the presentation.

Section: 1.4. Tools and Visual Aids

Now, you are going to add style and creativity to your presentation.

You can be creative with modern applications such as Microsoft PowerPoint and with access to excellent imagery you can professionalize and animate your presentation quickly and easily.

Creativity

A good creative presentation supported by colour can bring the discussion to life and introduce reality to a particular situation.

You have briefly covered illustrations, samples, examples and visual aids and you have seen them used often in the past.

See Touch Feel and Smell

Good presenters use real samples of their products for their audience, buyers, engineers and managers need to see, touch, feel and if appropriate smell the product.

Where possible you should illustrate your presentations with actual products, materials, photographs, documents, graphics, etc. and these should be of good to excellent quality. Never use poor quality graphics, illustrations or imagery in your presentation.

Visuals Assist the Memory

Visuals assist the memory and your audience is better able to remember those points you want them to remember and this covers a multitude of visuals from pleasant to shocking. A word of warning – as a general rule you must not use visuals or objects which may be shocking in a business environment, unless of course, it is your intention to shock your audience.

However, you must never use visuals or objects which may be inappropriate for your audience.

A Word on the Costs

There are many alternatives available and this is normally limited only by the cost of the presentation materials, however, a computer, a projector and your time are the rule. The venue if taken outside the company may have to consider the return on investment and the payback from the presentation.

Some Presentation Methods are as follows: -

Dry Wipe - White Board

This method is perhaps appropriate for short presentations and discussion work, to illustrate concepts and reach agreement or consensus quickly and where record is not necessarily required, it is often used typically in engineering, creative media or software companies where you will find a proliferation of white boards, which are used predominantly to aid discussion for smaller audiences.

Flipchart

A method used for the flipchart presentation, is that you write the heading only on the flipchart with the appropriate spaces to be filled in during the presentation, this will focus your audiences thought without them reaching a conclusion by reading ahead. Alternatively, you could:-

1. Draft the outline sheet ahead of time and place where you can read it easily without detracting from your presentation.

2. Write out the headings and the points you wish to make lightly in pencil on each page of the flipchart beforehand to remind you and then go over them with the felt tip during your presentation.

This method is useful for the smaller audience.

Quick Tip: *this method can also be used as standby visual aid – when the power goes out or the equipment did not arrive or has been damaged in transit.*

Sepia transparencies used with an overhead projector.

This method is pretty much obsolete in first world countries, these are overhead transparencies, made on a copying machine, they have the advantage that they are simple, quick to make from typed or printed matter and you can highlight key words or areas on the transparency while presenting and projected onto a white wall or screen.

35millimeter colour slides on a carousel projector

Again this method has limited use and although slides offer unlimited visual effects, text is limited and requires careful planning in advance of your presentation

If you make use of them you should use at a pace which does not lose attention. They are useful for changing the pace of a predominantly verbal presentation or lecture environment.

Computer generated presentation used with a large computer screen or an overhead projector.

Probably the most widely used presentation method and system is the Microsoft PowerPoint programme or similar, which is an excellent medium for both preparation and presentation. It is simple, easy to use programme and you get ready made templates with the programme for certain topics which you can modify to suit. The programme can be used to good effect to assist you with professionalizing your presentation format and timing.

Presentation or Graphics Agency

There are many agencies specializing in the production of high-quality visual, and audiovisual presentations at a relatively low cost that may be worth investigating for your major presentations or a presentation which is to be presented many times and high quality is a prerequisite.

There are currently some very exciting developments in visual and audio-visual presentations, as the technology in this area is changing rapidly with smaller, quicker, smarter and cheaper devices available.

Accessories

By the way, don't forget the accessories when you need to indicate a point during the presentation or at question time: -

- ❏ Retractable pointer.
- ❏ Laser pointer.
- ❏ A remote control projector.
- ❏ A microphone and sound system.

Venue

Whatever your preference you will need to pay close attention to the venue, power, lighting, light dimming, sound system for large audiences, seating, obstructions in line of sight, air conditioning, refreshments, bathroom facilities. Most importantly, everyone should be able to see and hear clearly.

Quick Tip: if possible, personally check the venue for these aspects by viewing your smallest and most complex slide and getting someone to listen to the presentation from the back seat of the audience.

A Guide to Presentation of Visuals

Whatever the type of visuals you decide to use, keep the following in mind when presenting.

1. Make sure everyone in your audience can see the visual.
2. Make sure everyone in your audience can hear you.
3. Do not allow your visuals to detract from your talk, show it when you are ready to talk about it and then switch it off or remove it if it is not being used. It helps if you introduce the 'visual' before showing it, in this way you focus attention on what you will be showing.
4. Never face the visual and end up talking with your back to your audience, apart from being bad manners; the chances are your audience cannot hear you.

5. Do not overuse visuals, use them to clarify a point or strengthen your argument.

6. Keep them simple, too much detail and lots of figures in tabular form, in particular, or vivid colour can detract from your message.

7. Be sure you know how the electrical and electronic equipment you are going to use operates and prepare yourself for breakdowns by having an alternate method available and/or have an 'expert' person standing by.

Remember, don't get sidetracked, your first priority is to spend the appropriate amount of time on the content and get that right first and use the visuals to enhance your presentation.

Section: 1.5. Analogies

Making a really effective presentation involves preparation and practice and then more preparation and practice to lead your audience towards a logical conclusion which ultimately supports your own view on the subject matter.

It requires research, writing, sequencing, more writing, editing and rehearsing and more writing; reducing the bulk of your research each time, down to key easily followed concepts.

You may not have a great deal of time to prepare for all of your presentations. Therefore by thinking through the preparatory work now and establishing a few good outlines for your presentations you will be making it easier and quicker for yourself in the future.

You have considered visual aids and how to give your presentation impact, it is important to hold your audience's attention in terms of their needs or your facts and figures may be lost. You have carried out an audience analysis and this is where the planning of your presentation and your examples play an important part.

Visual aids have their place and your objective is to make your presentation relate to your audience through your use of analogies, stories and illustrations.

Look for illustrations in the media, your local library, perhaps a book of quotations and creative or lateral thinking books. Look for events that have happened at work or in the street. You should collect a few quotations and analogies you might use from your experiences and a few news items that are current; to illustrate a point in a presentation you are planning and refine them through practice.

When you relate firsthand experiences and current events people tend to take more interest in what is being said. A good source is the current events in the newspapers or television. You could use a topical issue from the news as an analogy for a point you are making. By weaving a current topic into your presentation you could make the point more humorous or more sincere perhaps. This is not an easy area and it takes skill and practice so rehearse it ...... on as many people as possible, before your presentation!

A word of warning

1. Don't circulate your presentation before hand.
2. As a general rule, avoid telling jokes during a presentation as this takes a particular skill which if it is misunderstood by the audience it may be disastrous.
3. Don't be derogatory - in anything you say.
4. Don't embarrass anyone - either deliberately or inadvertently.
5. Don't use any facts or figures which cannot be fully supported by you.

Practice

For your own practice and rehearsal try your presentations out on someone who is prepared to give you feedback and the chance to practice.

Section: 1.6. The Body Language and How to Use it

You have now covered several important aspects of presentation work.

You have:

- ❏ Assessed your audience.
- ❏ Know the primary purpose of your presentation.
- ❏ Sequenced your key points.
- ❏ Looked at interesting ways to commence the introduction.
- ❏ Looked at ways of holding your audience's attention.
- ❏ Know how to logically present the facts.
- ❏ Looked at visual aids and verbal illustrations.

Next, you shall consider ways of making it easy for your audience to follow you and how to get audience participation.

Body Language

You often see people listening to someone intently on a fascinating subject, but it is guaranteed that the speaker did not stand still and speak in a monotonous voice from behind the podium!

The presenter has to be enthusiastic and passionate about the subject for the audience to get excited. Body language and vocal variety...... show enthusiasm.

Quick Tip: Your audience will believe what they see in your face, your manner and your attitude and your visuals far more than the words you speak.

The audience will see excitement, boredom, sincerity, pleasure. A good presenter therefore gives a performance very much as an actor would. A good presenter has to practice using expressions and gestures that show the audience a positive attitude towards the presentation content.

Your hands and gestures are important for illustrating a point: -
- ❏ They can indicate importance, futility, despair, excitement, anger, sorrow or determination.
- ❏ They can also show lack of involvement or commitment.

Your face and eyes should also portray your feelings about certain aspects or topics you are covering in the presentation if you are:
- ❏ Relieved through a solution presented - show it.
- ❏ Relating a humorous example - smile.
- ❏ Talking about an incident which annoyed you - show annoyance in your expression.

Some Don'ts
- ❏ Don't fidget.
- ❏ Don't hide behind the podium.
- ❏ Don't mumble; speak clearly and at your normal pace.
- ❏ Do not focus on one area of the audience; share your attention with different parts of the audience.
- ❏ Don't turn your back on the audience.
- ❏ Don't turn away from the microphone when speaking – the audience will not hear you.
- ❏ If using a microphone, ensure you can move it with you.
- ❏ Don't over animate or oversell.

Remember, you are also trying to illustrate with non-verbal behavior, so practice using body language and don't be concerned if at the beginning you feel awkward, with practice your gestures will become naturally fluent and spontaneous.

Body language is useful to help the audience to understand better, practice before hand on a captive audience, your girl friend, boy friend, wife, husband colleague, etc. If your animation and expressions are too much, modify them, rehearse them and practice again.

When your presentation is right, you will know.

Section: 1.7. A Summary

Summaries are important part of making presentations, whether it is on problem solving, identifying an opportunity, a new product launch or training your personnel on a new process. Summarizing what you have covered helps your audience group the information logically.

By grouping the information logically you can make statements during your presentation, which will assist your audience move from one topic to another easily.

For example:

❑ The profit margin graphs that support my statement on project 'xyz', are presented next these will give you an overview of the excellent year on year results so far.

❑ Now that you've seen the dramatic effect the change in the rates has on our raw material purchases, let's look at what we can do about it.

These types of statement are useful whenever you lead your audience into a new area of your presentation.

Let's look next at questioning your audience. Questions or statements similar to the following help you to build your presentation on the previous experiences of your audience. It also helps in situations where you are trying to sell an idea, a concept, a product or a benefit to your audience.

For example:

❑ Do you remember our last presentation?

❑ Where do you think things went wrong?

❏ Why should our subcontractors contribute to our research development?

❏ We have a computer system which will assist you with our cash flow forecasting problems.

The Benefits

The benefits should be those that your audience can relate to and are interested in.

Consider for a moment the benefits that will be received from the purpose and content of your presentation:

1. **Benefits that your audience:** would receive, that would make them interested in listening to your presentation and link this benefit to your audience's experiences.

2. **Benefits that your company:** would receive from your presentation.

For example: -

❏ A cost savings.

❏ A time savings.

❏ Shared knowledge.

❏ Assists cash flow.

❏ Training.

❏ Job enhancement.

❏ Etc.

Section: 1.8. Audience Participation and Understanding

When making presentations, there are two sorts of questions you could use, questions that do not really require an answer and those that do.

1.   Rhetorical

First, there is the rhetorical type of question, where you do not really expect an answer.

For example:

❏ Have any of you been in a situation where you have to make a health and safety critical decision?

What you are trying to do with the rhetorical question is to stimulate thought and you don't need an answer. Most people would nod or smile at the thought in their minds and this works well when you are addressing a larger audience.

2. A Question that does require an answer

The other type of question is the one that does require an answer.

Often in presentations, the presenter needs to know exactly what the audience thinks or feels on different issues.

This is more common to problem solving or selling type presentations, but can be used very successfully in other situations.

There are three questioning techniques, which you have reviewed previously, which can be used, they are: -

A. **Open ended questions** (exploratory).

> ❏ To ask an open-ended question will give you a useful and more specific response. It also helps to address your question to a specific person in the audience.
> For example:
> - John, how do you feel about this last issue?
> - John will feel obliged to answer, but help him by restating to issue to him if he starts to struggle.

B. **Multiple choice questions**.
C. **Problem solving type questions**.

> ❏ B. & C. are more suited to use with individuals in smaller groups, as the larger groups tend to give you too many opinions to cope with.

Questions add variety and pace to a presentation.
But like all the other techniques for making a presentation stimulating and interesting, **questioning must not be overdone**, and neither should it be the only technique you use. There should always be a balance in a good presentation.

Checking Understanding

It is imperative with smaller group presentations that you test the understanding of your audience. More so if the main objective of the presentation is to solve a problem or to create follow up action. Many company presentations are to clients or personnel, which are likely to be the smaller group presentations.

When you spend a great deal of time considering a complex idea or concept it can be misunderstood, the presenter can check the audience understands. However, with larger groups this is not always possible unless 'questions from the floor', are invited to get an idea whether there have been any misunderstanding.

To check understanding you need to start questioning and consider: -
- ❏ Which type of question?
- ❏ At what point during or at the end of the presentation?

Smaller group presentations are often more in the nature of a discussion with information sharing, followed by more presentation work. It is appropriate to check understanding at the end of each major point as there may be reasons for misunderstanding, particularly, if there are complex facts etc. being presented.

You could start off the discussion by commencing a question as follows: -

1. What do you think of the point on…..?
2. Do you foresee any problems with the installation of…..?
3. What other implications can you see on……?
4. How do you think *x*'s proposal as a solution can be improved?

Some of the above may bring disagreement out into the open but you will at least be able to test if the disagreement is valid and will give you an indication of possible misunderstanding on a particular issue.

Generally, it is best to structure your questions to seek the facts, benefits, or advantages towards the later stages of the presentation to keep the discussions positive. This will give you an idea of your audience's understanding of the facts.

Quick Tip*: remember in your outline presentation to insert one or two places where you could involve your audience in discussion and check for understanding.*

Section: 1.9. The Outline
Now, you are in a position to start putting the complete presentation together, so that you can rehearse and get your message across in a clear, logical and stimulating manner. Build all the points you have covered so far, into your presentation.

As a general rule, you should be able to fit your complete presentation outline on a separate piece of A4 paper using the following outline. Use the headings to encourage your thoughts: -

Outline for Presentation - Total Timing for the Presentation ___		
Introduction	**Body**	**Summary**
Total Timing for Introduction ___	**Total Timing for Body___**	**Total Timing for Summary___**
Present introduction to get attention and make your audience sit up and take note:	Present clearly and factually and support with evidence and facts – why, how, where, when, who:	Present major points briefly and reinforce using challenging or provocative statement to get action / commitment which relates to the audience:
Slide No.___/Timing ___	Slide No.___/Timing ___	Slide No.___/Timing ___
Note 1. ❏ Must be Interesting Introduction opening that involves audience ❏ Explain the Purpose of Presentation	**Note 4.** ❏ Present a Background one - Provide Facts & Examples ❏ Supporting information ❏ Check understanding ❏ Link up to previous parts ❏ Outline next area	**Note 8.** Include briefly:- 1.0. Purpose of Presentation 2.0. Background 3.0. Current status 4.0. Background 6.0. Proposed Solutions or Recommendations 7.0. Approvals & Action Required 8.0. Summary
Slide No.___/Timing ___	Slide No.___/Timing ___	Slide No.___/Timing ___

Note 2.	Note 5.	**End and thank the audience**
Present a Brief Background to the apparent problem or opportunity situation:	❏ Present a Background two (*if required*) - Provide Facts & Examples ❏ Supporting information ❏ Check understanding ❏ Link up to previous parts ❏ Outline next area	
Slide No.___/Timing ___	Slide No.___/Timing ___	

Note 3.	Note 6.	
❏ Present the Current status. ❏ A brief outline of presentation and the action required	❏ Propose a solution & recommendations ❏ Costs ❏ Timing ❏ Who ❏ When ❏ Etc.	
Slide No.___/Timing ___	Slide No.___/Timing ___	
	Note 7. ❏ Summarize to check understanding	

Quick Tip: *highlight where visual aids are required and number your visual aids in order of presentation. Alternatively, if a computer generated presentation is to be used, use the prompts from the presentation.*

Now you will be able to see your whole presentation at a glance and add in some of your own visual aids, where necessary.

The next exercise is to 'sleep on it' over night and then read it through again aloud, rehearse it, time yourself and your visual aid presentations and revise where necessary.

Section: 2.0. Quick Guide to Powerful Presentations

You have the following Quick Guide to use when you need to make presentations in the future.

Remember, professional and effective presentations are vital to getting your message across and they also improve your image. Broaden your experience by using them wherever you get the opportunity – to sharpen your skills.

1. **Before the Presentation**
   1.1. Clarify your objective.
   1.2. Decide on your audience.
   1.3. Analyze your audience.
   1.4. Plan in outline the major points.
   1.5. Plan to overcome objections.
   1.6. Plan visual aids appropriate to group size and venue.
   1.7. Practice how to use visual aids.
   1.8. Plan to use verbal illustrations, examples, anecdotes, analogies, etc.
   1.9. Get your facts right.
   1.10. Anticipate questions and have your answers ready.
   1.11. Book your venue, seating arrangements and visual aid equipment well in advance.
   1.12. Get your notes in order, rehearse and time your presentation.

2. **During the Presentation**
   2.1. You've done the preparation work ......Relax!
   2.2. Dress appropriately for the occasion. (Dress up - rather than down).
   2.3. Make use of body language and facial expressions bring your presentation to life and get excited about your subject matter.
   2.4. Get and hold your audience's attention immediately!
   2.5. Use your tone of voice and volume.
   2.6. Speak at your normal pace.
   2.7. Do not slow down too much or speak faster than normal; as this can upset your timing.

2.8. Project your voice to the back of the room or group.

2.9. Keep your audience sat-up and listening!

2.10. Focus on your audience - and not on your notes or visual aids.

2.11. Don't stand in front of your visual aid when your audience is to look at it.

2.12. Use your voice, pitch and modulation, to emphasize points.

2.13. Don't turn away when using a microphone while speaking; your audience will not hear you.

2.14. When moving ensure you stand in a position that your audience can see you at all times.

2.15. When ending the presentation, genuinely thank the audience for their contribution and participation.

3. After the Presentation

3.1. Document any agreements.

3.2. Note any areas still to be resolved or followed up.

3.3. Write follow-up reports, letters or meetings, if appropriate.

3.4. Obtain feedback from different members of your audience and if you receive less than enthusiastic feedback; thank them for the critique, write it down and work on it.

3.5. If you receive a positive and enthusiastic response from your audience, acknowledge it, and thank them for their contribution.

Get out there.... Present.... and Enjoy!

Chapter 14: Managing Your Health and Stress Levels

The Twelfth Rule of Smart Management:
Reduce your stress levels and improve your health
and wellbeing when you are under pressure.

Section: 1.0. Some Thoughts on How to Manage Stress

If you want to excel in business it helps if you are physically and mentally fit. This chapter is presented to provide you with some final thoughts on how to manage your present health, wellbeing and stress levels.

The following may help you address some of the frustrations and reduce the stress levels in your job. If you are under pressure then it is important to reduce your present stress levels, improve your health and wellbeing and get back on track, don't risk burn out and take control of the situation right away.

You have to cope with stress at various levels and failure to cope with stress lays you open to inefficiency and worse. Only when your mind is clear and your thoughts are organized can you realise your full potential and achieve effective management. More importantly, your productivity and stress levels are directly proportional to your ability to relax.

Remember.........

Management Wisdom

To keep the body in good health is a duty ....otherwise we shall not be able to keep our mind strong and clear.

*Buddha

Most people, when looking at the early signs and the results of stress often tend to ignore them or explain them away!

Unfortunately, the effects can be serious; at the very least it affects your nervous system and at worst it makes you susceptible to serious health problems and even death. If this sounds a little dramatic – it isn't!

When stress continues unabated over time your ability to manage stress is reduced and your body starts to exhibit the symptoms and debilitating effects of stress. The symptoms of stress often involve circulatory, gastrointestinal and respiratory systems; resulting in high blood pressure, migraine, stomach ulcers, allergies, fatigue and executive burnout.

Section: 1.1.Origins of Stress the Fight or Flight Reaction

In primordial times safety and physiological needs were primary concerns; when primitive man was threatened the immediate reaction was to fight or run! This reaction is accompanied by physiological changes made within the body to prepare for a 'fight or flight' response which includes increased breathing and heart rate, an increase in oxygen to the blood, increased sugar and hormonal output. This 'fight or flight' response still remains today, as one of the body's defense mechanisms.

Anxiety can also produce identical physiological reactions and there is often no means of ensuring this tension is dissipated. In other words, when you are anxious or feel stressed in your work environment you may not have to physically fight or run to dissipate the tension, the problem here is that you are left with the physiological changes that your body naturally produced to get you into 'fight or flight' mode. These changes in the body can also be produced by being exposed to intermittent and continuous stress and environmental changes, rather than the stresses due to a direct physical threat to your safety.

Stress can come to you in many different forms and you can be exposed to different levels of stress, from:

- ❏ Direct physical danger.
- ❏ Personal environmental changes.
- ❏ Daily work anxiety at various levels every day.
- ❏ All of the above make you potentially susceptible to the accompanying disorders.

Importantly: one of the ways to reduce stress..... is that you need **time** to recover. Rest and relaxation can restore you and provide relief, but this is also dependent upon taking the time to relax and reduce the level and the duration of stress.

Remember.........

Management Wisdom

Healing is a matter of time, but it is sometimes a matter of opportunity.

*Hippocrates.

Stress Experiments

There have been many stress related experiments and research carried out to consider the extent of damage that stress can cause and these have confirmed that continuous levels of stress and anxiety are dangerous to your health.

Dealing with even the minor stressful events of your life can lower your resistance to illness, it is therefore important to you and your family that you address the issue of lowering your stress levels in your work environment, particularly if you are working in a fast paced and highly stressful environment

Quick Tip: in order to avoid a problem - you must first acknowledge that you may have a problem in the future.

Section: 1.2. Symptoms of an Overstressed Person

The following are the typical symptoms related to stress and anxiety when a person is under continual stress:-

1. **Lack of enthusiasm**

    1.1. No drive.

    1.2. No energy.

2. **Poor interactions**

    2.1. Over or under reacts to situations.

    2.2. Dampens the enthusiasm in others through complaining.

3. **Inability to solve problems**

    3.1. Poor concentration and lack of confidence.

3.2. Reluctance to make decisions and take action.

4. Inability to communicate

4.1. Written and verbal communications tend to be vague or even incoherent.

5. Apparent irresponsibility

5.1. Indiscreet statements.

5.2. Outbursts.

5.3. Irresponsible actions.

5.4. Excessive disciplining of personnel.

5.5. Excessive arguing with colleagues.

5.6. Heavy drinking or drug use.

5.7. Displays emotional extremes.

6. Failure to delegate

6.1. Delegation is unplanned, sporadic and uncoordinated.

7. Obvious physiological indicators

7.1. Clammy palms or perspiration.

7.2. Rapid and erratic hand, head and eye movements.

7.3. Shortness of breath.

7.4. Inability to concentrate, sleep and relax.

Section: 1.3. Take Control of Your Work Environment

When you are in a highly stressful and continuingly stressful situation it is imperative that you take control of the situation and your work environment.

A Word on Responsibility, Authority and Stress

Responsibility comes with every job; it gives managers a feeling of usefulness and pride in their work. But when managers lack the appropriate authority the result is that they may feel unable to take control of the situation and their work environment to meet the assigned responsibility. This creates further heightened stress, anxiety and dissatisfaction.

Important Note: Stress, anxiety and dissatisfaction levels can be reduced and sometimes avoided by the manager who has the appropriate level of authority to take control of the situation and modify their work environment, be it the ability to allocate additional resources, extend deadlines, or bring in external resources to assist etc. the appropriate level of authority is therefore important to reduce the level of stress from the assigned responsibility.

Section: 1.4. Factors Influencing Stress and a Healthy Life

Reduce Stress through understanding the factors which can cause stress. When discussing your health, your life and the management of stress, there are certain factors that can either work in your favor or against you.

1. **Age**
    1.1. Unfortunately, you cannot turn back the clock, so not much can be done to change your age. You should be aware that from the age of about 40 onwards your ability to manage stress may reduce; however, there are some things you can do about this. You can take steps to reduce your exposure to stressful situations and take control of your work load and environment; take on less responsibility, lower your workload, increase your support resources or change your job etc.

2. **Weight**
    2.1. Being overweight, means your heart must work harder to carry the additional weight.
    2.2. Overweight people are at a higher risk than those who are at their optimum weight.
    2.3. If you believe you are overweight, watch your food intake and join a gym or start a moderate jogging or exercise regime.

3. **Drinking**
    3.1. It is said, that drinking in moderation can relax you.
    3.2. Excessive drinking can kill you and at the very least it will stop you from becoming the best manager in your chosen industry.
    3.3. Moderation is the cue here.

4. **Blood Pressure**
    4.1. High blood pressure or hypertension is probably one of the most common illnesses of our time. It places an extra load on your heart and causes circulation problems.
    4.2. If you have or suspect high blood pressure, get a check up and seek medical advice.

5. **Physical and mental fitness**
    5.1. If you do not exercise and believe you are not physically fit, make the time to join a gym or start a moderate jogging or exercise regime.

5.2. Alternatively, any physical sport will give your body and mind the exercise it needs, and the more demanding the sport - the more it will take your attention away from work and help you relax.

6. **Smoking**

6.1. Smoking increases blood pressure and pulse rate and reduces your inclination to exercise.

6.2. If you want to excel in business it helps if you are physically and mentally fit, so, stop smoking. Lung cancer, emphysema, heart disease, etc scares most people - don't wait for it to scare you!

7. **Gender**

7.1. Historically, women may have tended to live longer than men.

7.2. Stress has no boundaries; both men and women who have got to the top of their fields in businesses are both susceptible to stress related health issues.

Quick Tip: in business, it is imperative for your long term wellbeing to take time out and relax; to stand back and switch off from the work, and bring clear thought and a refreshed outlook back to the work at hand.

Remember.........

Management Wisdom

A calm mind brings inner strength and self confidence that is very important for good health.

*Dalai Lama

Section: 1.5. Personality Types

Firstly, how do you see yourself are you a Type 'A' or a Type 'B' personality from the following: -

1.0. Type 'A' personality

Type 'A' is characterized by having a distinct sense of urgency and appears; driven, ambitious, competitive and aggressive. Type 'A' personalities continually react with their work environment. The Type 'A' personality typically has a higher: blood pressure, incidence of diabetes, concentration of blood fats.

2.0. Type 'B' personality

Type 'B' personality on the other hand is characterized as being easier going. It is interesting to note that the Type 'B' personality may still have *all of the characteristics* of a Type 'A', but the physiological reactions are at much lower levels.

Comparison of personality types 'A' and 'B' in stressful situations

Type A personality	Type B personality
Leaves the office feeling anxious, irritable and frustrated. Thoughts of work are carried home; relaxation is difficult and sleep is intermittent.	Leaves the office feeling satisfied. Thoughts of work are left behind, with enough energy to devote to family and leisure or sport activities.

Benefits of Lower Physiological Reaction Levels

❑ The lower physiological reaction levels taking place within the body results in a lower incidence of coronary problems.

❑ Low physiological reaction levels can increase productivity over the short term.

Stress vs. Performance

If stress levels continue unabated or increase excessively the physiological reaction to stressful situations can increase changing the reaction from productive to destructive!

Coping with Stress

Each person has a different ability to cope with stress. You have a certain type of personality, it may be a Type 'A' personality or a Type 'B' personality or somewhere in between; you are a product of both your personality traits and your environment which determines your reaction to stressful situations, but the good news is you can learn to reduce your stress levels.

The key to coping with stress is the ability to recognize and assess the stressful situation and the will to take the necessary action to reduce it.

People who handle stress well: -

❑ Recognize the potential for stress in different situations.

❑ Break down the stress situation and analyze it methodically in order to reduce or eliminate it.

❑ Understand their reactions to a stressful situation.

❏ Take action to reduce the stress in a stressful situation.

❏ Alternate their actions to different stressful situations.

Remember.........

Management Wisdom

Learn from yesterday, live for today, hope for tomorrow

*Albert Einstein

Section: 1.6. How to Reduce Stress

Here are some ideas on how to reduce stress that may work for you: -

1. **Engage in a sport or hobby essentially to take your mind off work**
    1.1. A physically demanding sport.
    1.2. An outdoor activity.
    1.3. An engrossing hobby.
    1.4. Coach a sport.
    1.5. Community affairs.
    1.6. Reading.
    1.7. Art.

2. **Ensure you get physical exercise regularly.**
    2.1. Join a gym or walking club.
    2.2. Take up yoga.
    2.3. Set aside a moderate daily exercise period.

3. **By getting regular sleep and exercise you will build up a resistance to tension and stress.**
    3.1. Ensure you get *at least* six hours restful sleep per day.

4. **Analyze the stress producing situation and change or reduce it.**
    4.1. Clearly define your major result areas.
    4.2. Ensure you have the correct levels of authority for your job responsibilities.
    4.3. Determine what your responsibilities are.
    4.4. Don't worry about things you cannot change.
    4.5. Don't try to control things which are outside your control.

4.6. Accept less perfection.

4.7. When work builds up, delegate a portion of the work.

5. **Separate work and home life.**

    5.1. Learn to work effectively - at work.

    5.2. Leave your work problems at work, make a list of what you have to do the following day and leave it on your desk - do not take the work or the list home!

    5.3. Don't discuss work at home.

    5.4. Don't take after-work calls at home.

6. **Take regular breaks - withdraw physically from the situation temporarily.**

    6.1. Get away for a beak - for a weekend or a week.

    6.2. Find out where the 'off button' is on your mobile phone, laptop and email and switch them off regularly and particularly when you take a break!

7. **Work smarter - not harder**

    7.1. Delegate a portion of your work.

    7.2. Work longer hours if you must, but only when it is absolutely necessary.

    7.3 Don't take work home, but if you must only as the exception - not the rule!

    Quick Tip: compensate yourself and your wife, husband, girlfriend or boyfriend with a dinner, show or a movie for any additional work you do working late or taking work home.

8. **Talk a problem through with a colleague to get another opinion.**

    8.1. Arrange for informal discussion with a colleague over coffee or tea.

9. **Talk a problem through with your wife, husband, girl friend or boy friend.**

    9.1. A word of warning, do not over burden your partner with great amounts of detail.

    9.2. Keep these talks off the cuff and to a minimum.

    9.3. Keep these talks as the exception rather than the rule.

10. **Take a break or change to a different work task or job activity.**

    10.1. Stop what you are working on and take a break or multiple breaks.

    10.2. Tackle something completely unrelated to the work at hand.

11. Get a health check

11.1. Once or maybe twice a year get a full medical checkup.

11.2. If a health problem starts to develop - prevention is far better than cure!

This is what most successful executives do to reduce stress. Consider what is applicable to you and plan how you will address stressful situations by adapting one or more of the above for your own benefit.

Remember.........

Management Wisdom

All work and no play, makes Jack a workaholic.

*Unknown

Section: 2.0. Quick Guide to the Effective Management of Stress

Stress management is a serious business and you should review the situation perhaps twice a year, the following Quick Guide will assist you with this.

A Quick Guide for Stress Management:

1. What stressful situations are you encountering right now?

1.1. What physiological reactions are being experienced?

1.2. How are you managing your stress?

2. Are you moving towards a Type 'A' or a Type 'B' personality?

2.1. Which situations are causing the shift?

2.2. How can you control or change your environment?

3. Have you been ill recently?

3.1. What do you feel about your current health?

3.2. Is your general health and fitness on the way up ... or on the way down?

3.3. Are you eating healthily?

3.4. Are you exercising regularly?

4. How far are you to your break point - right now?

4.1. Do you believe you are managing your current workload?

4.2. Are you handling your stress level?

4.3. On a scale of 1 to 10 maximum how stressed do you feel right now?

4.4. Are you relaxing and recovering properly from a recent stressful situation?

5. **What about your personnel?**

5.1. Are any of your personnel overloaded with work?

5.2. Are any of your personnel exhibiting stress related symptoms?

5.3. Do you notice any significant behavioral changes in your staff?

5.4. What can you do to assist them?

6. **What control do you have over your work environment and stress factors?**

6.1. Do you have the appropriate authority level to change or control your current work environment?

6.2. Can you change or reduce the stress levels through moving the deadlines, additional support, delegating or additional resources etc.?

7. **What specific things are you doing right now to reduce your stress levels?**

7.1. What are they?

7.2. Are they working?

7.3. Should you change them?

7.4. How?

Effective managers carry out regular reviews in this area.
And use the Question Model of Management to assist you in keeping stress under control:-

1. **Why** do I need to take action in a particular area?

2. **What** objectives, action plan shall I set?

3. **Who** will be involved?

4. **When** are my objectives and action plan dates?

5. **How** are my objectives and actions, to happen?

6. **What if** a problem develops, what will I do?

7. **Where** should my objectives and action plan take me?

Remember.........

> ## *Management Wisdom*
>
> Success in business requires training and discipline and hard work.
> But if you're not frightened by these things, the opportunities are just as
> great today as they ever were.
>
> ***David Rockefeller**